Good Thinking, and Bad

Using the Science of Cognition
to Make Better Decisions

Good Thinking, and Bad

by

KJP Sheedy

Copyright 2018 KJP Sheedy

All rights reserved. No part of this publication may be reproduced, stored in a retrieval system or transmitted in any form or by any means electronic, mechanical, audio, visual or otherwise, without prior permission of the copyright owner. Nor can it be circulated in any form of binding or cover other than that in which it is published and without similar conditions including this condition being imposed on the subsequent purchaser.

ISBN: 978-1-9996238-0-7

This book is produced by **Navidus Consulting** in conjunction with **WRITERSWORLD**. It is available to order from most bookshops in the United Kingdom, and is also available globally via Internet book retailers.

Navidus Consulting

www.navidusconsulting.com

WRITERSWORLD

2 Bear Close Flats, Bear Close, Woodstock, Oxfordshire, OX20 1JX

☎ +44 1993 812500

www.writersworld.co.uk

Copy edited by Ian Large : Cover design by Jag Lall

The text pages of this book are produced using an independent certification process that ensures the trees from which the paper is produced come from well managed sources that exclude the risk of using illegally logged timber and allow the use of recycled paper.

Contents

Prologue 7

Introduction 11

How This Book Works 17

PART 1: THINKING ABOUT THINKING **23**

1.1 Certainty & Doubt 25

1.2 Rational and Reasonable 34

1.3 Auto-Thinking vs Effort-Thinking 41

1.4 Emotional Thinking 47

1.5 Probably Just Luck 54

1.6 Moral Thinking 63

1.7 Social Thinking 70

PART 2: THE COGNITIVE PROCESS **75**

2.1 Intelligence 77

2.2 Thinking Style 87

2.3 Creativity 96

PART 3: THINKING ABOUT DECISIONS **103**

3.1 Thinking Quality 106

3.2 The Decision Process 111

3.3 Triage Thinking 119

PART 4: A TAXONOMY OF THINKING PARADIGMS 127

4.1 Constructing Paradigms 134
- The Framing Paradigm 137
- The Narrative Paradigm 147
- The Confidence Paradigm 156
- The Intuition Paradigm 168

4.2 Reducing Paradigms 176
- The Availability Paradigm 179
- Incomplete Information (WYSIATI) 186
- Full Knowledge (WYKEK) 193
- Confirmation Bias 198
- The Ownership Paradigm 204

4.3 Heuristic Paradigms 209
- The Substitution Paradigm 214
- Rules of Thumb 219
- Models, Maps & Metaphors 226

4.4 Experience Paradigms 234
- Risk Reward Paradigm 237
- Creative Memory Paradigm 245

CONCLUSIONS 251
- THINKING ABOUT THE FUTURE 254
- LEARNING BY TEACHING 260

APPENDICES 263

THINKING PARADIGMS QUICK REFERENCE 264

Constructing: THE FRAMING PARADIGM 268

Constructing: THE NARRATIVE PARADIGM 270

Constructing: THE CONFIDENCE PARADIGM 272

Constructing: THE INTUITION PARADIGM 274

Reducing: THE AVAILABILITY PARADIGM 276

Reducing: INCOMPLETE INFORMATION (WYSIATI) 278

Reducing: FULL KNOWLEDGE (WYKEK) 280

Reducing: CONFIRMATION BIAS 282

Reducing: THE OWNERSHIP PARADIGM 284

Heuristic: THE SUBSTITUTION PARADIGM 286

Heuristic: RULE OF THUMB 288

Heuristic: MODELS, MAPS & METAPHORS 290

Experiencing: THE RISK REWARD PARADIGM 292

Experiencing: CREATIVE MEMORY PARADIGM 294

Contents

- TOOLS FOR THINKING 296
  - MANAGING OPTIONS...299
    - Divergent Thinking – Expanding Your Options 301
    - Convergent Thinking – Making Choices 304
  - PRIORITISATION TOOLS 309
    - The Two-by-Two Priority Matrix 309
    - The Decision Matrix 311
  - CHARACTERISTICS OF A GOOD MODEL............................315
  - RISK MANAGEMENT 318
  - STANDARDS OF EVIDENCE TOOL 323
  - ADAPTER DOGS AND INNOVATOR CATZ TOOL 325
  - PROSPECT THEORY: A Summary and an Extension 328

REFERENCES AND ACKNOWLEDGEMENTS............................341

Prologue

I wish that I had been taught more about thinking when I was younger. It was not until I was a young adult that I began to come across snippets of information about how people think, mainly gained from reading about psychology. These insights were both fascinating and useful. They generally made me more effective at whatever I was doing. I am still learning about cognitive psychology now and it continues to be useful as well as interesting. I am convinced that learning is something that we can do at any age. I am also sure that learning about thinking makes you better at thinking, so that you can learn more and apply that learning to better effect. It is a virtuous circle.

A little over two years ago I was flicking through one of my battered books on cognitive psychology. I was looking for a half remembered chapter on thinking fallacies as I prepared for a meeting. It struck me that I should really get my collection of notes on the subject of thinking into some kind of order. It consisted of a shelf of dog-eared books, various articles with my own notes in a scruffy folder, and a collection of web page bookmarks. It was less than pristine and not very user friendly. I thought how great it would be to be able to search for the various insights I had gleaned over the years in one logically organised volume. Then, I thought, other people would find these insights useful too. Surely someone has done this already? I searched and I researched, but no one title offered me the single source, easy to understand reference book I needed. The idea for this book was born.

Prologue

I thought that writing this book would be a big job and that I would have to be very determined to get through it. I was wrong. It was a *very* big job, but I did not need a steely determination. It was fun. I discovered a lot of new things as I updated my understanding and I got to speak to some fascinating people. This impetus also inspired me to complete my work developing new perspectives on some of the more exciting and challenging elements of this science. This book is a result of all of that effort.

While writing this book, my original point kept coming back to me; how much better equipped I would have been to make life's more challenging decisions if I had been taught at a much younger age how good thinking leads to good decisions. Wouldn't it be wonderful if 'thinking about thinking' was included as a subject in every educational curriculum? That is a big ask but I decided that I could make a first step in that direction. I resolved that, if this book proved to be popular, I would try to send a free copy to any school library that wanted it. I imagine a curious teenager, similar to myself at that age, coming across it on the shelves and starting, a few years earlier than I did, to teach themselves about thinking.

Thank you for choosing to read this book. I hope that you will find it entertaining, interesting, and even useful.

Kieran Sheedy.

This book is dedicated to my whole family,

you know who you are.

My thanks to you all

for your enthusiastic support.

Introduction

Introduction

> ***"From the brain, and from the brain only,***
> ***arise our pleasures, joy, laughter and jests, as***
> ***well as our sorrows, pains, griefs, and tears."***
>
> *Hippocrates – Philosopher*

Brains are greedy. Your brain is about 2% of your total body weight, but it consumes roughly 20% of the energy you use. Scientists recently discovered that as humans' brains evolved our muscles weakened, to allow the energy-hungry brain a greater share of scarce food resources.[1]

The reason our brains succeeded in the competition with muscles for energy is, of course, the profound competitive advantage that brain power represents. Yes, humans are the dominant species on Earth but perhaps it is not so obvious that this is largely because we used our intelligence to interfere with standard selective evolution. Before the humans were smart enough to interfere, standard evolution waited for good accidental mutations which proffered advantage and would therefore continue. Humans however, are smart enough to invent and implement changes which are designed to create advantage, simulating the process of standard evolution. There are myriad examples of this *conscious evolution* by humans, from selective breeding of plants and animals to the eradication of smallpox using vaccines. Some of the most important of these conscious evolutionary changes are behavioural changes in humans and the powerful, viral concepts that have changed the way humans interact. The division of labour and the creation of money are two powerful examples of these viral concepts.

A better example in the context of this book is the way we humans are constantly improving our thinking performance by studying how we think. We have brain power which is improving brain power in a virtuous circle. This is powerful stuff.

As well as being greedy, brains are complicated, very complicated. The number of synaptic connections in your apparently average human brain is about 100 trillion (10^{14}), which is greater than the number of stars in the Milky Way, our home galaxy. Your brain is also exceptionally efficient. The world's most powerful supercomputers, which are substantially less powerful than your personal allocation of grey matter, typically take up thousands of cubic meters of air-conditioned space, and guzzle electrical energy at a phenomenal rate. By comparison your greedy brain is a model of efficiency.

So what do we know about how this little miracle of evolution works?

Your complicated, powerful brain does get a lot of attention. We humans have invested a lot of effort trying to understand how it works. This effort has been put in mainly because we are smart and curious creatures, but also because we want to improve our use of this powerful instrument. We have not yet gone very far in this important effort to understand, but we do know quite a lot of stuff. Looking at what we know it is worth breaking this question into two parts:

i) How does the brain work?

ii) How do we think?

Introduction

The very difficult question of how the brain works on a biochemical level will continue to keep a lot of very smart people occupied for a very long time. (See the box for an example of why.) To manage your expectations I should say that this book does not address the 'how does it work?' question. It makes only a few references to the connections between our biochemistry and the way we think.

> *Scientists have recently discovered that human breast milk has components that humans can't digest. Instead, these feed the symbiotic bacteria in our gut, which in turn have biochemical impacts on the brain which measurably affect our moods.*[2]

It is not surprising that the study of human thought and the brain has drawn the attention of great scientists, philosophers, sociologists, and economists. The subject is extraordinarily broad and there is a lot of very interesting debate, but very few solid conclusions. This is great if you want to immerse yourself in what might be the greatest scientific investigation of all time, but it doesn't help if you want to get to the pragmatic 'so what?' questions.

- ✧ So what does all of this mean in practical terms?
- ✧ How can I use this stuff to make me smarter and to help me to be more effective at thinking and to make good decisions?

This book is inspired by the pure science of how our brains work, but is focused on applied science, on the more practical question:

'How do we think?'

Humanity has made some very useful progress on the practical question. While there is a lot more work to be done, there are already a lot of really valuable insights into how we think. These are what you will find in this book. We can use these discoveries to improve the quality of our thinking and to improve our performance in any area where we choose to focus our most powerful tool. Whether the driver is personal, social, business, or intellectual, there are discoveries and thinking techniques that can make us smarter, and which can also improve our capacity to understand other people's thinking.

I expect that some of these insights will be familiar to the reader, for example Confirmation Bias (the way it is easier to find evidence which supports our views) and Framing (where the subtle setting of expectations can influence outcomes). Others are not so well known but equally interesting and powerful, such as Prospect Theory, which explains how expectations of gains or losses affect our judgment of risk.

All of these patterns, or 'Thinking Paradigms', have both advantages and disadvantages. They support Good Thinking, and Bad. Once we are aware of them we can support the good thinking effect and subvert the bad.

This book has two objectives: It is a user-friendly overview of where science is right now on the 'how we think' question. It is also designed to be a handbook which organises what we currently know about how we think into a clear structure with tools and tips

Introduction

that you can use to improve your thinking performance. This will enable you to better utilise the phenomenally complex and fantastically powerful tool that each one of us is casually carrying around with us every day, and which we apply, often unconsciously, to solve all of our problems, great and small. The measure of this improvement will always be the quality of the decisions that we make. Good decisions are what really matter. It is decisions that make Good Thinking concrete and actionable, and this is where the real consequences of Good Thinking, and Bad, are manifest.

It is all about that virtuous circle. Just about all of the best stuff that humanity has done has been because we can think. Because we like to think about thinking, we are getting better at thinking over time. The better we get at thinking, the more we can use the brains we have to their full potential. Then we can do even better stuff. This virtuous circle applies to humanity in general and to each one of us. So read on and find out how you can be even smarter than you already are.

> *"The world as we have created it is a process of our thinking. It cannot be changed without changing our thinking."*
>
> *Albert Einstein – Scientist*

How This Book Works

"Taxonomy is described sometimes as a science and sometimes as an art, but really it's a battleground."

Bill Bryson – Author

This book is designed to be a reference, a toolbox for thinking. The author hopes that, unlike many toolboxes, the reader will find that it is organised in such a way that you can find the tools you are looking for when you need them. Even better, this book will guide you to the tools that you might find useful based on what you are trying to do. For example, you might be trying to generate potential solutions or to choose a course of action from a list of options. For this reason, the book has a structure that reflects a particular taxonomy of thinking.

Structured Thinking

The taxonomy used in this book is inspired by the current science on the subject and it makes sense to the author. This taxonomy also makes sense to the various smart people whom the author has tested it on, and developed it with. However, as you will find by reading the chapters on Heuristic (Modelling) Paradigms later, no taxonomy is a true reflection of reality. No taxonomy works for everybody. If you find this taxonomy works for you, excellent. If not, you might want to search the same tools on the Good

Thinking, and Bad website. You may also find the website, with its search capability, a more convenient resource. I love the search capability of the Internet, a miracle of modern information management. But I also really like books, and this book is designed to be read both sequentially from start to finish to get an overview of the subject of thinking (good and bad), as well as to be reread, digested, dipped into, and bookmarked as a reference for day-to-day use.

At the highest level, thinking can be divided into:

- **Constructing** – where thoughts and ideas are created.
- **Reducing** – where analysis is used to break problems down in order to solve them.
- **Heuristics** (Modelling) – where structures like metaphors and pictures are used to help to understand complex concepts and the place of things in their wider context.
- **Experiencing** – where responses to events and feelings are collected to classify our thoughts.

Pattern of Paradigms

Each of these thinking activities contains a set of Thinking Paradigms. These are patterns of thinking that are consistent across humans and through history. By definition, their evolutionary origin means that any Thinking Paradigm that persists in humans is more than likely a very valuable tool which enables efficient and effective thinking – Good Thinking.

However, these paradigms can also sometimes lead us to errors and wrong conclusions – Bad Thinking.

The principle that this book relies on is that any Thinking Paradigm found consistently in humans can deliver both Good Thinking, and Bad, depending on the context. Understanding the context, and the effect that it has on the various thinking paradigms being deployed, will enable the Thinker(s) to deliver Good Thinking more often.

These paradigms are sometimes referred to as 'Thinking Fallacies' to point out that they may often cause undetected errors. This use of the word 'fallacy' refers specifically to the negative outcomes of the Thinking Paradigm in question. If the paradigm can also deliver Good Thinking that leads to positive outcomes, then it is not logical to name it as a Thinking Fallacy. Furthermore, this naming practice gives a negative perspective on the paradigm, which can be both unhelpful and misleading. The word 'paradigm' is chosen because it is neutral. This better frames each thinking pattern as being equally useful and dangerous.

Take, for example, the Incomplete Information Paradigm, also known as 'What You See is All There Is' (WYSIATI).[3] This paradigm can lead to Bad Thinking when it discourages us from looking for further data, which might be a critical input, prior to making a decision. However, it also enables quick decisions, which is often the essence of Good Thinking. An experience of mine neatly illustrates this.

I was walking through a theme park in Spain with my ten-year old. "Look Dad!" I could hear excitement in the voice. "A black panther!" I glanced over to see the big cat less than ten feet away with no bars between us and its ferocious jaws. A millisecond later I was in full flight, dragging my confused child by the hand, oblivious to the shouts of, "It's behind the glass!" It was a first for me. The zoo kept many big cats in glass enclosures so that visitors could get up close.

I will not easily live down the embarrassment of my real terror when the actual danger level was zero. But the decision to flee based on the data available was reasonable. It was Good Thinking. In the same situation in the wild, seeking further information before reacting would have been Bad Thinking, with potentially fatal consequences.[4] The WYSIATI Paradigm can result in Good Thinking or Bad Thinking. It is a matter of context.

A Toolbox for Decision Making

Choosing the right tool for the job in hand becomes much easier when you know what the tools are for, and how to use them. Sledgehammers can be very useful, but not when you want to crack a nut. Each of the chapters is a tool in the Good Thinking, and Bad toolkit, and the book acts as the instruction manual for the tools. Like any really useful tools they can be used to create or fix a wide variety of different things.

There are a number of devices used in the book to ensure that we are focused on improving our thinking when it is most important, when it matters. For this reason there is a strong focus on decisions and decision making. Of course, it is true that much valuable thinking is done away from decisions. Musing, speculating and dreaming are not moments of decision and it is important that the pressure to decide does not limit this kind of creativity in thinking. However, unless we start considering alternatives, choosing hypotheses to test, and actions to take, our thinking will have little or no impact on ourselves or anyone else. It is at decision points where Good Thinking becomes essential and has the most beneficial impact on outcomes. For this reason our focus is on good outcomes, by concentrating on how to deploy Good Thinking at decision points.

One chapter is dedicated to the description of a typical decision process based on the DECIDE model[5] created for use in the medical field. This model is then used throughout the book in order to narrow down the paradigms being considered to those that are most relevant to where we are in the decision process.

A second device to maintain focus is Triage Thinking. Good Thinking has high costs in time and effort. It is important not to spend these resources on thinking that is not high value. Focusing on risks and impacts, triage is a simple technique to prioritise decisions and therefore to focus effort on the thinking that matters.

The first half of the book is an introduction to the subject of meta-cognition. This is followed by a series of chapters dedicated to each Thinking Paradigm. Each paradigm is described with enough scientific detail to ensure the reader understands what it is, as well as when and why we instinctively deploy it. The pros and cons of the paradigm are then considered, with some tips and tricks which can help us to use it effectively. Each paradigm is mapped to the decision process (the DECIDE Model) to highlight where in that process it is most relevant. Finally, some checks for context are provided, which can be used to test if this paradigm can be expected to deliver Good or Bad Thinking at this point in the decision process.

Ideally, the reader will quickly develop personal 'rules of thumb' which suggest which Thinking Paradigms are relevant, and how they can hinder or help Good Thinking throughout the decision process. In time these rules should be internalised and become subconscious, in the same way driving becomes 'natural' for an experienced driver, who can then focus on and enjoy the environment they are driving through to get to their destination. Even better, a team of people who share the language and approach to Good Thinking in this book should be able to effectively communicate using the concepts set out in later chapters and hence work together to efficiently produce better decisions.

> *"We become what we behold. We shape our tools and then our tools shape us."*
>
> Marshall McLuhan – *Professor*

This book is complemented by a website at
www.good-thinking-and-bad.com
which includes updates on the applied science of thinking.

Part 1

Thinking about Thinking

Part 1: Thinking about Thinking

In this section we look at some general concepts that affect the way we approach thinking. We will answer questions like: 'Can we be certain that a truth is true?' and 'How do we deal with the influence of luck when taking decisions?' These questions are hard and complex but our focus is on finding practical ways to deal with them rather than determining absolute solutions.

These chapters address aspects of thinking that have an impact right through the decision process. They are a pragmatic foundation to our study of the more specific Thinking Paradigms that we will focus on later.

> **"We can not solve our problems with the same level of thinking that created them."**
>
> *Albert Einstein – Scientist.*

1.1 Certainty & Doubt

> *"Doubt is an uncomfortable condition, but certainty is a ridiculous one."*
>
> *Voltaire – Writer and Philosopher*

One way to describe thinking is as the mental activity that moves us from doubt towards certainty. For example, moving from 'I wonder where is the best holiday destination for my family?' to 'I'm sure we will have a great time on the holiday in Florida that I have just booked'. The problem is, how close can you get to being certain that this holiday will be perfect, that the Earth moves around the Sun, that the Higgs Boson Particle exists, or that good is better than evil. This is where the professional thinkers, the philosophers come in.

First Philosophy

Philosophy has a way of getting very complicated very quickly, so it is better to get this over with at the start of any book that is about thinking but is not about philosophy.

When we talk about thinking we must also talk about philosophy, i.e. 'the study of the fundamental nature of knowledge, reality, and existence, especially when considered as an academic discipline', or literally in Greek, 'the love of wisdom'. We can find evidence of both Good and Bad Thinking from philosophers, but our focus in this book is the process of thinking as it typically occurs, rather than the conclusions of those who are professional thinkers. There are certainly overlaps. Philosophers study pure logic. Being able to spot the logical error in a syllogistic fallacy will surely help you towards Good Thinking (see box below). Likewise, a quick study of the subject of certainty from a philosopher's perspective is a useful foundation to manage the ambiguity inherent in Good Thinking.

In logic, a syllogism is a form of deductive reasoning consisting of: a major premise, a minor premise, and a conclusion. The structure is a series of statements: A is true in relation to B, and B is true in relation to C, therefore A is true in relation to C. This can be a correct construct. For example, "Mammals are warm blooded, dolphins are warm blooded, therefore dolphins are mammals."

But the form can produce apparent logic from nonsense. A favourite example is "God is love, love is blind, Stevie Wonder is blind, therefore Stevie Wonder is God." When it is this obvious that the logical conclusion is flawed it cannot be described as dangerous. However, when the flaw is a little less obvious there is a high risk of Bad Thinking. For example, "Staff in that organisation are corrupt. This person works in that organisation. Therefore this person is corrupt." The first statement is correct but does not specify whether all *staff or only* some *staff are corrupt. Therefore, the last statement might correctly be either "this person must be corrupt" or "this person may be corrupt".*

Also known as 'categorical arguments' this structure is often used by demagogues and others who mislead by accident or design.

Getting to Certainty

The bottom line is that nothing is absolutely certain. From ancient philosophers, such as Pyrrho of Elis (c.360-c.270 BCE) in Greece (who apparently learned this from gurus on the Indian subcontinent), to modern era philosophers like Karl Popper (1902-1994), there is a general agreement that humans can prove nothing beyond any shadow of doubt. The problem from Pyrrho's perspective is that all human perception happens in the brain, based on input from the senses. As the brain only creates reality based on this second-hand data, it can easily make mistakes. The brain can even hallucinate realities that don't exist. Have you had any interesting dreams recently? The debate continued in intellectual circles throughout history. The Scottish sceptic David Hume (1711-1776) supported Pyrrho and argued that to predict that the Sun would rise again tomorrow was not rational as we could not be certain of that fact. His contemporary, the Englishman Thomas Bayes (1702-1761), subscribed to a different view. He believed that an all knowing god had established an order in the Universe but that mankind was probably not smart enough to understand it. He came up with one of the founding principles of statistics: Bayes' Theorem, which essentially suggests that, as we gather more data, we refine our views of the probability of an event, drawing ever closer to a certainty, but not necessarily reaching it. Every day that the Sun rises improves the probability of its predicted appearance tomorrow. This very pragmatic approach underpinned scientific research for the next few centuries.

In the early 1960s Karl Popper took this Bayesian approach to scientific thinking to a new level with his idea that no scientific statement can be proven to be true, but it can be falsified.[6] He realised that the closest we get to a truth is a statement made in a way that presents the opportunity to prove it wrong (falsified). Once we establish that it is falsifiable, then we can treat it as the truth unless/until it is falsified. On this basis, he established, for your information, that neither Psychoanalysis nor Marxism are actually science. For me these two achievements are excellent reasons to believe that scientific philosophy does have some real practical uses.

So uncertainty is the norm. Fortunately these clever guys, and many other philosophers, managed to find ways to get on with life without being paralysed by this unfortunate insight.

Practical Pragmatism

The vast majority of us get by by being pragmatists, without even being aware that this is our philosophy of life. William James (1842-1910) gave a pretty clear explanation of the pragmatist's approach to knowing something when he said, "Useful ideas copy practical realities". His example goes something like this:

Think of a (mechanical) clock hanging on a wall. You can easily imagine it, and its function. Unless you are a clock maker, its working parts are summed up in your mind as 'clockworks'. But even a clock maker will have a cursory idea of a spring, compared to a physicist. What is important is that you have a practical, usable idea of what a clock is, in the same way a clock maker has a practical and usable idea of what a spring is. You might find, on closer examination, that the clock is battery operated. But it is still a clock. Or you might find that it has stopped. Then it is still a clock, but in this case its function has changed. It has become a wall decoration in the shape of a clock.

Taking a pragmatic approach means framing concepts and ideas in a way that makes them useful. It means accepting that you cannot occupy your mind with the full detail of things, and that it is perfectly acceptable to ignore the unfortunate insight of uncertainty, provided that you don't actually forget it.

Standards of Evidence

A useful term to use in pragmatic conversations about certainty is the word 'truth'. The word truth suggests an opinion sincerely held on the basis of fact. Furthermore, it suggests confidence from someone who declares something to be true, but does not claim absolute certainty.

A pragmatic tool to deal with truth when we are thinking about thinking is to use a variation of the legal concept of degrees of certainty. These standards of evidence, from less certain to more certain, are set out below. I have added a vernacular translation and some remarks on how they can be used when challenging a Thinker when they say something is true.

Legal Standard	Common Term	Notes
no credible evidence	**Guess**	*No attempt has been made to test veracity. If it is an attractive guess which might lead to clarity, begin to test it.*
some credible evidence	**Idea**	*Enough evidence is readily available to make it worth examining and refining.*
a preponderance of evidence	**Hypothesis**	*Enough evidence pro and con has been gathered to suggest this may be true. Use with caution in your thinking process.*
clear and convincing evidence	**Theory**	*An evidence-based assumption which is coherent and reasonable. Use as it is, but keep an open mind.*
beyond reasonable doubt	**Truth**	*Treat this as true, searching for contradictory evidence is no longer useful. Ideally it will be represented as a falsifiable statement. Accept that it might some day be disproved.*
beyond any shadow of a doubt	**Belief**	*i.e. Undoubtable – recognised as an impossible standard to meet – which is used only as a device to terminate the legal list. Take anything represented this way as suspect. If it is an important component of the thought process, test the impact of the opposite belief.*

So we can agree that nothing is absolutely certain, and that this doesn't really matter. Instead, accepting uncertainty is a useful reminder to be sceptical. When it comes to good quality thinking, it is of roughly equal importance that we can trust our ideas to be true as it is to challenge the truth of our ideas.

Doubt and Doublethink

Much of being good at thinking comes from accepting that a current valid answer might still be wrong. Unless we accept that an answer might be wrong we will not be open to testing it effectively. At the same time we must take action as if the current answer is correct. This ambiguity could be described as Orwellian doublethink but in reality it is much more pedestrian and commonplace than the mind games described in *1984*.

Flan O'Brien, in his absurdist comic novel *The Third Policeman*, elaborates a theory about the molecular exchange between a policeman and his bicycle, which means that each becomes in some way a part of the other. Anyone who has studied a little science will understand that this page is made up of atoms, a complex collection of vibrating particles, and made far more of space than of mass. However, we can deal with it effectively as a solid and simple page. This is similar to the pragmatism of the clock example from William James mentioned above.

The world is full of such ambiguity. We conceive of money as a physical thing with a reliable value, while it is in reality a social contract with a solid value that is based on nothing more than belief and trust. We think of WiFi as Internet connectivity to mostly free stuff. Really it is one step in a chain of capabilities, both technical and commercial, which are integrated by written and unwritten agreements between millions of people to give us access to information which in turn is gathered and presented by means of another complex web of co-operation and co-dependencies. We think of ourselves as a consciousness, an individual thinking creature, at the same time as we see ourselves as one element in a social whole of family, nation, of humanity. Yet we are only 45% human. The other 55% is made up of bacteria and microbes. I am a system, not an individual, the total genes in my bugs' genomes amount to perhaps 150 times the number in my human genome.[7] To keep it simple, I am pragmatic, I might feed my bugs with pro-biotic yoghurt, but I will still act and decide on the basis that there is one of me and I get to decide things.

> *"The test of a first-rate intelligence is the ability to hold two opposed ideas in the mind at the same time, and still retain the ability to function."*
>
> *F. Scott Fitzgerald – Author*

This unnoticed doublethinking ability is one of the many ways our sophisticated brain pragmatically helps us to get through the complexity of life. Just like breathing, it can seem a little odd if you focus your attention on it. When we start to challenge our thinking processes this uncertainty becomes evident. The vibrating atoms metaphor applies to the outcomes of our thinking. We need to simultaneously see them as made up of complicated collections of Thinking Paradigms, and as solid facts that support the decisions that we make and the actions that follow. You might personally find the resulting ambiguity disturbing (psychologists call it 'cognitive dissonance'). The sensation may be either exhilarating or stressful, or it may alternate between the two. It varies with the individual and with the context. To see why people respond in different ways to this dissonance we will look at thinking styles in another chapter.

The capacity to consciously process our usually invisible doublethinking is necessary for Good Thinking. It requires us to be pragmatic as well as both reasonable and rational. The good news is we do this doublethinking already, and we do it a lot. We just need to become aware of this ability and focus on it until we understand it well enough to be able to forget it again. A bit like working on your golf swing or learning to play the piano.

> *"If you would be a real seeker after truth, it is necessary that at least once in your life you doubt, as far as possible, all things."*
>
> *Rene Descartes – Philosopher.*

1.2 Rational and Reasonable

Rational: *Based on or in accordance with logic.*

Reasonable: *Having sound judgement; fair and sensible.*

www.dictionary.com

In the chapter on Certainty and Doubt, the legally defined 'degrees of certainty' tests were suggested as a usable framework to decide what is true. It is interesting to note also that the test of what is true in a courtroom is 'beyond *reasonable* doubt', not 'beyond *rational* doubt'. As you would expect with lawyers involved, this choice of words reflect an important distinction. It is also a distinction well worth exploring when we are thinking about thinking.

Let's be Reasonable

The bottom line is that rational thinking is not enough to produce Good Thinking. If we want our thinking to be effective and deliver good outcomes, we need a dash of reason as well. The word 'reasonable' means someone who is generally open to hearing alternative points of view; who is in tune with reality, and who will not act against their own best interests.

In common language, using the word 'rational' to describe someone does indeed suggest a reasonable person. The words are often treated as equivalent. However, that is not the meaning of rational in the strict sense, when one is taking a meta-cognitive perspective.

From this perspective rational means only that the thinking described is internally consistent. Rational thinking is logically coherent thinking, whether or not that thinking is reasonable.

For example, a survivalist, who believes that an imminent doomsday event like a global plague or major asteroid strike is a highly likely scenario, might invest the majority of their wealth in a bunker, a stash of weapons, and stocks of non-perishable food. They would describe long-term investments in the status quo, such as contributing to a pension scheme, as irrational. Their investment in small arms and tinned food is logically coherent and internally consistent. The survivalist is imagining a future where the typical pension investor is begging for access at the door of the fallout shelter while the world descends into chaos. Meanwhile, the pension investor imagines a future sipping chilled white wine on a cruise liner in the Med. Both are being rational; one is certainly being unreasonable. The jury is out as to which one that is.

You might decide that the survivalist is not reasonable, but you can see that we should not confuse this with being irrational. Being irrational is a very different behaviour. When someone draws conclusions which are not logically coherent with the defined facts, they are irrational. If they have sight of information which contradicts facts that are core to their rational thinking and refuse to reconsider, they are being irrational.

Another important distinction to note is that irrational thinking is not the same as thinking based on intuitions. Generally, intuitive thinking is accepting that there are important facts which cannot be determined in time to support a rational decision, yet requires making a decision with an awareness of these gaps. Usually the gaps are closed by guesswork or beliefs to get to the decision. Intuitive thinking may be categorised as unreasonable + rational thinking by anyone who makes a different guess or who subscribes to different beliefs. We will look into this in more detail in the chapter on the Thinking Paradigm called 'Rules of Thumb'.

It is also worth remembering that reasonable but apparently irrational thinking can be very useful to us humans and is pretty fundamental to our success in the world. This is nicely illustrated by the Ultimatum Game experiment.[8]

Economists invented the Rational Agent Model, which expects that people are rational, selfish, and consistent. It also assumes that they have full knowledge of all the facts. The model says that, given access to full information, a person will take the course of action which delivers the most benefit to them. At face value this makes good sense. Knowing that there are two loaves of bread of equal quality for sale, we will buy the cheaper one. This theoretical personality type, christened 'Econs' by behavioural economist Richard Thaler, is at the foundation of many important economic theories in use today. The Ultimatum Game experiment was designed to prove that the majority of people behave as Econs, but it brought to light a very different discovery.

The game is quite simple. There are two players, A and B. Person A is given $100 to play with. Person B is given $0. Person A must offer Person B a share of the $100. If B accepts the offer, they each get their share of the $100. If B rejects A's offer, they both get nothing. For example, if A offers B $20 (the ultimatum of the title) and B accepts, A get $80 and B gets $20. If B is an Econ they will accept *any* offer from $1 upwards because by accepting the offer they gain $1, whereas a refusal gets them nothing. However, the experiments show that the typical B rejects 'unfair' offers and typically will not accept any offer less than $20. On the face of it, B is being irrational but there is an explanation. We humans have what might be called a 'justice gene' which rejects what are seen as unfair ultimatums.

There have been many versions of the Ultimatum Game experiment looking at the results by culture, gender etc.[9] Entertainingly, the experiments show different results when A and B are Male to Male, Male to Female, Female to Male, and Female to Female. Males make aggressively low offers to other males and generous offers to females. Females in general made generous offers to both males and females and so more often than not they do get their cash and come out ahead. It is amusing to see that the Ultimatum Game experiments have delivered reliable statistical evidence to support the statement: "In the game of life, women are the fairer sex... but men have a justice gene too." We have yet to see experiments looking for measurable differences for transgender or gay participants. We do know that intoxicated participants have an enhanced drive for fairness.[10] I'm sure that there will be more fun findings on human nature to come.

This consistent irrational behaviour must deliver some evolutionary advantage; otherwise it would not be present in the vast majority of humankind. The best explanation is that this is a component of humans' sociability. If you let another take unfair advantage of you for your short-term gain, you will undermine your status in the group. This leads to less effective inter-group sharing to the extent that it reduces survival chances of the group's genes. In the rough and tumble of life, teamwork does work and natural evolution always drives the genome to survive, if necessary even at the cost of the individual. It is not surprising that experiments with our close cousins the monkeys[11] have demonstrated the same 'justice gene' in action.

If this evolutionary explanation of the justice gene is correct, and Person B was aware of it, you can say that the refusal to accept an unfair offer is a rational decision. However, in general Person B does not have this awareness. B just feels annoyed at the unfairness they perceive and behaves in a reasonable, but irrational, manner.

When looking at the quality of our thinking, it is worth holding in the back of our minds the counter-intuitive idea that reasonable + irrational thinking is both a natural trait of humankind, and can sometimes be very useful.

As an aside, the failure of the Ultimatum Game experiment is a nice example of good science using Karl Popper's falsifiable statements, which we mentioned in the previous chapter on certainty. A falsifiable hypothesis (that the experiment would show that the ultra-rational Econs existed) was indeed found to be false. However, that evidence led to new insights. These insights were also tested as falsifiable hypotheses. For example, experiments were run to confirm that there would be measurable differences in male and female behaviour when playing the Ultimatum Game.

This picture is a useful way to remember the distinctions of rational and reasonable thinking. Also I find the use of a '+' sign joining the two words is a useful device to show how each kind of thinking is made up. For example, the Ultimatum Game is an example of reasonable + irrational Good Thinking.

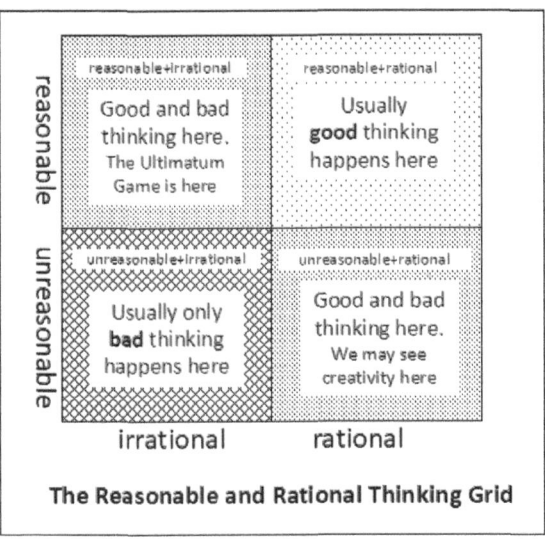

The Reasonable and Rational Thinking Grid

These distinct kinds of thinking, reasonable versus unreasonable, and rational versus irrational, are very important in the pursuit of Good Thinking. They are important because thinking that is very rational has the effect of appearing to be very reasonable. This assumption that 'rational' and 'reasonable' are exactly the same thing is the result of the impacts of a number of the Thinking Paradigms which we will discuss in some detail later. In particular, the Narrative Paradigm (it is a good story, it seems reasonable) and the Substitution Paradigm (answering easy questions in place of hard ones) come into play here. A good thinker is sensitive to the distinctions and will try to identify and to declare the key facts, assumptions, guesses, and beliefs that a rational train of thought relies on. Highlighting these foundations is a very powerful way of identifying which Thinking Paradigms are in play and where they are having an impact on the quality of the decisions being made.

The likelihood of Good Thinking is improved by:

- ✧ Checking if a decision is genuinely rational, that it is internally logical.

- ✧ Identifying and separating the rational and reasonable components of the thinking.

- ✧ Accepting that reasonable + irrational and unreasonable + rational thinking both occasionally have value.

With any combination of reasonable and rational thought, different modes and styles of thinking may be used. These are addressed in other chapters.

> *"So convenient a thing it is to be a reasonable creature, since it enables one to find or make a reason for everything one has a mind to do."*
>
> Benjamin Franklin – Polymath

1.3 Auto-Thinking vs Effort-Thinking

*"A general 'law of least effort' applies to
cognitive as well as physical exertion.
Laziness is built deep into our nature."*

Daniel Kahneman – Psychologist

Emotionally, the word 'fast' is usually a good word and 'slow' has negative connotations. However, 'jumping to conclusions' certainly feels bad, and 'carefully considered decisions' are often assumed to be better ones. As with many aspects of thinking, both quick and considered thinking have value. It is all about context. People do think in different modes in different circumstances and it is important to recognise these two different modes, and sometimes to choose one over the other.

Automatically Avoiding Effort

Thinking fast and slow are scientifically quite different to each other. There is not a continuum from lightning fast innovations to slow steady elucidations. In his rather brilliant book of the same name, Daniel Kahneman[12] explains that slow, 'effortful' thinking is a glucose greedy, energy sapping activity where attention must be paid and which humans will avoid wherever practical. He calls this 'System 2' Thinking. Quick, 'automatic' thinking on the other hand is the easy, lighting fast thinking that lets you know that New York in is the USA, and reminds you that you should assume that yellow cab drivers do not know their way around, the green man means you can cross the street in reasonable safety, and you should jump for your life if you hear a car horn blare behind you. Kahneman and Tversky named this 'System 1' Thinking. For clarity, and to stop myself getting confused, I choose to call these two types of thinking 'effort-thinking' and 'auto-thinking'.

Auto-thinking is highly efficient and leaves you with the spare intellectual bandwidth to spot anomalies as they happen, benign or dangerous, out of the corner of your eye. It includes your instinctive reactions to loud sounds and strange smells but it is important to realise that it can also be trained. This trained auto-thinking is an incredibly useful tool. It enables us humans to deliberately develop an automatic thinking capability for new and complicated processes. A skilled musician can play a complex piece of music with a band while paying attention to other performers' improvisations and the audience reaction. This is because they originally spent many hours of *effort-thinking* with their full concentration on playing each note as they learned the skills which they can now access unconsciously.

Think of the difference between a learner driver panicking at a busy road junction compared to an experienced driver who can react instinctively and confidently to any sudden danger. Perhaps the most powerful example is a top class athlete in a team sport who is auto-thinking the physical techniques of the game as well as the strategy and positioning of all the players on the field. When we say a player carried out a spectacular feat of instinctive sportsmanship 'without thinking', what we really mean is that they used auto-thinking, without any need to invoke effort-thinking.

Automatically Wrong

However, this wonderful auto-thinking also has some pretty fundamental flaws. Because it is an unconscious function it is particularly susceptible to the Bad Thinking that can be caused by the negative side of every type of Thinking Paradigm. One of the most common of these problems is the Substitution Paradigm. We will look at this paradigm in more detail in a later chapter but it makes a good example here. When an advertisement asks: 'Is this new car attractive to you?' your brain in auto-think mode responds by substituting an easier question. 'Is the person in the car advert attractive? You come up with the answer: 'Yes. Attractive.' In fact you have answered the substitute question suggested by your brain in lazy auto-think mode but the answer 'Yes' is now attached to the original question. This is just one example of how the brain in auto-thinking mode is more likely to slip into Bad Thinking. It is a familiar trade off. What you gain in speed you lose in accuracy and quality.

Joining the Circus

Effort-thinking is at its most useful when the subject being considered is a demanding one. It might be new, or complex, or both. If the impacts of the decision that you are making are important, then the time and energy focused into the effort-thinking process will be well rewarded. However, effort-thinking is not a guarantee of quality. When you are effort-thinking, the paradigms that can undermine the quality of auto-thinking are a little less dangerous, but they still present risks to the quality of your thinking. For example, even a careful and considered review of an important life decision, like choosing the right job offer, can overlook the deceptive effects of the Framing, Accessibility, and Confirmation Bias Paradigms among others. The familiarity of your current job, the framing effects of your career plan, and your risk aversion feeding into a confirmation bias might mean that you remain an excellent accountant. It might mean that you will never get to feel the wind in your hair as a star trapeze artist in the Russian State Circus. Just because it is slow and considered doesn't mean effort-thinking is Good Thinking. But it does have some real advantages. A quick auto-thinking response that has you packing your best Lycra leotard and your Russian language phrasebook in response to this tempting job offer may be even worse thinking. Good Thinking and Bad happen in both auto-thinking and effort-thinking modes.

Perhaps the biggest downside of effort-thinking is that it is a bandwidth hog. There is a limit to how much a human brain can process in real time. Effort-thinking requires a lot of the brain's available processing power and crowds out other thinking. The best and most famous example of this is the gorilla on the basketball court experiment (see box). This shows that effort-thinking can make us blind, and can even make us blind to that blindness.

When engaged in an intense bout of effort-thinking it is always a good idea to check for blind spots by stepping back and running your thinking through the paradigms described later in this book.

> *Chabris & Simons described a classic experiment in their book, The Invisible Gorilla.*[13] *They asked their subjects to pay attention to a short film of two teams of players passing basketballs. The subjects were asked to count the number of passes the team in white shirts made while ignoring the ball passing of the black shirts. While engaged in this effort-thinking task, 50% of the subjects did not notice a woman in a gorilla suit walk onto the court and spend nine seconds on camera thumping her chest before walking off court. Even more interesting, the 50% who were told that they missed the gorilla were very sure it had not happened, and when they watched the film a second time they initially thought the film had been substituted.*

It is always good to keep your eyes peeled for those gorillas.

Part 1: Thinking about Thinking

The table below is a useful visual summary of the differences between auto-thinking and effort-thinking.

Auto-thinking		Effort-thinking
Fast	⊘	Slow
Low Energy Use	🖥	High Energy Use
Low Bandwidth	📶	High Bandwidth
Unconscious	🗣	Conscious
Everyday Familiar Decisions	❗	Important Unusual Decisions
Approximate – Error prone	⊕	Accurate – More reliable

For Good Thinking it is important to choose the mode of thinking appropriate to the decision you need to make and be alert to the default mode of thinking.

> *"The strokes of the pen need deliberation as much as the sword needs swiftness."*
>
> *Julia Ward Howe – Poet*

1.4 Emotional Thinking

> *"Could a greater miracle take place than for us to look through each other's eyes for an instant?"*
>
> *Henry David Thoreau – Writer*

Albert Einstein did some spectacularly Bad Thinking on the question of the Tectonic Plates Theory, also known as Continental Drift. It appears that he did this because his thinking on the subject was emotionally driven. There were people involved who had a lot at stake in relation to this idea, and that tends to lead to emotional thinking. There are only a few subjects we think about where people are not part of both the question and the answer. For example, mathematical proofs and theories in physics exist in this abstract zone. Because the outcomes of these thoughts don't directly affect people they might appear to be unaffected by emotions. On the other hand the people doing the thinking can be affected by the outcomes, so even for these examples it is not quite true. The thinkers will have emotional attachments to a theory or a tradition which can affect the quality of their thinking. And, of course, the battles between academics contesting different perspectives can be deeply personal and get pretty ugly. It is somehow reassuring to know that even Albert Einstein's thinking could be bad, sometimes.

The Continental Drift Theory that we now take for granted to be true had a troubled genesis. In 1912, Alfred Wegener, a

31-year-old meteorologist, presented it to the Geological Society in Frankfurt. He was ridiculed for half a century for his novel idea that the continents float and drift. In 1955, Albert Einstein wrote an enthusiastic preface to a book written by his acquaintance Charles Hapgood, criticising Wegener's theory.[14] Mr Einstein was not alone in his scepticism. In 1964, the *Encyclopaedia Britannica* included the Continental Drift Theory but suggested that it had "grave theoretical problems". When it was introduced, Wegener's theory challenged the world views of scientists in geology, geophysics, zoogeography and palaeontology. Even the possibility of Continental Drift was a huge threat to the established authorities in each of these disciplines. The geologist R. Thomas Chamberlain, set out the risks: "If we are to believe in Wegener's hypothesis we must forget everything which has been learned in the past 70 years and start all over again." A variety of irrational defences were used by scientists keen to ignore the facts that supported the theory. Fossils common to continental edges separated by enormous distances across the sea were explained away by fantastically long 'land bridges', which had subsequently disappeared without trace. A Trilobite found in Europe, and also 3,000km away on the European side of the island of Newfoundland, was not to be found a mere 300 km away on the other side of the island. Thinking Paradigms like the Ownership Paradigm and Confirmation Bias prevented an objective acceptance of the evidence and this Bad Thinking was fuelled by emotional thinking. But it is possible in retrospect to understand the resistance. A lot of people had a lot to lose.

Even very smart people who have set out their stall as scientific thinkers are essentially emotional beings with reputations to defend and who are used to being right. We need to be aware of this fact and to understand how those emotions are driven. The majority of really interesting or important subjects that we think about will have some people involved in them. If people are directly affected, emotions can cause Bad Thinking, and emotional bad thinking can have high impacts.

For Good Thinking, where people are involved, it is important not to let your views be distorted by any antipathy for your opponents, or for their positions in the debate. It is equally important to avoid unintended bias driven by sympathy. To manage these biases in yourself and others, it is very helpful to have an understanding of the mechanics of empathy.

Empathy is a combination of three factors:

1) *Identification:* The ability to understand and/or share the feelings of another human being. The degree to which you can 'put yourself into another's shoes'.

2) *Response:* Sympathy or Antipathy for the other person's feelings and motives. It is very important to avoid the common error of thinking that antipathy is the absence of empathy and sympathy is synonymous with empathy.

3) *Mode:* There are two types of empathy processing that we use. Emotional Empathy and Cognitive Empathy. A normal person will naturally use a mixture of both. A

psychopath or severely autistic person might only have a cognitive empathy capability. A young baby will only have the emotional mode available.

Empathy is best understood as the intersection of these three dimensions. This is called the Identification/Response/Mode model, or Empathy_IRM.[15] I find it easier to understand as a picture, as in the diagram below. For Good Thinking it is enough to have an overview of the model so that you can use it to map the empathy position of yourself and others. This enables us to understand how emotional drivers are likely to affect thinking quality.

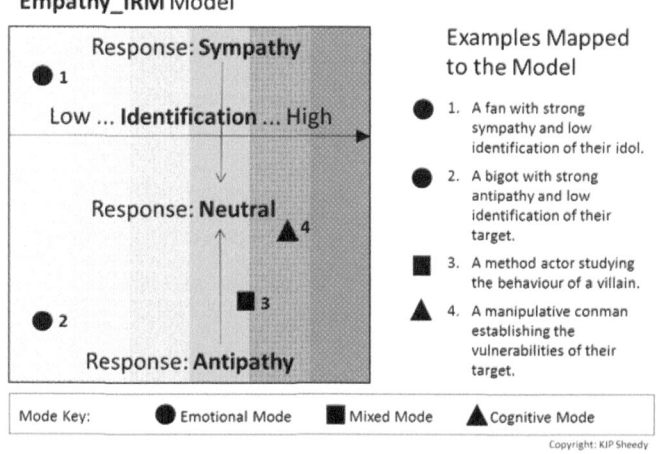

Identification is quite obvious and is on a continuum. The extreme of zero identification is very rare. Humans are pretty good at identifying with others because we are a social animal. Therefore, full identification is more common than zero identification. Very close partners in a clearly defined and understood situation can have very high levels of identification. For example, two members of a sports team during a match, or two parents at their child's graduation. The measure of identification is: Can you describe the emotional, social, and physical point of view of the subject in a way that they would agree with?

The **Response** axis: Sympathy/Antipathy is also quite straightforward. There we have two extremes and a neutral middle position. It is a measure of your 'moral' reaction to another's actions. For example, you might well understand why someone who is very drunk might begin to fight with ambulance staff trying to help them, while at the same time you would have absolutely no sympathy with their actions.

The intersection of Identification and Response dimensions are where the model becomes useful. A low level of identification combined with strong sympathy is sentimentality. Low identification with strong antipathy is prejudice. A high level of identification despite antipathy is real empathy.

The third dimension of **Mode** examines how the identification level has been achieved. Emotional empathy (also called affective empathy) is the unconscious 'feeling your feelings' that we experience when we see someone get hurt or when we yawn in response to another person yawning. Cognitive empathy on the other hand is when we deliberately imagine another person's perspective. For example, combining body language clues with previous experience and what we know of another's personality, we create a view from their perspective of the situation they are in.

Referring to the previous chapter on quick and slow thinking, the emotional mode is always an auto-thinking function, whereas cognitive mode can be either a learned, auto-thinking ability or it might require effort-thinking. Finally, empathy mode is very rarely binary. It is a good rule of thumb to assume both modes are working and to identify the dominant one.

Feeling this Way

The diagram is a graphic representation of how the three dimensions that make up empathy interact. It can be used to map the position of individuals or groups. Their location will indicate the position they are taking towards others affected by the decision being considered. For example at '1' a well-intentioned response may be misguided by a lack of understanding of the other person's real position. Whereas at '3' antipathy may not prejudice the individual because it is based on a high level of understanding of the other's position.

Emotions will always affect thinking. Even if you have the dubious advantage of being a true psychopath who starts at a neutral response and has to work a little harder to identify with others, once you have reacted with sympathy or antipathy to another person, it will affect your judgment. Of course, when it comes to considering yourself, a sympathy response is more likely than antipathy, but either will change your thinking in ways that are not immediately obvious.

For clarity it is worth mentioning here that intuitive thinking is *not* the same as emotional thinking. Intuitive thinking is just another term for the auto-thinking we looked at earlier. Auto-thinking is very susceptible to emotional drivers because it is unconscious. However, emotional thinking, driven by empathy, is a very powerful context and driver in effort-thinking. We go into more detail on this in the chapter focused on the Intuition Paradigm.

So, it is very useful to establish where you are on the Empathy_IRM map, and how you got there. This will help to identify which thinking paradigms are most likely to impact your thinking and how sensitive your thinking will be to the paradigm identified. The locations of other people affected by, and involved in, the thinking process are also worth mapping and considering in the same way. Locations of people on the map will change, and can deliberately be changed, by gaining information about, and insight into, other perspectives.

> *"When you choose to broaden your ambit of concern and empathize with the plight of others, whether they are close friends or distant strangers – it becomes harder not to act; harder not to help."*
>
> *Barack Obama – US President*

1.5 Probably Just Luck

"In God we trust, all others must bring data."

W Edwards Denning – Quality Engineer

A recent survey showed that more than 95% of UK MBA graduates would rather have root canal treatment than read a chapter of *Introduction to Statistics & Data Analysis* by Heumann, Schomaker and Shalabh (2016). That is pretty convincing data. It confirms our suspicion that even MBA graduates who use statistics quite frequently don't enjoy the subject. It may even confirm our suspicions that UK graduates will have a frank and humorous, irreverent, even British reaction to a question like this, more than other nationalities might.

Nobody Likes to Read Statistics Textbooks

You might be familiar with the expression 'there are lies, damn lies, and then there are statistics'. There is a little bit of truth in this aphorism. The survey of UK MBA graduates referred to above is not inaccurate. However, it does use some questionable methodology. The survey sample size is 1 (the individual surveyed is the author of this book). If the individual surveyed happened to be a fan of statistics and dentophobic, they would have chosen to read the chapter over the painful dental treatment. The results would have been exactly the opposite, but equally legitimate. In that case we would have concluded that MBA graduates are profoundly boring and are not tough enough to handle a bit of necessary dental work.

This reflects the law of small numbers, i.e. that small sample sizes create extreme outcomes. Taking the example further, you can see how a sample size of two could show either of the results above, or show that about half of MBA graduates prefer physical pain to statistics. Assuming a population of 10,000 UK MBA graduates, this doubling of the sample size means that the margin of error drops from +/- 19.5 to +/-14. It only takes a sample size of 15 out of 10,000 to get a very convincing margin of error of +/-5.

The fact that the survey might have legitimately given two contradictory but quite persuasive answers reminds us that humans are very rarely intuitively good at statistics. It also reminds us that we have the Narrative Paradigm ready and waiting to creatively join the dots in the data to deliver convincing stories with minimal effort. By the way, about 65% of UK MBA graduates are not UK nationals. Any irreverent reaction to the survey question is very unlikely to be based on their nationality. The single subject of our original survey, the author, is in fact an Irishman who happens to be a UK MBA graduate.

Why should we care that statistics can be misleading? We should care because a lot of decisions are advised by data analysis, by statistics. You may be thinking about now, "OK wise guy, statistics can be misleading. That is not exactly new news. So what can we do about it?" That is a fair question. Let me give you my take on how to reduce the 'stats risks'.

Do Not Study Statistics!

I'll begin with the good news. Studying statistics to doctorate level will not help very much. The majority of scientists who need reliable statistics to run their experiments choose sample sizes by guesswork, and generally get them badly wrong.[16] This is despite the fact that calculating a reliable sample size is pretty trivial maths, and there are many readily available online sample size calculators (like the one on surveysystem.com). We do need to know our means from our medians, but a deep study of the subject is not an efficient solution to reduce stats risk. So, if we are off the hook in terms of becoming statistics wonks, what can we do to reduce the risk that a poor understanding of stats can lead to Bad Thinking?

Below are a set of simple test techniques which will help to reduce stats risks depending on the degree to which the decision is influences by statistics.

If there is a single piece of data analysis which is very powerful or influential in a decision but where there are alternative reference points:

1) **Omit the Data Test**. Test the decision without using that data analysis. If the same decision looks like Good Thinking with that data analysis omitted, you are probably on the right track.

2) **The Data Narrative Test.** Unpack the data analysis and pick out the key points in the narrative that supports it. Then test the narrative's reliance on the focus points by reversing or challenging them.

If the decision is based primarily on, or relies very heavily on, data analysis:

3) **Alternative to Data Test.** Carry out the thought experiment of asking: "If we had no access to this data, how would we make the decision?" This will hopefully produce some suggestions on how you might cross check what the analysis is suggesting against some simpler information.

4) **Falsifiable Test.** Use Karl Popper's Falsifiability approach (described in the chapter on Certainty & Doubt) to restate the basic premise as a statement which can be disproved. Then attempt to disprove it. If it survives this test you can be reasonably confident that what the data says is true. In any case, undertaking the Falsifiability exercise will provide insights into the decision process.

5) **Independent Expert Test.** If you can't see any solid way to test or validate the proposed decision without the data analysis, get some outsider with no interest in the outcome of the decision and who deeply understands statistics to try to break or contradict the data analysis conclusions, using the same data set.

Bill Gates Gets it Wrong, Sometimes

These tests do require quite a lot of effort-thinking and we know that we all have a natural inclination to avoid that effort, especially when it is linked to statistics. To inspire you to invest that effort let me share a final example that shows how even very smart people can make big mistakes because of 'stats risks'.

The Gates Foundation spent $1.7bn in the late 1990s on supporting small schools, including breaking up larger schools into smaller units. This was based on statistics gathered to answer the question: "What are the characteristics of the best performing schools in the USA?" These stats showed that there were four times as many small schools in the top 50 schools than there was on average in the total. Hence the Gates Foundation made large investments into small schools. Unfortunately, these investments did not produce the expected results. You may have identified the problem based on our MBA graduates example. If the opposite question had been asked: "What are the characteristics of the *worst* performing schools in the USA?" the analysts would have also observed an unusually large incidence of small schools in the 50 worst schools. What the stats really show is that small schools (with small numbers of pupils) have more extreme results than larger schools. It is the law of small numbers again! Wainer and Zwerling, the statisticians who published a paper in 2006 that pointed out this expensive glitch, were fairly polite in their critique.[17] After all, it is a very human mistake to make and, who knows, maybe Bill is sensitive about this kind of stuff.

Be Lucky is Good Advice

My father has spent many years working hard at his hobby, the search for the perfect betting system for horse racing. Fortunately, he invests relatively small sums in his search for this gamblers' Holy Grail. He does invest a lot of time, but he really enjoys it. He is sure that some clever combination of data relating to previous races and horses will deliver a sure-fire way of making a fortune. He has often been excited by an unusual run of good results he was recording from his latest fiendishly clever betting system, but eventually the pattern would break and the results would go the other way. He always sees this 'reverting to the mean' as a bit mean spirited. However, he is a smart man and a large part of him is well aware that horse racing is about luck. The bookies who take the bets usually drive more expensive cars than the punters do. It is an interesting contradiction that he simultaneously needs to believe he will be lucky enough to find the winning system, and somehow not believe that the results of every race have a very large component of luck. Another example of the natural doublethink we saw in the chapter on Certainty and Doubt.

The simple definition of a lucky event is any outcome that defies the law of averages. Averages by their nature are notional things which only exist because they are overshot and undershot by about the same amount over time, on average! An excellent example of this is the way that 'passive' stock market funds (which simply track the market indices) over time will beat actively managed funds (in which fund managers attempt to beat the market by selecting particular stocks). The fund managers who sell and manage the active funds are mathematically literate and will generally agree that, in an open market with regulated information flows, active funds will revert to the mean. However, they will make a (doublethink) exception for the fund that they are currently selling.[18]

As you might expect, humans are likely to underestimate the influence of luck in their own success and the failures of others.

Likewise, we exaggerate the effect of luck on our own failures and in the success of others.[19] This rather unattractive human trait is driven by a combination of the good old Narrative Paradigm with a generous helping of Confirmation Bias. We will look at both in more detail later.

An excellent example of this underestimating of luck and overlooking the influence of a good narrative is the rise and fall of the best-selling business book *In Search of Excellence*, published in 1982. At first it topped the best sellers' lists until 1984, when a story in *Business Week* magazine was published, which made the front cover, called *Oops Who's Excellent Now?* Of the 43 companies which were celebrated in the book for their excellent fundamentals, one third had fallen from grace by reverting to the mean. The star companies appeared to be stars at least partly because they had a good run of luck. The expert authors of the original book had identified eight success factors which explained their success. None of the eight was luck. Incidentally, the original book is still in print, has four stars on Amazon, and appears to be selling well. We can't argue with the authors' luck.

You are (Probably) Already Lucky

Fortunately, there is a more positive view on personal luck which it is worth touching on. We all understand that, consistent with a reversion to the mean, some people are just luckier than others. Some of this is random; if you are born in a rich, democratic country you are luckier than a person born in a despotic, poor country. However, personal luck is not entirely random.

Experiments by Prof Richard Wiseman published in 2003 [20] suggest that there are four behaviours common to people who see themselves as lucky.

People who are lucky:

- ✧ Are skilled at creating and noticing chance opportunities.
- ✧ Make lucky decisions by listening to their intuition.
- ✧ Create self-fulfilling prophecies via positive expectations.
- ✧ Adopt a resilient attitude that transforms bad luck into good.

Essentially the science says that feeling lucky is the same thing as being lucky, being open to good luck will probably increase your luck, and noticing when you are lucky makes you more open to good luck. So don't just count your blessings, celebrate them.

In so far as it affects the quality of your thinking, the bottom line is that any run of luck is exactly that. Enjoy it, make the most of it, but be aware that the question you need to address is not *whether* this luck will run out, but *when* will this luck run out.

What does this mean in the context of Good Thinking, and Bad? Always check for a bit of luck (good or bad) that might be creating a bias in your thinking and tilting the playing field. Be sceptical of out-of-the-ordinary data points (positive or negative), especially if your hypothesis relies heavily on these very points. Ask the Thinker(s) these test questions:

1) If the measure of these data points had been close to average instead of out-of-the-ordinary, would it change my decision?

2) Is a return to an average performance in the future a reason to either:

   i) move quickly, and to take advantage of this anomaly while you can?; or

   ii) change the decision to account for the downside of an expected return to 'normality' later?

In this chapter we have looked at probability and chance in a fairly general sense. When the probabilities of wins or losses affect us directly, our reactions are not entirely rational. They vary greatly according to both the level of probability and the size of the impact. We look at this in detail in the Risk Reward Paradigm.

> **"I would prefer to have a general who is lucky rather than one who is good."**
>
> *Napoleon Bonaparte – Emperor*

1.6 Moral Thinking

"What is moral is what you feel good after and what is immoral is what you feel bad after."

Ernest Hemingway – Writer

The author was brought up a Catholic. When he was at school, 'good' and 'bad' thoughts had some very specific meanings. These had nothing to do with the quality of the analysis or the clever use of Thinking Paradigms. They were more to do with avoiding the awakening of natural impulses that all teenagers experience. You will be relieved to hear that this chapter, and no other part of this book, has anything to do with that subject.

While we are focused in this book on Good Thinking, and Bad in the sense of the quality of outcome, thinking about good and bad from a moral perspective has a useful and important place in this discussion. Whether a decision is right or wrong in a moral sense may be the most important measure of its quality. Adopting morals into the scope of cognitive psychology is a relatively recent change. Most people give the evolutionary biologist Robert Trivers the credit for this change; based on some papers he published in the early 1970s, in particular his work on the evolutionary advantage of altruism.[21] He proposed the scientific study of human nature by bringing the disciplines of moral philosophy and ethics into the scientific realm, and linking it closely to the study of evolution and biology. This gives rise to the new field of Moral Psychology. This is a broad and fascinating area of discovery and experimentation that is the subject of many books by luminaries such as Stephen Pinker and Richard Dawkins. However, we must be satisfied here with just a summary of the primary ideas and an understanding on how discoveries in this field can impact both Good Thinking, and Bad.

I need to set down two caveats before we move on. Before we get to finding out which are the key discoveries in Moral Psychology that we should be conscious of, and which we should try to understand in terms of how they impact on thinking quality, these caveats are:

> **Morality is Civilisation, and Vice Versa.** In the interests of brevity, this chapter is built on the premise that our morality (every religion, philosophy and cultural norm that humans have come up with) exists as it does because it provides evolutionary advantage through social cohesion. People feel good when they do the right thing because that right thing is in the best interests of humanity.

> **A Word of Warning about WEIRD People.** This new discipline of Moral Psychology has mainly been developed by, and tested on, WEIRD people. That is, White Educated people from Industrialised Rich and Democratic societies. It is at least possible that some of the conclusions reached will evolve substantially, or be changed completely, when the science includes a more diverse sample. Having said that, people are very much the same when you strip back the

cultural layer. I do believe that the results are good enough to work with for now. We can take them as being true.

Consequences or Principles? You Choose

Our perception of morality has two basic drivers: Consequential Morality and Principled Morality. If we choose an action knowing there are more negative consequences for other people than the alternative, most people will consider that an immoral choice. There are also some principles that humans generally agree are wrong. Don't kill people is a good example. The famous trolley car thought experiment sets up the quandary of choosing to kill one innocent to save a few other innocents. There are many variants of this question but they all bring consequential and principled moral thinking into sharp relief. In real life, the contrast is rarely so obvious and experiments show that humans are very flexible about unconsciously choosing the appropriate moral construct to suit their objectives.

In German politics the phrases 'ethic of conviction' and 'ethic of responsibility' (Verantwortungsethik and Gesinnungsethik) are household words to describe Principled Morality and Consequential Morality. Family dinners in Berlin must be very erudite. The terms come from a speech made by the sociologist Max Weber in January 1919 after Germany had lost World War I. The current Chancellor, Angela Merkel, was seen as the ultimate exemplar of an ethics of responsibility perspective, but she invoked the ethics of conviction when she opened Germany's borders to refugees in September 2015. This was a very human response in the way she changed her moral construct to suit the circumstances. Also, it was very human in that she did the humane thing.

David Pizzaro at University College Irvine in the USA designed and ran a series of experiments to show the power of this effect.[22] Two alternative scenarios described some innocent civilians being killed in a military operation to take out senior terrorists, which would in return save many more lives than were lost. The civilian collateral casualties were described alternately as foreigners or Americans and the participants in the experiment were manipulated to be in a 'patriotic' or 'multicultural' mind-set before being given the scenario. They were then asked the question: "Is this morally justifiable?" The participants with a multicultural mind-set tended to support the action using consequential morality when the innocents were American. They argued against the action using principled morality when the innocents were foreigners. The participants who were framed as patriots did the opposite. This showed that the participants would use the approach to morality which suited their objective. Follow-up questions were asked about whether race or nationality had, or should have, played any part in their response. This was very consistently denied, usually vehemently. Despite their denials, it is obvious that empathy has a big impact on the practical expression of morality.

This unconscious flexibility in our approach to moral reasoning makes complex questions easier to answer and gives us more confidence in the answers we come up with. Peace of mind and a clear conscience apparently deliver more of an evolutionary advantage than agonised self-doubt. No real surprise there.

Proximity and Empathy Affect How Morality is Perceived

Imagine a scene. You are walking the short-cut to an important meeting in your best outfit when you see a small child struggling in the dirty water of a pond. It looks like the child will drown. Do you wade in and save the child, sacrificing your best outfit and missing your meeting? Yes! Yes of course you do. Even if that outfit cost you £1,000 you go ahead and do the right thing. Any other course of action and you would see yourself, and be seen, as an immoral monster. On the other hand, what will you do if someone asked you not to buy that £1,000 outfit and instead to send the cash across the world to save some children in dire need? If you decide you do want to buy the suit most people will say, "You're not perfect, but that is not an evil act." That is the most common reaction to this morality test. We have already established that most people's morality is relative, and now we can see that it is selective too.

This selectivity is not surprising, but it is something to be aware of when testing the quality of your thinking and that of others. The more sympathetic empathy there is, the higher the value people will put on the consequences to the people affected by decisions. Benefits to the in-group outweigh the same level of benefits to an out-group. It is not hard to see the evolutionary advantages in this innate bias to your own team.

The combination of our unconscious flexibility between consequential and principled morality to support our views, combined with the different weighting of benefits we assign based on levels of empathy, can easily make a choice feel morally right when it is, at best, neutral.

How should we take account of this when we are managing our thinking to get to the best possible decisions?

1) Where the ethics of a decision are important, establish whether the justification being presented is based on consequential or principled morality. Whichever is being used, challenge the Thinker(s) to deploy the opposite morality to justify the decision again. If it makes sense from both perspectives you can feel pretty confident it is the right way to go. If not, the exercise will be a valuable route to new ideas and insights.

2) Review a benefits analysis which compares benefits to different populations or groups from the point of view of each of the groups. This can be done using a thought experiment of putting the Thinker(s) in each group's shoes. (Refer also to the chapter on Emotional Thinking for more details on the components of empathy.) Even better, if time and resources allow, bring representatives of the groups affected by decisions into the process.

I think that is Disgusting

Physical disgust is a very visceral emotion and its strength is a useful way to naturally keep us safe from infection and poisoning. It also leaks over and affects our thinking more than we might realise. There is a close correlation between our sense of moral purity and the sensation of disgust. An offence to our sense of morals leads us to feel the emotion of disgust. The reverse effect also works; when we experience the emotion of disgust, we are more likely to condemn others for a lack of morals. This has been established by experiments measuring moral judgements made by people who have been framed in advance by seeing disgusting images, compared to a control group.[23]

Even working in an environment which provokes disgust, like a very dirty office, will affect people's judgements. There is no need for the disgust stimuli and the thinking stimuli to be logically related for this to work. Seeing a video of someone vomiting will make us more likely to condemn someone accused of stealing. People who are measurably more sensitive than average to feelings of disgust therefore have different world views and politics than people who have a higher tolerance of disgusting stimuli. People with conservative political views generally have a higher propensity to disgust than liberals.[24] This is a physical example of the Framing Paradigm at work. The lesson for Good Thinking is: be alert to the framing effect of the disgust reaction on moral thinking. A clean and orderly environment will keep moral standards high.

Keeping your office reasonably tidy may actually be good for your soul.

> *"Moral excellence comes about by a force of habit. We become just by doing just acts, temperate by doing temperate acts, we become brave by being brave."*
>
> *Aristotle – Philosopher*

1.7 Social Thinking

"It is not what subjects do but for whom they are doing it that counts."

Stanley Milgram – Psychologist

The science says that it takes approximately five 'no occasion' bouquets of flowers to make up for one forgotten birthday.[25] There are rules to social engagement and these rules affect thinking just as much as other activities. This is not a surprise. Humans are a social animal and pretty much everything we do is designed to promote the good of our social in-group and to maintain or improve our place within that group. There have been many psychological observations based on experiments to measure the impact of others on our thinking. A favourite of mine is the work by John and Julie Gottman who discovered that, on average, it requires a ratio of five positive interactions to one negative one to maintain a stable positive relationship between two people. The Gottmans were focused on married relationships, but the rule applies to relationships in general and it explains why we all moderate our thinking to avoid social discord. This moderation of thinking is affected by both obedience (perceptions of authority) and conformity (the influence of peers).

Stay with the Group

The classic proof of the effect of conformity is an experiment by Solomon Asch where the subject was surrounded by apparent peers who persistently gave the same wrong answers to simple questions like: 'Which of these lines look longer than the rest?' The lone experimental subject showed signs of significant stress, which only reduced as they began giving wrong answers which matched the group's opinion. This is called 'Groupthink'.[26]

Yes Boss

The experiments which famously demonstrated how social thinking conforms to authority were the series of experiments to measure obedience carried out by Stanley Milgram, starting in 1963 at Yale University.[27] The subjects were prepared to (apparently) inflict severe, even potentially fatal, electric shocks to a peer because an authoritative experimenter told them it was required. While no human actors were injured in the running of these experiments, we should all be disturbed by the fact that 100% of subjects were prepared to inflict shocks rated as dangerous, and 65% went to the maximum level, labelled as '450V Danger Severe Shock'. The experiments have been repeated in other, less WEIRD, cultures with similar results.

It is easy to get worried about human nature based on these two forms of negative social thinking. It might seem that once other people are involved we all become sheep without a moral compass. However, social thinking based on compliance and respect for authority has very substantial advantages to us all, both as individuals and as members of groups.

The Good Side of Gangs

First and foremost we humans are very powerful when we cooperate. From hunting as a pack 50,000 years ago, to barn-raising, to working in companies which create wealth and benefits for the planet, the division of labour requires social Good Thinking and it is the primary driver of civilisation. This is enabled by compliant social thinking, giving us a unity of purpose and, crucially, the willingness to follow leaders. There are far more good examples of humans following leaders than bad ones, despite the fact that bad leaders make better headlines (c.f. the Availability Paradigm). Also, accepting that one person or group has authority in respect to a certain subject means, for example, that courts of law and a justice system can work.

Second, accepting that knowledge and ideas held by the majority is most likely to be true, means that we can all share the benefits without reinventing wheels, perhaps literally. Stopping at a red light is both compliant and boring, but it is a very useful convention. This is despite the great stories we all love about the lone genius who fights against the received wisdom of the crowd to have a powerful and beneficial insight accepted. From Galileo to Elon Musk, we do all love an intellectual rebel. However, the vast majority of the time the lone rebel simply has the 'wrong end of the stick' and the story is lost to history. This is such a commonplace and dull outcome that we will almost always ignore it. The chapter on Innovation and Adaption says more about how people's preference to be compliant, or not, affects the way that they address challenges. In summary, both approaches have real value. A combination of both modes of creativity is usually best.

Fitting in by Standing Out

So if social thinking is endemic and compliance and obedience are the human defaults, we have a question to answer. How can we tell if compliance and obedience are contributing to Good Thinking by avoiding unnecessary distraction, or actually trapping us in a rut of Bad Thinking? Honestly, we cannot, at least not at a glance. However, there are some tests that we can use which help to make that distinction with a little effort:

The Devil's Advocate: Taking a contrary view, being the 'Devil's Advocate' and deliberately spending some time thinking the unthinkable is a useful exercise. What if nobody ever stopped at red lights? Well, we would have to zig-zag through the traffic on the junction to avoid accidents. How could that be OK? Well, if cars were fitted with sensors and computers that avoided collisions on junctions even at high speeds, then no one would ever have to wait at an empty junction on a red light. Or if the traffic lights could even detect when there was no cross traffic, we would at least not waste our time at unnecessary red lights. This simple example shows how a little time as the 'Devil's Advocate' can be constructive. For Good Thinking it is important to commit fully to the Devil's Advocate role, but only for a short time. Then take a step back and ask, 'Is this helping to solve the problem?'

The Angels' Advocate: To address the situation where your thinking is naturally bringing you to non-compliant and disobedient positions, first check if your default thinking mode is to be an Innovator. (See the quick 'Dogs versus Catz' test in the chapter on Innovators and Adapters.) If you are a default Innovator (and that is not automatically a good thing) get an Adapter type involved and listen carefully. If you are Thinker working alone, role play an Adapter for a bit. You might learn a lot as the 'Angels' Advocate'. Look hard for a solution inside the generally accepted norms. Then, if you really can't find one, go ahead and rebel! At the very least, you will have a better understanding of the objections the rest of the world will come up with in response to your brilliant but disruptive ideas.

In group situations where groupthink has the potential to drive Bad Thinking, establish whether the group as a whole are being Devil's or Angels' Advocates and:

> Look for any individuals who might have an opposite view but who are being socially pressurised to stay with the group. Give that person a voice. An anonymous feedback format may work.

> If there is no one else in the group inclined to take the contrary view you have two options. Either be that person for a while to challenge groupthink. Or, if the team is large enough, split the team at random and have a short formal debate pitching the opposing perspectives.

> ***"It would be absurd if we did not understand both angels and devils, since we invented them."***
>
> *John Steinbeck - Author*

Part 2

The Cognitive Process

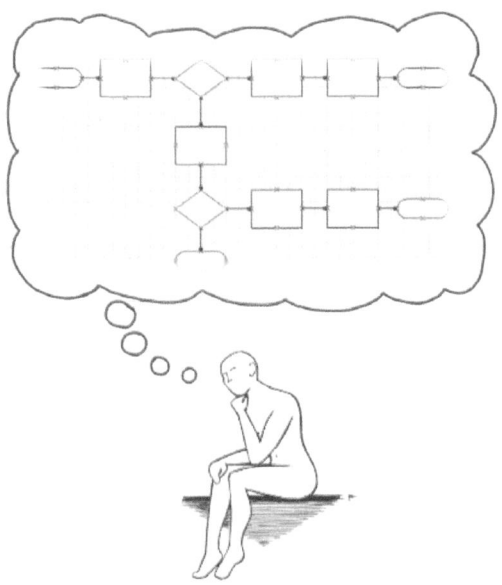

Part 2: The Cognitive Process

How smart we are, what quality of information we have access to, and the skills and experience we have all contribute to the quality of our thinking. This section of the book takes apart the first of these. We examine 'smart' by looking first at raw intelligence, then we consider our default thinking style, finally we get into creativity. We will look at two different types of creativity, one of which, adaption, is underrated and often overlooked.

Good Thinking is delivered by all three components of the cognitive process. No matter how smart you are, applying the wrong type of creative thinking for the problem at hand leads to Bad Thinking. Also, understanding your natural thinking style, and knowing how to exploit other styles, can produce better thinking. It is often faster and more effective than sticking to what you feel most comfortable with.

> *"By three methods we may learn wisdom:*
> *First by reflection, which is noblest;*
> *Second by imitation, which is easiest;*
> *Third by experience, which is bitterest."*
>
> *Confucious – Philosopher*

2.1 Intelligence

"Intelligence is something we are born with. Thinking is a skill that must be learned."

Edward de Bono – Psychologist

You guessed it; high intelligence is reliably correlated with high quality thinking and good decisions. Also, intelligence is largely determined by genetics and environment. Once you are adult there is not a lot you can do to increase it. Of course there are a few ways to reduce it but I'm going to assume that the readers of this book are unlikely to abuse recreational chemicals like alcohol to the extent that it permanently reduces their intellectual capability.

So, once we accept the premise that our intelligence is pretty much a constant, how can an understanding of intelligence help us to make good decisions? The obvious and most important answer is to ensure that other intelligent people are involved in the decision-making process. Two heads really are better than one. In later chapters we will look at thinking styles which ensure that a thinking team is balanced for maximum effectiveness. In this chapter we are looking at intelligence itself so that we can be knowledgeable about how we measure and think about the raw material of good thinking. We will look at IQ, EQ, and Risk Assessment. Then we will touch on technology augmented intelligence.

IQ – Be Smart About It

Intelligence Quotient (IQ), which was created by William Stern in 1912 as a base measure of intelligence, has been around for long enough to have been in and out of fashion a few times. IQ is essentially a measure of logical thinking. You will remember from the chapter on being rational and reasonable that logical ability alone does not produce Good Thinking.

IQ has at various times been described as simplistic, statistically flawed, and even racist. A fun point is that the evidence suggests that Northeast Asians and Jews both score higher than non-Jewish Europeans on IQ tests. This may be due to environmental influences. But if IQ is racist, at least is not white supremacist. However, the broad consensus is that it is statistically reliable.

It is possible to take a quick online approximate IQ test[28] and it is entertaining and useful (and perhaps even humbling) to know where you rank.

What can we do to take appropriate account of IQ in the thinking process?

Don't Ignore IQ, but don't give it too Much Attention

It is not necessary to measure the IQ of the thinkers in a team. It is very unlikely to be a selection tool used to choose team members. You will generally be selecting members on very different criteria, like stakeholder status. However, it is worth keeping in mind the idea that the level of logical reasoning ability varies between individuals. While there is no such thing as an average individual it is interesting to note that different professions typically have different IQ levels (see table). Note also that there is no evidence of a difference in IQ between the sexes. In terms of simple IQ, no matter how many times you will hear it said, women are just not any smarter than men! In any case, we should always assume that there is a variety of IQ levels in every team and we should always remember that a lower IQ may be accompanied by other valuable mental aptitudes, skills and abilities, which can be much more valuable than simple IQ in a particular thinking challenge.

Average IQ of various occupational groups: Kaufman 2009[29]

Accomplishment	IQ
Professional and technical	112
Managers and administrators	104
Clerical workers, sales workers, skilled workers, craftsmen, and foremen	101
Semi-skilled workers (operatives, service workers, including private households)	92
Unskilled workers	87

In the IQ Measure 100 = An average IQ, but the IQ points are not percentage points.

Approximately two-thirds of the population scores are between IQ 85 and IQ 115.

About 5 percent of the population scores above 125, and 5 percent below 75.

Part 2: The Cognitive Process

Let's look at the other types of intelligence which may be even more important that IQ, depending on the nature of the decision to be made.

People (with EQ) Matter

Emotional Quotient (EQ) is properly called Emotional Intelligence (EI) but the EQ term is more popular. EQ is defined as the measure of a person's ability to use emotional information to guide thinking and behaviour. For the *Star Trek* fans among us, if Spock is the IQ guy, then Dr 'Bones' McCoy is the EQ guy. Developed by Michael Beldoch in 1964, EI did not make its way into popular use until 1995 when it was the subject of a bestselling book.[30]

There are two parts to EQ; observing emotional information, and then using that emotional information to advise thinking. This links strongly to the chapter on Emotional Thinking. There are very few important decisions that don't involve people as sources of information, interested bystanders, as those directly affected by the outcome, or all of the above. It is a fairly reliable rule of thumb to say that, if fewer people are involved, then the outcome of a decision will be less significant, and the decision will be less complex, and vice versa.

It's relatively short life means EQ has not had quite as much negative criticism as IQ, but neither does it have quite the same statistical rigour behind it. The significance of EQ on the success of individuals as leaders or in becoming wealthy, for example, is still up for debate. It is very difficult or even impossible to extricate the impact of EQ from other factors, like IQ! However, the existence of EQ as a different and complementary aspect of intelligence to IQ is very widely accepted and is a valuable concept when working towards Good Thinking.

How do we ensure that EQ has an appropriate place in our thinking process? The following actions will help:

Close any EQ Gap. If you have concerns that the team don't have a useful insight into the thinking of the stakeholders involved in (or who are affected by) the decision, then expand the team to include this skill.

Identify Thinkers who have Better EQ. Identify, and make space for, the people who have high EQ in the team and ensure they are heard in the thinking process.

Carry out Basic Stakeholder Analysis. There are many techniques. A simple and effective one is the stakeholder map. This positions individuals and groups on a grid, comparing their support for a decision against the impact the decision will have on them. A useful enhancement is to add a visual code for relative influence. This usually becomes more relevant closer to the end of the decision process, but is worth doing periodically as the stakeholder map evolves as the thinking process unfolds.

Stakeholder Map
Example Outsourcing Project

A 2×2 matrix with axes "Support for Change" (Low to High, vertical) and "Impact of Change" (Low to High, horizontal):

- Top-left (High Support, Low Impact): ■ *Shareholders*; □ Senior Exec Team
- Top-right (High Support, High Impact): □ Project Manager; □ Outsourced Management
- Bottom-left (Low Support, Low Impact): ■ *Retained Staff*
- Bottom-right (Low Support, High Impact): ❖ Outsourced Staff; ■ *Redundant Staff*; □ Outsourced Executives

Key
- □ HIGH Influence
- ❖ MEDIUM Influence
- ■ *Low Influence*

The example Stakeholder Map for a project to outsource a company function shows that there can be differences in the level of support, impact and influence of groups, which will suggest how they may behave. Individuals can also be mapped. The best use of this type of map is to identify supporters and objectors and to consider how they might be moved to different parts of the map to change that behaviour. For example, the executives to be outsourced could be given incentives to move them into the support zone.

Judging Other People's Judgment

Brains evolve over a lifetime, so the quality of decisions will vary with the development stage. This is not just the obvious point that a young person with less experience has fewer resources at their disposal to support Good Thinking, although this is certainly true. There is also a substantial biological component. Young people really do think differently, from a biochemical viewpoint.

Neurons in the brain multiply and are then pruned back at different stages of human development. Myelination – the growth of myelin sheaths which enhance the communications between neurons – starts at birth and continues through to early adulthood. In that period there are two bursts of synaptic pruning, where the number of synaptic connections is reduced and the brain becomes more efficient, one in early childhood and one in adolescence. At 15 years of age basic thinking abilities more or less match an adult brain. Processing speed, which improves from age 5 to 15, levels off at mid-adolescence. Through late adolescence and into the early twenties improvements occur in other areas; selective attention, memory, and meta-cognition. Evidence of improved meta-cognition familiar to all parents include a more sophisticated sense of humour (nice) and a developing appreciation of sarcasm (real nice!) These biological changes are driven by variations in the levels of hormones like dopamine, glutamate and serotonin. These variations, by the way, can cause mood swings in adolescence ranging from the simply annoying to diagnosable but, thankfully, usually transient, mental illnesses.

This process has an important impact on decision making because every decision has an element of risk management. Adolescents can identify risks and rewards in the same way that adults do, but they typically place a higher value on reward over risk. One experiment that established this is called the BART test.[31] In the experiment, developed in the USA in 2002, adults and kids inflated a set number of balloons, receiving more money depending on how much the balloon was inflated before they stopped to take the cash. If the balloon burst they lost the money. Adolescents burst a lot more balloons than the grown-ups.

Other experiments show that adolescents' attitude to risk is similar to adults when the outcomes are clear but their risk tolerance increases when the outcomes are uncertain. They have a higher tolerance for ambiguity.[32]

This means that young people take more substantial risks, more often, than adults. This is a great reason to have them on any thinking team that needs to be creative and deal with ambiguity. It is also something to be aware of when there are differences of opinion across age groups in the thinking process. There is evidence that this risk-friendly behaviour is more common in young men than young women. Car insurance claims back this up pretty convincingly.

By the way, many evolutionary psychologists subscribe to the view that these differences in the behaviour of younger members of the social group helps to break family bonds and replace them with friendship bonds among their peers. This is useful for social cohesion across the group and encourages wider mixing of genes. Teenagers and sex. It is not exactly a new thing. It also may be very useful that young men, who were battling the young men of other tribes, have a high tolerance of risk. They make better warriors, win more resources and are more expendable than young women.

Personally Computing

A relatively new enhancement to humanity's thinking power, measured in decades rather than millennia, is computing power. You can have a supernatural memory by using a good note-taking application with a decent search function. You can have immediate access to the thinking and experience of millions of other people via the Internet. Commonly available software like spreadsheets provide even a basic user with powerful calculation and numerical analysis capabilities that were limited to a tiny minority of people just a couple of generations ago. The mental capability of one IT literate, connected person is extraordinary compared to even a few years ago.

This process of enhancement of human thinking capability will continue and intensify in the immediate future. For example, when artificial intelligence techniques like deep thinking are readily available in cheap computer programs, we will start thinking in different ways. Also, as interfaces to computing like voice and movement evolve we will access more information more often, and more efficiently. This will improve thinking effectiveness. Humanity really is getting better at thinking.

How do we ensure we are exploiting these enablers of intelligence and therefore of Good Thinking?

Individual Thinkers:

Every individual Thinker should have a sense of their IQ and EQ capabilities compared to average and their immediate peers.

We should be quick to seek help to augment and complement these capabilities if we have any doubts about our capabilities to address the thinking task in hand. Erring on the side of modesty is a good approach.

Anyone who does not already have IT skills, at a minimum should get into the habit of using a good notetaking software, learn to search the Internet effectively, and get familiar with the basics of using a spreadsheet. If you can already do those things, keep in touch with developments. There is always something new to use.

Thinking Teams:

A team needs the right balance of IQ and EQ, of risk takers and conservatives, and including at least one person who is technically literate is a good strategy.

Using technology to share data and for collaboration is very powerful, provided all of the team members are at an equivalent level of IT literacy. To be effective, the team must set its team level technology for information sharing and collaboration to the lowest common denominator. This maintains engagement. Of course, in parallel, individual team members can still continue to exploit their preferred technical thinking tools to their maximum ability.

> *"Too often we forget that genius, too, depends*
> *upon the data within its reach,*
> *that even Archimedes could not have devised*
> *Edison's inventions."*
>
> Ernest Dimnet – Author, The Art of Thinking

2.2 Thinking Style

*"All styles are good except
the tiresome kind."*

Voltaire – Author

If you have worked in a professional corporate environment you have probably been through the psychometric testing part of a team-building process. You have been informed of your preferred thinking style, your skills in relation to communication, etc. The first time this experience was probably engaging. On a third or fourth repeat, with a range of different tests, probably a bit of 'so what?' boredom had set in. Potentially there was even a little cynicism about the real scientific validity of these psychologically significant approaches.

Doing the Psycho Stuff

Scepticism about psychometric testing is partly justified. They are useful, but not as useful as they are made out to be. The vast majority of these tests are based on a set of well understood, and useful, standard psychological types defined by Karl Jung and his followers. However, the premise that a person's default thinking style is consistent across different circumstances is still contested by the experts. Fortunately however, the tests are usually enough to give us a good indicator of cognitive style, which can be used to inform and to guide Good Thinking both individually and in teams.

Which models of cognitive style and associated tests are better than the others is not a debate that I, nor any reasonably sane person, would want to get into. The most popular are probably the MBTI: Myers Briggs Type Indicator; the FFM: Five Factor Model; and the KTS: Keirsey Temperament Sorter (an MBTI offshoot). There are myriad alternatives and variations on these. If there is a test that you, and all of the people that you do your thinking with, will normally use, then that is exactly the one you should use. Most are adequate, and the switching costs of becoming familiar with a new test are high. Otherwise I would recommend the Myers Briggs Model because, in order of importance; there is a free online equivalent resource anyone can use,[33] it is (fairly) robust, it is widely known, it is easy to understand, and it is fairly well understood.

The Myers Briggs Type Indicator (MBTI)

The first time this author received feedback from a formal Myers Briggs Test with a trained assessor I was delighted at how well I had done and at how positive my thinking style was. I commented to the psychologist assessor that I had enjoyed the process. Their somewhat amused response that 'most people do' only became clear to me some time later. People like to talk about themselves, and people like to hear positive feedback about themselves. That is the secret of the success of the Myers Briggs Model.

A quick reference to the structure and meaning of the MBTI is set out in the table below. A Myers Briggs test result consists of four letters, each referring to a preferred behaviour in four cognitive function areas. We should note that the Thinking/Feeling measure is strongly associated with decision making.

Key	Cognitive Function	Style	In practice will prefer
I/E	Gaining Energy	I:Introverted	Inner world, ideas and concepts
		E:Extroverted	External world, people and experiences
S/N	Absorbing Information	S:Sensing	Information received via the senses
		N:Intuitive	Information gained from insights and patterns
T/F	**Making Decisions** *(The cognitive function we are focused on)*	**T:Thinking**	**Decision based on facts and principles**
		F:Feeling	**Decisions based on human perspectives**
J/P	World View	J:Judging	Structure and discipline
		P:Perceiving	Flexibility and adaptability

A Myers Briggs result can be any one of 16 combinations of four letters. These combinations have been given various user-friendly names to help with interpretation and retention. A diagram showing a list of commonly used MBTI names is given at the end of this chapter.

> **Criticism of the MBTI**
>
> *The MBTI comes in for quite a lot of criticism. For example, it is true that 50% of people will have a difference in their results, even in a second test taken just a few weeks apart.[34] The main issue with the MBTI is that it is made up of four polar indicators. Rather than position the test taker on a spectrum for Introvert to Extravert, it chooses one or the other. Obviously, if you are just into the I or the E by a small margin, a retake might put you on the other side of the line. This is a valid criticism. But it is only relevant of you think an MBTI score is absolute. The users need to understand that each of the four dimensions is a spectrum, and that taking the test at another time, in a different mood, may well produce a different result. The 'I' in MBTI means 'Indicator' for a reason. The merit of using four bi-polar measures is that it simplifies the test results so that they are easy to understand.*

The author is a fairly consistent ENTP (this combination is called the Inventor). So I typically gain energy from the people and world around me, I like to find patterns in the data I use, my decisions are based on facts and basic principles, and I enjoy a relaxed working style. My opposite type, an ISFJ (The Protector), will get their energy from within, will trust their senses as their information source, they will take the views and feelings of others into account when making decisions, and they will enjoy working in a structured environment where people respect discipline. We would find it difficult to work together. You will notice that both types are described in positive terms. This is the key advantage of the Myers Briggs Test and one of the reasons why it is so well accepted. The other 14 types, like these two, are also presented as contrasting set of positive styles. This balance encourages us to accept other people's styles as legitimate and useful. Obviously, most people think their cognitive style is positive and probably better than average. The more opposite another person's style is to yours, the more difficult it is to work with them effectively. It is also true that opposites will usually find it more worthwhile to work together than people who have the same default thinking type.

The MBTI has many more subtle nuances to it than I've mentioned so far. For example, each Cognitive Function is not measured as a split; someone who is an 'E' is not 90% E:Extravert vs 10% I:Intravert. It is possible to be an E who is 55% E and 45% I. This means that the person has good capabilities in both styles and will easily switch styles to respond to the context and the problem being addressed. By all means dig a little deeper if you are interested, but there is enough here to be able to exploit cognitive styles to enable Good Thinking.

The insidious and all too common temptation is for the Thinker(s) to spend far too much time navel gazing and focusing on how they think. There is a plethora of material online relating MBTI types to everything from *Game of Thrones* characters to American Presidents.[35] It is much better to tightly time-limit this task and get on to the job of actually doing the thinking.

It's The Way That You Think It

If you prefer to use a different measure of cognitive styles, you should check if it is based on the same fundamental Jungian types as the MBTI. If so, the rest of this chapter will be easy to relate to the alternative test. If not, the general principles will still apply.

In teams the MBTI has two uses. First, the process of measuring the cognitive types in a team gets a conversation started about achieving a team balance and what capabilities the team needs to focus on to be successful. Equally importantly, it teaches the members respect for each other's cognitive type and creates a common language to address cognitive style issues.

The MBTI is also useful when you are thinking on your own. Knowing your default style will make it easier to critique your thinking. Also, modelling an alternative style in each Cognitive Function is a good way to get new perspectives. For example, deliberately switching from a F:Feeling to a T:Thinking style will ensure that your decision is not overly influenced by emotion, while the opposite switch can check that people's potential reactions have been taken into account before a decision is finalised.

Finally, the execution stage of Good Thinking, the getting things done part, almost always involves persuading others of the merits of the decision you have arrived at. If you understand the cognitive style of the person or people to be persuaded, you can construct a case in a way that matches their preferences. For example: Delegating authority further down the hierarchy of an organisation can be explained to a J:Judging world view with an emphasis on the checks and balances which will be put into place. On the other hand, a P:Perceiving world view will appreciate an emphasis on how this will harness the imagination and energy of junior staff.

The sixteen MBTI types can be organised at a higher level into four 'Temperaments' (see the diagram below). This is done by choosing one Cognitive Function (or pair of Letters) as the primary perspective. This example used the third 'Making Decisions' function as the primary dimension. A popular variant when looking at learning styles is to use 'Absorbing Information' (the second Cognitive Function) as the primary dimension. This version is the basis of the 'Kiersly Temperaments'.

This summary view can be useful when looking at large groups to identify potential cliques, and to highlight which styles are common to different groups. For example, the Human Resources Department will often have quite a few Facilitator Types (FJ), while the IT Departments will be well endowed with Builder Types (TP).

For smaller groups (10 people or fewer), using the sixteen Role Variant names is a more useful way to discuss cognitive styles across the team. Note that the further up the tree that two people need to go to meet up, the wider the difference in their default thinking style. The Generals (ENTJ) are a long way from the Artists (ISFP).

Part 2: The Cognitive Process

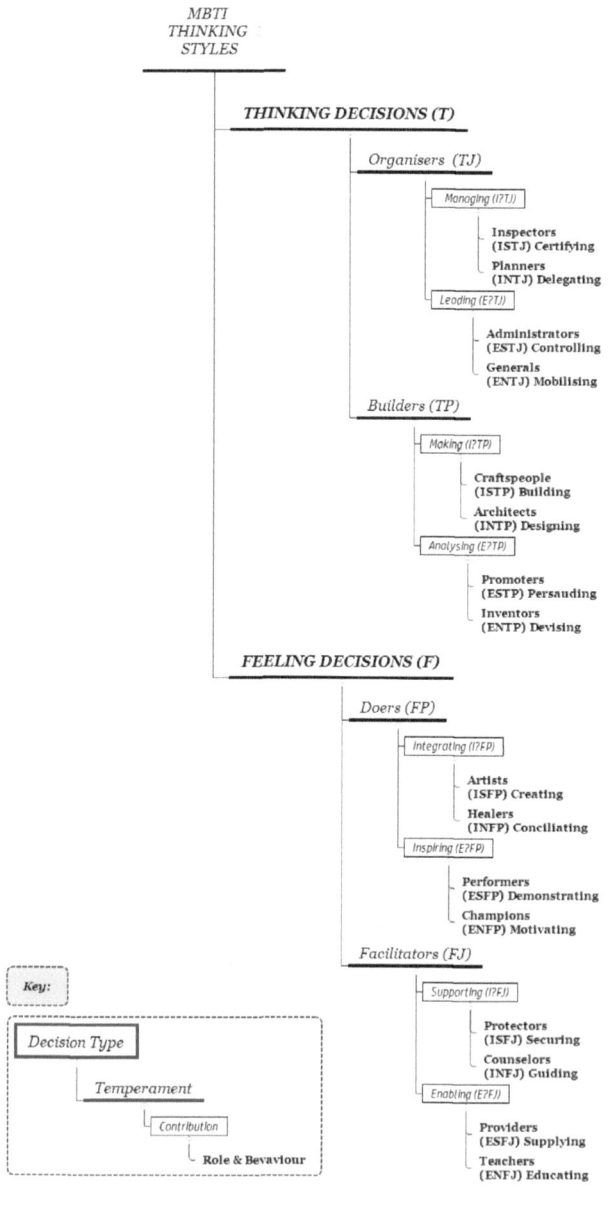

As an individual Thinker, it is well worth while learning your own default thinking style. It is also useful to consider which style you can expect from others you engage with.

> ***"To be a real philosopher all that is necessary is to hate someone else's type of thinking."***
>
> *William James – Philosopher*

2.3 Creativity

> *"A key ingredient in innovation is the ability to challenge authority and break rules."*
>
> *Vivek Wadhwa – Businessman*

It is a classic example of the Substitution Paradigm that the question 'Is that person smart and creative?' is often substituted with the question 'Is that person innovative?' Innovation is a highly available word with very positive associations. Innovation gets good press. Everybody wants to be innovative and come up with the kind of 'out of the box' and 'disruptive' ideas which will change the world and make millions, or even billions, of dollars. In contrast, the alternative creative thinking mode (called Adaption), if it is recognised at all, is seen as dull and uninspiring. It is sometimes described as the contrast between Making Better Things and merely Making Things Better. But this bias against Adaption is both unfair and short-sighted.

The distinction between the innovative and adaptive creative styles was defined by the British Psychologist Dr M.J. Kirton, who developed A-I Theory and the KIA (Kirton Innovation Adaptation) Inventory in the late 1970s.[36] The key achievement in Dr Kirton's approach was the separation of preferred creative style both from intellectual capability and from default thinking style.

> **How the KIA Inventory Works**
>
> *The KIA Inventory is a 32-item questionnaire which measures creative problem-solving style on a scale of 32 to 160. The distribution is a normal bell curve. An Adaptive problem solver will score between 60 and 90. An Innovator will score between 110 and 140. Between 90 and 110 the problem solver is seen as capable of both approaches.*
>
> *It is interesting to see that the Innovators have the higher scores and are on the right-hand side of the scale. This has an Intensity Matching effect which, ironically, will make most of us see Innovators as more valuable that Adapters. (See the section on Heuristic Paradigms.)*

From Heretic to Hero

The term 'innovator' was not always so popular. In the Middle Ages the word was synonymous with the term 'heretic'. Being an Innovator could get you jailed, tortured, or even burnt at the stake. In the creativity of the Industrial Revolution it gained in popularity along with its more popular cousin, the word 'Inventor'. In 1939, a definition offered by Austrian economist Joseph Schumpeter dramatically improved its status. He defined invention as an act of intellectual creativity undertaken without any thought given to its possible economic import, while innovation happens when firms figure out how to craft inventions into constructive changes in their business model. Thus, innovation is 'applied inventive thinking'. The use of the word 'innovation' overtook the words 'inventor' and 'creativity' in the '50s, passed 'invention' in the late '60s and has not looked back since. It continues to climb while creativity has levelled off. See graph below (courtesy of Google Ngram).

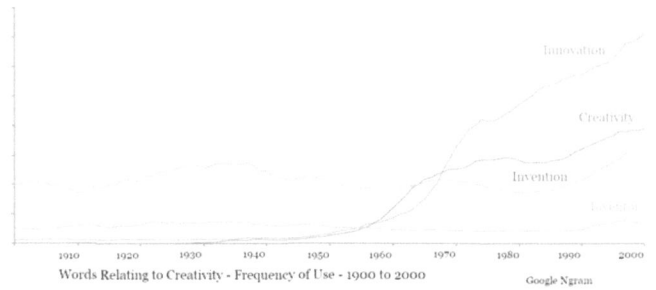

Words Relating to Creativity - Frequency of Use - 1900 to 2000

However, as Kirton pointed out, there is more to applied creative thinking than innovation.

Adapting to Succeed

The difference between Innovation and Adaption is the difference between two types of creative problem solving. According to Dr Kirton, Innovators solve problems by ignoring the rules and norms and taking a novel perspective on the issue to be addressed. Adapters, on the other hand, will take account of the complexities of the environment and come up with a solution that works through and around the existing rules. Sometimes the context or environment is very difficult to change, and sometimes that environment can be a very valuable creation in its own right. In these circumstances, a 'break-the-rules' innovative solution can cause more problems than it solves. This is where Adapters are the type of creatives that you need to deploy.

It is safe to say that the majority of creative activity in the world is Adaption. It is also worth saying that you are always better off with a very smart Adapter than with a not so bright Innovator.

The problem context and the mix of KIA types in a group of Thinkers will both affect creative style. The team members who are relatively outliers on the Innovator or Adapter ends of the spectrum will be perceived as extreme Innovators and Adapters and will naturally behave in that way. People who score in the middle can use both creative modes and can bridge between the two styles in the problem-solving process. By understanding the mix we can anticipate the team's creative style in response to the problem.

In the same way as knowing the Thinker(s) default thinking style, it can be a useful investment to carry out formal KIA Inventories on the members of a team, especially if they will work together for a substantial period and/or on a particularly difficult problem. The KAI testing process and the exposure of different creative styles afterwards are very useful ways to make people aware of other styles and to ensure those with different styles respect each other's contributions. (Full online tests are available from kaicenter.com.)

Catz and Dogs

For shorter projects with less complex decisions it is still very useful to use the concept, and a rough self-assessment to get an understanding of, and respect for, different styles of creativity.

The Dogs and Catz framework below (developed by the author) is an unscientific, tongue in cheek way to get the idea across and to get a discussion started.

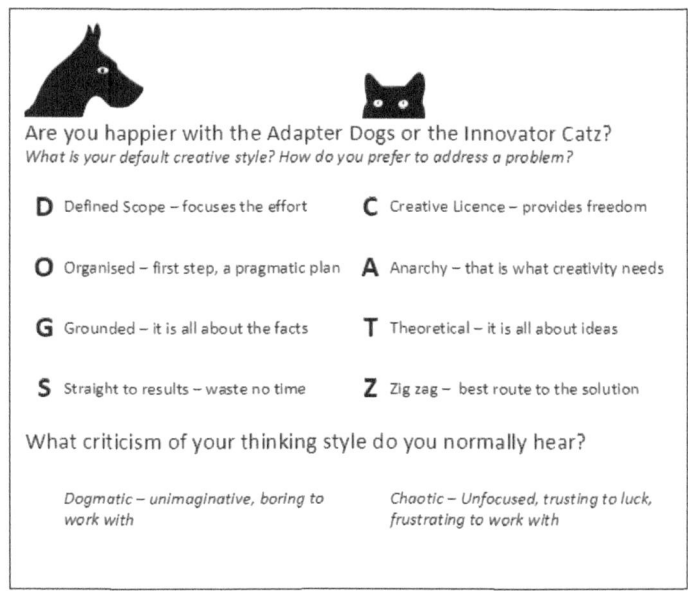

(There is an explanation on how to use the Dogs and Catz tool in the Appendix.)

The author's KIA Inventory score puts him firmly on the Innovator end of the continuum. So I'm with the Catz. However, experience has taught me the value of behaving like an Adapter when it is appropriate, and of supporting the Adapters in the team when the circumstances are right.

From the Innovator – Adapter Theory we can see that a mix of creative styles is valuable in general problem solving. When problems seem intractable, a burst of Innovator thinking can break out of assumptions and norms that might be unimportant but stifling. On the other hand, when negotiating in a complex environment you may not have the time, or any good reason, to disrupt it. That is when getting a bit of ingenious Adapter thinking going to find the best path through is the right response. When working alone or in very small teams the trick is to switch your own thinking mode deliberately.

To switch modes successfully the Thinker(s) requires first you need to recognise their default creative mode. Using the default mode is generally pretty easy, just relax and address the decision as you normally would. To get away from your default mode, the best way is to work with someone who is naturally on the opposite end of the KAI spectrum and deliberately encourage them to take the lead. If you don't have easy access to an opposite style thinker, there are some techniques below to help you to shift your style. If you are a mid-continuum neutral style you can use the techniques below to switch to either end as required.

Moving into Adapter Mode

Apply project management techniques to help focus: Define the scope of the issue and agree the characteristics of a successful outcome, identify and gather relevant data, establish time constraints, write down a plan… and follow it.

Have regular 'bullet-proofing' sessions where the latest solution is tested to destruction, ideally in a group. This will bring out the pragmatism. These are the opposite of the more familiar 'brainstorming' sessions. (See details in the Appendices.)

Moving into Innovator Mode

Remove the constraints on ideas. Try asking how we would solve this if money was no problem, if time were not an issue, if no one could object, if we started from a blank sheet of paper.

Real 'brainstorming' sessions are very effective. That is, brainstorming sessions where the only response allowed to any idea presented is a build like: 'It would be even better if…' (See details in the Appendices.)

Despite their differences, both Innovators and Adapters will naturally cycle through divergent and convergent phases at the same points in their thinking process. It is just that Innovators are in their comfort zone in the divergent phase and Adapters excel when they are converging. There is more detailed information on this in the section on Managing Options in the Appendix, where brainstorming and bullet-proofing are also discussed in more detail.

"Intelligence is the ability to adapt to change."

Steven Hawking – Scientist

Part 3

Thinking about Decisions

When I decided to write this book it was the culmination of a great deal of research and thinking about the subject of Cognitive Science, a little on Game Theory and Decision Theory, and a lot of thinking about how to improve my own thinking day to day. On reflection, it was the decision to write this book that really mattered. Without a decision, all of that other contemplative thinking has little impact. Whether a decision is a conclusion after a long cogitation, or a plan of action chosen from a set of alternatives, it is the decision that makes the thinking real and means that it might have a real impact (however large or small) on other people and on the world.

Deciding to Daydream

As we noted in the Introduction, much good and valuable thinking is done away from decision points. Albert Einstein famously came to many of his greatest breakthrough concepts in Physics while daydreaming. He is not alone in this. Mendeleev's Periodic Table and August Kekulé's Benzene Rings also provide evidence of unconscious processes and playful musing delivering breakthrough ideas. Musing, speculating and dreaming do not lend themselves to conscious analysis of the processes that drive them. In fact there is a substantial risk that the quality of such open-ended creative thinking would be substantially impaired by making the Thinker conscious of the process. This type of thinking is not yet well understood by science so this book will not suggest ways to improve or interfere with this most human, and almost magical, thinking ability. Most of our thinking is a little more pedestrian and commonplace than these rare flashes of genius and insight, but it is this commonplace thinking that gets stuff done.

We are also fortunate that the science of thinking is better developed from that point where we start to translate the spark of an idea into a set of outcomes. We do this through the decision process.

Decisions and Decision Making is a whole field of study in its own right and we can only take a quick glance at that wider subject here. We are simply exploiting a little of the good science work done on decision making in order to focus our investigation of thinking on its practical outcomes. This section chooses a decision process model to use (one of many available), it looks at how we can decide which decisions are worth our thinking efforts, and it talks a little about some valuable, easy to use decision tools.

> *"Nothing is more difficult, and therefore more precious, that being able to decide."*
>
> *Napoleon Bonaparte – Emperor*

3.1 Thinking Quality

> *"If anyone on the verge of action should judge himself according to the outcome, he would never begin."*
>
> *Soren Kierkegaard – Philosopher*

Applied thinking is all about consequences. It is the study of the questions asked, the decisions made, the actions driven by those decisions, and the outcomes created by these actions. We need to understand how we can best measure the quality of applied thinking.

The end often justifies the means. This is certainly true when it comes to Good Thinking. Thinking has various modes; from musing over an interesting conundrum where the outcomes of your Good or Bad Thinking is inconsequential, to making a snap decision that might mean life or death. Underpinning the approach and the structure of this book is the principle that all thinking worthy of our attention and effort leads to decisions. Thinking that reaches no conclusions may be fun, or it may not be, but it is neither good nor bad because it has no real consequences.

There will be Consequences

Questions are very important. Good questions are an essential input to the thinking process to ensure good answers. Asking the right questions well defines the issues and therefore dramatically improves the chances of Good Thinking. However, measuring the inputs to any process will not tell you much about the quality of the outputs. Therefore, measuring the quality of questions that start the process is not the best way to measure Good Thinking. But we will come back to questions later in this chapter.

In terms of thinking, actions are essentially a type of decision. Actions taken are choices between alternatives. Therefore, the choice of action is a decision, hopefully a good decision, arrived at by Good Thinking.

Sometimes we are deciding not to decide. Thinking that does not obviously deliver a conscious and concrete decision usually delivers a default decision to delay; to come back to the question later when there is either more time available, more data available, or both. This delay may well be the best decision available at that time. But it is certainly a decision.

Logically, the best measure of thinking quality must be the outcomes it delivers. Ultimately, it is the final consequences that matter. But there are challenges with using outcomes as the measure. It is a truism that the ultimate measure of a decision's quality is the effects that it has. However, these impacts may be far into the future, or the outcome may be affected by other parties or other factors. Also, it may be that a decision which was perfectly good at the time it was made unintentionally contributes to bad outcomes due to other factors that could not have been anticipated at the time the thinking was done. If a good decision can sometimes deliver poor outcomes, despite being based on Good Thinking, and outcomes are not usually available as a measure when thinking quality needs to be tested, we need a way to measure Good Thinking that does not rely on outcomes.

This leaves us with the quality of decisions when they are made as the best measure of Good Thinking, and Bad.

A Quality Decision

Decision quality is a short-term indicator that acts as a measure of Good Thinking and predicts good outcomes. So how is it possible to measure the quality of a decision at the point when it is made? First, it is necessary to examine it without using outcomes as the criteria. This measurement can be done by proxy. Assessing the quality of the thinking activities that support the decision provides a very good indicator of the quality of the decision, and therefore of the outcomes that can be expected. This slightly circular perspective means that, if Good Thinking delivers good decisions, then the way to measure good decisions is to measure the quality of thinking that contributed to them. The good news is that this assessment of the thinking activities is itself a contributor to Good Thinking, creating a positive feedback loop.

For these reasons, you will find that that the terms 'decision' and 'thinking' are used more or less interchangeably in this book about applied thinking. In the chapter on the Decision Process you will notice that the 'DECIDE' Model is also used to describe the thinking process, and used throughout the book as a framework for Good Thinking.

So we are saying that the process of testing decision quality is the same process as testing for Good Thinking. It involves mapping the thinking being done to the stages of the decision process and testing at each point for positive and negative influences of the Thinking Paradigms, which are described in detail later.

But let's not forget about the inputs, the importance of questions.

Great Question

Clear questions are key to clear decisions. Decisions are often best understood and communicated as answers to questions. Indeed, the process of formulating the right question is an important element of Good Thinking.

A famous example of asking the wrong question is the Lydian king Croesus asking the Oracle of Delphi if he should cross the River Halys to attack the Persian king Cyrus. In reply, the Oracle said that a great empire will fall if Croesus would cross the River Halys. Unfortunately, Croesus did not ask the supplementary question, "Which empire would fall?" and assumed that it was Cyrus' Persian Empire. Instead, he lost the war and his Lydian Kingdom, and, ultimately, the Greek Empire that it was a part of was the empire to fall.

This very old example is simply a process question with implied outcomes which should have been replaced with a very precise outcomes question. "Will I defeat Cyrus if I cross the river and attack him?" This would have made for a very much less interesting story but it would have been a question based on better thinking.

Other common problems with formulating the right questions are described using the Thinking Paradigms that are set out in detail in the later chapters. In particular, the Confidence Paradigm and the Substitution Paradigm tend to influence us when we come up with the wrong questions.

Testing Questions

The best way to challenge the quality of the question that you are setting out to address is to reframe it from the perspective of different parties who have an interest in the outcomes. Had Croesus considered the question from Cyrus's perspective, he might well have come up with the more useful phrasing, "What will be the outcome of an attack by Croesus from across the river Halys?" The Stakeholder Map tool described in the chapter on Intelligence is a very useful tool to establish different perspectives on a question.

> ***"The riddle does not exist. If a question can be put at all, then it can also be answered."***
>
> *Ludwig Wittgenstien – Philosopher*

3.2 The Decision Process

*"The most difficult thing is the decision to act.
The rest is mere tenacity."*

Amelia Earhart – Aviator

So, I had an important decision to make early in the process of writing this book. I had to choose which model of the decision process to use. Which of the many models out there would be the very best foundation for Good Thinking? Which would also act as an effective framework for testing thinking to identify and avoid Bad Thinking? And of course, I didn't yet have that process tool in place to help me to make that vital decision. You will probably have guessed, as you are reading this, that I managed to get around this fiendish 'Catch 22'. How did I do that? I just made a decision. I'm labouring the point here, but none of us need a decision process model to make the many choices that we must and do make every day. They are only useful when we are getting 'meta' with our cognition, when we are thinking about our thinking.

Decisions come in many forms and sizes. When we start considering alternatives, choosing hypotheses to test, and actions to take, this is when our thinking starts to have impact on ourselves and others. It is at decision points where Good Thinking becomes essential and it has the most beneficial impact on outcomes. It follows that we should focus on better outcomes from thinking by concentrating on how to deploy Good Thinking at the key points in the decision process. By the way, the important question of deciding which decisions to focus on is the subject of a separate chapter on Triage Thinking.

There are many models of the decision process which have been developed over the years by decision theorists. These serve different purposes for scientists studying decisions and the people making them. I finally chose the DECIDE Model as the basis for a framework suited to the application of Thinking Paradigms to improve thinking quality. This is not simply because it has an excellent acronym, although that is certainly a useful characteristic. (It exploits the Availability Paradigm to make the model more memorable, and hence more useful and compelling.) It also has the merit of being quite simple and practical to use. It does not rely on any complex scientific language or esoteric meta-cognition concepts to understand it.

The DECIDE Model was designed in 2008 by K L Guo at the University of Hawaii-West Oahu to improve medical practitioners' decision making.[37] It is used to make medical practitioners aware of the steps in their treatment decisions with a view to making those decisions better, i.e. to deliver Good Thinking in life and death situations. I have taken the liberty of developing and adapting the DECIDE model to broaden its application to decisions relating to activities relating to solution creation, as well as the 'diagnose, act, review' context that inspired its creation. However, I would certainly not be crazy enough to try to change its excellent name.

DECIDE is the acronym of six activities in the decision-making process:

D = Define the problem, or Design the Desired outcomes;

E = Establish the criteria to measure a successful outcome;

C = Create alternative routes to the outcome;

I = Identify the best alternative;

D = Develop a plan of action and Do it;

E = Evaluate and monitor the solution and feedback on the outcomes.

A Visual Representation of DECIDE

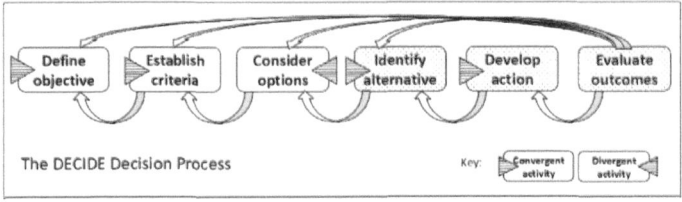

Like every useful model, DECIDE is a simple approximation of an immensely sophisticated reality. (See the chapter on Models, Maps & Metaphors for more on this.) It works well in the context of challenging one's thinking throughout the decision process. Of course, if the reader has an alternative model of the decision process that they find more useful for any reason, they can easily map the DECIDE model to it and the rest of this book will work just as well.

In reality, these decision activities are not discrete, and they are certainly not a simple sequence as suggested in the diagram. The human brain is far more capable than this. The activities will happen in various orders, in parallel, and even all in unison. The decision process is also iterative. At any point a switch backwards or forwards to another activity may improve the outcomes. However, this model is a useful device to clarify the complex process to the extent that we can map the various Thinking Paradigms to the process in a way that enables us to observe and challenge our thinking process and so to improve it. These maps are shown in detail in the chapter of Thinking Paradigm Quick Reference summaries. Simple maps are also used in relation to each Thinking Paradigm so that we can quickly see to which points in the decision process the paradigm is most relevant.

Another advantage of the clear visibility of the decision process which the DECIDE Model provides is that it can be used to highlight procrastination and short-cutting. Where any of the activities are being omitted, or given only cursory attention, there is a good chance that the decision process is not being effective or may even be stalled. Deliberately stepping through each activity and confirming that it has been completed at least once to a reasonable standard will identify the location of the blockage in a stalled decision. This is particularly useful when constant reiterations of some decision activities are creating noise, which in turn hides the fact that other activities have been omitted.

We need to focus a little more on each of the activities in the model to ensure that its purpose is clear. At the highest level the DECIDE activities can be grouped into the first three 'design activities' followed by three 'execution activities'. Note also that some of the activities are divergent, in that they create a variety of ideas or options. Others are convergent in that they reduce variety.

Looking at the six activities in turn:

THE DESIGN ACTIVITIES

D = Define the problem, or Design the Desired outcomes

A constructive and convergent activity.

This activity is very important, as a poorly defined problem will rarely be satisfactorily resolved unless we return to it in iterations which refine the problem definition. Focusing on the design of the desired outcomes is often more effective than focusing on precise problem definitions. If the definition seems very difficult it is best to continue through the other steps. Addressing the other steps will always enable an evolution of the problem definition. A loop between the first two activities of defining the problem and establishing the success criteria is an excellent way to get Good Thinking started.

E = Establish the criteria to measure a successful outcome

A constructive and convergent activity.

Time spent in defining how success can best be measured is always well spent. Not only does agreeing which measures will be reliable measures of success result in a better definition of the desired outcome, it will also make the execution activities more focused.

C = Create alternative routes to the outcome

A constructive and divergent activity.

The essential point here is considering *all* of the alternative routes to the desired outcomes. This particular activity is where both adaptive and innovative creativity can be equally important. (See the chapter on Creativity.) Creating the maximum number of feasible possible routes to the desired outcomes increases the choices in the following Identify activity.

Note that there is an exception to the broad rule that more alternatives lead to better decisions. This is generally where time is of the essence and is discussed in detail in the chapter on the Intuition Paradigm.

THE EXECUTION ACTIVITIES

I = Identify the best alternative

A reductive and convergent activity.

This is the key Execution Activity. This convergent activity is obviously where many sub-decisions are made. These sub-decisions might be simple or they might be important and/or complex enough to require their own DECIDE analysis. The process can be 'nested' as many times as is required, but any more than three levels of nesting will probably be more confusing than it is helpful. If it gets this complex it is a good idea to focus in on a lower level question until it is answered. Then the Thinker(s) can move up to the larger question based on a more solid foundation.

The evaluation measures decided in the second DECIDE activity are a very useful tool in this activity to test the relative merits of alternative routes.

D = Develop a plan of action and Do it

This is an Execution Activity which has a convergent outcome but, like the previous activity, it can become a full set of DECIDE activities in its own right. For a complex route to more substantial outcomes, the planning of the actions can involve a lot of decisions in itself. Again, the same rules of Good Thinking will apply in any 'nested' decision process.

E = Evaluate the solution and feedback on the outcomes

Somewhat surprisingly, this is the forgotten activity in many important decisions. Measuring whether the decision process is delivering (or has delivered) the outcomes defined at the start of the decision process can often suggest better decisions in the future. More importantly it can support a decision to abandon a solution and go back to the drawing board to get an outcome that actually works.

The DECIDE Model is equally useful as a personal tool to focus the Thinker(s) on completing the full decision process, and as a framework to bring a team of Thinkers through a decision with unity on what thinking activities need to be done and how to do it.

Part 3: Thinking about Decisions

In both cases, it really comes into its own when the quality of thinking in each activity is challenged and improved by applying knowledge of the Thinking Paradigms which most impact each activity. As I mentioned, the later chapters on the individual Thinking Paradigms in this book are mapped back to the DECIDE process to facilitate this process of challenging thinking.

> *"It takes vision and courage to create.*
> *It takes faith and courage to prove."*
>
> *Owen D Wilson – Diplomat and Businessman.*

3.3 Triage Thinking

"Action expresses Priorities."

Mahatma Gandhi – Politician

Florence Nightingale was one tough lady. Not only because she was a woman who worked very effectively in the man's world of the second half of the 1800s, although this is certainly true. One of her greatest achievement, alongside improvements to hygiene in the dreadful hospitals serving the Crimea War wounded, was the systematic application of Medical Triage.

The term 'triage' probably came from the Napoleonic Wars from the work of Dominique Jean Larrey. The word has a French origin, 'trier' meaning to sort or to sift. The method had a long history even before it had a name, but defining and formalising it made it more useful and it quickly became a standard response to critical medical resource shortages, which continues in use today.

In a war zone, triage means sorting patients into four categories of need:

0. No Need: Those who are likely to die, regardless of what care they receive.

I. Severe: Those for whom immediate care might make a positive difference in outcome.

II. Moderate: Medical care is required but not immediately.

III. Minimal: Those who are likely to live, regardless of what care they receive.

In this way scarce resources could be deployed, first to Category I, then continuing in sequence to get the best outcomes. The first triage category is also called 'Expectant' or 'Presumed Deceased' in various classifications. These less clear terms show that even military process designers are uncomfortable with giving up.

Before Florence got involved, the wounded were usually sorted by class and rank with lightly wounded and incurable NCOs and officers being treated before injured enlisted men who might be saved. Florence made sure that the expected outcome for the patient, regardless of rank, was put first. This was done despite initial resistance from the doctors, who were all upper or middle class (and always male). The results of this change meant that more lives were saved. It also meant more injured soldiers made it back onto the battlefield to fight again, very important to the generals. The latter benefit helped her win her case for using triage. She was a tough one, the Lady with the Lamp.

This triage approach is now used in all medical emergencies where resources are constrained. The approach has also spread to many other situations where resources are inadequate to address all of the demands on them. It is interesting to note that, despite its wide adoption and the proven value of the approach, it is often criticised as being brutal and simplistic. Looking closely at these objections they are generally driven by doubts of the ability of the people making the triage decisions to judge the true potential of the triage subjects. The quality of judgement is obviously key to effective triage. We will look at some tests of this later in the chapter.

Not Just Life and Death

The limited resource challenge is also a feature of problem solving and decision making. Hopefully we will not very often be making decisions that are literally a matter of life and death. However, as a problem solver – as an individual or as a part of a team – it is important to be selective about where limited time, energy and other resources are invested to get the best returns. In a final high school year the days spent deciding what to wear to the senior prom dance might be better spent on deciding which college course to target.

In applying Good Thinking to solve problems, the triage categories for problems to be addressed are:

0. Unsolvable: Problems which are unsolvable, regardless of the importance of the outcome.

I. Urgent: Time critical problems where investing in finding a solution will have positive outcomes.

II. Important: Problems which can be delayed, but solving them is worthwhile.

III. Irrelevant: Problems where the impacts are not significant, whether they are solved or ignored.

The most important action in the triage process is establishing and agreeing the Category Zero issues. These will often linger because they appear to have urgency and, were they to be solvable, high value outcomes. Understanding the value of the triage approach, and recognising the natural reluctance we all have to abandon investment in lost causes, will help with those difficult decisions. See also the chapter on the Ownership Paradigm, which includes a section on 'sunk cost analysis'.

Unsolvable vs Hard

Classifying a problem as Category Zero: Unsolvable, is an important decision. Once done, the issue will immediately be removed from the list of problems to be addressed, but it will usually remain as a context for other, related problems. It is very important that the judgement of a problem as unsolvable is credible and defensible. It must not be an answer to the alternative question: 'Is this a very difficult problem to which I see no solution at the present?' See also the chapter on the Substitution Paradigm.

Some useful questions to challenge and test the Category Zero classification are:

- ⬥ Has this problem (or a very similar one) been solved by anyone else? If so, can you exploit that solution?

- ⬥ Has this problem had any initial effort invested to test for possible solutions? If not, is a time boxed brainstorming session a good investment?

- ⬥ Is this problem outside of the experience and skills of the problem solver(s) who are deployed? If so, would involving an appropriate expert resource make the problem solvable?

✧ Would the solution to this problem be a breakthrough, i.e. a solution which would remove or solve many related problems? Again, consider a limited and focused investment of energy using the techniques in the Tools section at the end of this book.

These questions can also be used to challenge any inclination to keep an unsolvable problem on the table by describing it as a Category I or II.

Wicked Problems

This is a good place to mention what are formally called 'Wicked Problems'. Defined by Rittel & Weber in 1973,[38] a Wicked Problem is a problem that is difficult or impossible to solve because of incomplete, contradictory, and/or changing requirements that are often difficult to define. Because of complex interdependencies, the effort to solve one aspect of a Wicked Problem may simply reveal or create other problems. In other words, the first two activities in the DECIDE process, designing the outcomes and establishing the success criteria, become a never-ending loop. (c.f. the chapter on The Decision Process.) Therefore, Wicked Problems will often be triaged as being category 'Zero: Unsolvable'. This might make sense if your resources are limited or the benefits of solving it are not worth the costs. However, sometimes we have no choice but to address a

Wicked Problem. If that is the case, it is very important to choose the right approach. The options are set out in the following table.

Approaches to Wicked Problems	Pros	Cons	Use only when…
Authoritative: Give responsibility and authority to a few.	Cuts through confusion and complexity	Will not address all stakeholders' needs. Can create resentment.	Time is of the essence. and/or the possible solutions are closely matched for benefits.
Competitive: Set up opposing teams, a deadline, and a decision board.	Gets to a solution by exposing contradictions and comparing benefits	Can create long-term divisions and encourages all sides to suppress any data that they disagree with.	Maximising benefits are important to all sides. Evaluating outcomes is easy.
Collaborative: Engage all stakeholders in one team.	All views are aired. Solutions and outcomes are agreed.	Resource intensive and slow.	Time is not critical. Agreement is more important than other outcomes.

From work by Nancy Roberts 2000[39]

Whichever of the three approaches is being used, it is good practice to have a regular review to decide if the problem is (or has become) unsolvable. Or has become irrelevant.

Using hybrid approaches to Wicked Problems is a bad idea as the parties involved will generally assume that only the approach that suits their agenda is being used, and therefore the thinking will be dysfunctional.

Relative Values

A first cut triage of problems as described above may be enough to support resourcing decisions, or it may be all that time allows. However, there are often more Category I and II issues than can be resourced. Assuming that we have enough time, judging the relative urgency and value of solving different problems then becomes important. As an aid to the comparative judging process we can use a two-dimensional classification matrix comparing the value of the outcome with the urgency of the issue. This two-by-two matrix is very helpful in the process of making relative comparisons of the problems competing for attention and resources on the dimensions of value, urgency, and complexity.

The relative complexity of each problem can also be indicated by using different icons. However, the relative value and urgency take precedence in the categorisation. Resist the temptation to make the matrix a three-by-three grid with low-medium-high. The mediums become 'maybe zones' whereas the essential value of Triage Thinking is to force a yes/no decision and to drive action.

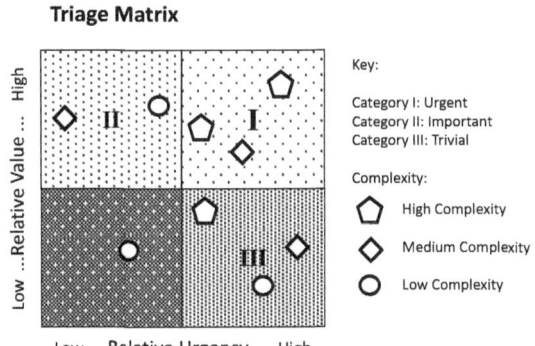

Placing all of the problems to be addressed on to the matrix so that there is a relatively even spread in the vertical and horizontal dimensions forces a distribution. The process of positioning the problems on the matrix, especially in a group discussion, will make a substantial contribution to the understanding of the problems and give confidence in the choice of priorities made.

There are other decision-making tools that can be used with this problem triage tool, or on their own. Some simple and useful examples of these are described in the Appendix. But, now that we have the tools to choose which problems we need to address, we can move on to look at the Thinking Paradigms that we will use when thinking about these problem decisions.

> *"...during the task execution more knowledge is acquired which leads to changes in resource allocations, schedules, and priorities."*
>
> Jay R. Galbraith – Professor

Part 4

A Taxonomy of Thinking Paradigms

Part 4: A Taxonomy of Thinking Paradigms

This section of the book is dedicated to Carolus Linnaeus. Born in Sweden in 1707 he gave the world the idea of taxonomy as a scientific tool. Linnaeus, starting with his first book of a mere 14 pages in 1735, pretty much organised all of life on Earth in a way that still drives scientific debate today. He was arrogant enough to suggest that his tombstone should say 'The King of Botanists' but he was a brilliant analyst and classifier of all living things. He was the first person, for example, to group whales with cows as quadruped mammals. That was almost 300 years ago. He is the exemplar for the influence of a good taxonomy on Good Thinking.

Why Thinking *Paradigms* and Why do we Need a Taxonomy?

Creating a taxonomy is one example of the Models, Maps, and Metaphors Paradigm in the Heuristic Class of Thinking Paradigms. Creating a map is about applying a structure to unstructured or complex information so that it can be better understood and more easily referred to in the thinking process. Using the Mapping Paradigm to create a structure that then helps us to understand the place of Mapping in the landscape of thinking is certainly circular, but it is very useful.

The patterns of thinking that we are examining have often been called 'thinking fallacies' by current cognitive scientists and writers on the subject. As we have already declared in the Introduction to this book, this negative framing is both unhelpful and misleading. Any Thinking Paradigm that has appeared and survived in common use by humans has proven its value by evolutionary selection. We can be sure that it will have value to add in our thinking processes. The fact that it may also deliver some disadvantages is important to know, but the logic of evolution tells us that the benefits delivered by each Thinking Paradigm will outweigh the downsides.

Paradigms Define and Celebrate the Edges

We are describing the different ways of thinking in this book as 'Thinking Paradigms'. A paradigm is defined as 'a typical example of something' or 'a model which confirms the correlation between things'. The identification and classification of Thinking Paradigms creates a little order in the complex, overlapping collection of ideas, concepts and models that add up to the many ways that we think.

The word paradigm is also used by Thomas Kuhn in this seminal book *The Structure of Scientific Revolutions*.[40] Kuhn's 'Scientific Paradigms' term describes the grouping together of all of the thinking that stems from, and supports, a particular scientific perspective. Kuhn's key point in his book is that creativity and scientific breakthroughs occur when different paradigms collide and a 'paradigm shift' creates a new scientific perspective. When we refer to 'Thinking Paradigms' we are using the phrase in the simpler 'typical example' sense. However, it is useful to think that when Thinking Paradigms collide, it will often lead to new insights in just the way that Kuhn described.

Part 4: A Taxonomy of Thinking Paradigms

Taxonomies Deliver Insights

In the Introduction I said that the book is based on the idea of classifying Thinking Paradigms into a taxonomy to help us to understand and use them better. Following the example of Linnaeus, this is a long-established and honourable scientific method. Most science started out first as collections: of plants, of animals, of anything that we found interesting. When a collection is big enough it is possible to identify sub-groups in the general mass. The process of explaining why these sub-groups are logical, and why they exist, drives us to create scientific hypotheses. These hypotheses become scientific theories as our understanding develops. The evidence for Darwin's Theory of Evolution came out of his passion for extensive collecting, cataloguing and classifying natural things.

For a more recent example we can look to the heavens. The classification of the astronomers' recent collection of exoplanets (planets circling suns other than ours, discovered by the Kepler telescope) identified a gap in the range of sizes of these heavenly bodies. The gap appears in the range of sizes between rocky Earth-like planets and so-called 'mini-Neptune' gas planets. To answer the question, 'Why does this size gap exist?' scientists combined the Kepler data on planets with the Keck Observatory collection of data on stars and came up with evidence to support the idea that there is a critical mass of a planet that has enough gravity to hold onto its gases in the face of solar radiation. Below this size the planet loses its gases and becomes more Earth-like. This insight explains the size gap and will now accelerate the discovery of more Earth-like exoplanets by focusing the search efforts of the various new telescopes now being launched.[41]

The evolution of taxonomies is evidence of the advance of science. When Pluto lost its place in the planets of the solar system it evoked a light-hearted and sentimental campaign to 'save' it. However, this change in Pluto's classification was a sign that our thinking had advanced. The taxonomy of thinking used in this book will certainly change and evolve, and some people will already disagree with it, but clear thinking about thinking will be easier for us with a taxonomy in place as a foundation.

At the highest level, Thinking Paradigms are grouped into four classes according to their primary use:

- ◆ **Constructing** – where thoughts and ideas are created;
- ◆ **Reducing** – where analysis is used to break problems down in order to solve them;
- ◆ **Heuristics** (Modelling) – where structures like metaphors and pictures are used to help to understand complex concepts and to position things in their wider context;
- ◆ **Experiencing** – where responses to events and feelings are collected to classify our thoughts.

We can map these four classes of paradigms to the DECIDE Model activities to provide a visual clue that helps us to find which class of paradigms it will be most useful to focus on at different stages in the decision process. At this top level of the taxonomy we can see that the activities **D**efine Objective and **I**dentify Alternatives are impacted by more of the paradigms. You can also get a sense of how the paradigms have a wide application across the whole decision process. We notice that the Creating Paradigms and the Experience Paradigms are, relatively speaking, more important than the Reducing and Heuristic Paradigms. (A darker colour at the intersection of the decision activity and the paradigms indicates that these paradigms are more influential in that decision activity.)

Level 1	DESIGN ACTIVITIES			EXECUTION ACTIVITIES			
D.E.C.I.D.E. Decision Steps	Define Objective	Establish Criteria	Consider Options	Identify Best Alternative	Develop Actions	Evaluate Outcomes	Overall Importance
Creating Paradigms							
Reducing Paradigms							
Hueristic Paradigms							
Experience Paradigms							
Relative Importance							

At the next level down, the individual paradigms in each class can be mapped to the DECIDE Model. This shows when in the decision process the paradigm has the most potential to deliver both Good Thinking, and Bad. The picture here is actually a summing up of the mappings of individual paradigms at the level below. There is a full description of this mapping for reference in the section 'Thinking Paradigms: Quick Summary' in the Appendix.

Does Search Trump Taxonomy?

One function of taxonomies is to organise data and therefore to help us to find things in a large mass of information. Some have suggested that with the current advances in search tools taxonomies are redundant, and even limiting. There is no doubt that this search capability of taxonomies is less important now, in this era of Google and computers with natural language search capabilities. But enabling search was only a bonus feature of taxonomies. Computer scientists are still big fans of taxonomies and have even taken them to a new level to improve what they call vertical search in a vertical domain. Taxonomies are as natural to human thinking as the branching trees of our circulation system or as the bronchi, bronchioles and alveoli of our lungs.

> *"In a museum, if you take away the taxonomy,*
> *you are left with a lot of bric-a-brac."*
>
> *Anon*

Part 4: A Taxonomy of Thinking Paradigms

4.1 Constructing Paradigms

It makes sense to start with the Thinking Paradigms classed as Constructing; the ones we use to create thoughts and ideas. These paradigms are obviously particularly important at the start of the decision process, as described in the chapter on the DECIDE Model. However, they will also appear throughout any thinking process. They will deliver hypotheses large and small during both the effort-thinking and auto-thinking we talked about in the chapter comparing quick thinking and considered thinking. When most of us think about thinking we will tend to focus first on creativity and the Constructing Paradigms.

It is probably fair to say that these are the most powerful of all the Thinking Paradigms. Therefore, they are the most useful to enable Good Thinking and also present the highest risk of causing Bad Thinking. If we want to apply a 'quick and dirty' check on the quality of a decision made or we need to inject some Good Thinking to help solve a difficult problem, the Constructing Paradigms are the right place to start.

The Constructing Paradigms in this section are:

Framing Paradigm: We create cascades of conscious and unconscious associations between any stimuli we encounter. Even if the stimulus and the associations are unconscious they will influence our reaction to further stimuli. This capability to frame our thoughts allows us to access the millions of data points in our minds efficiently, improving the speed of both effort-thinking and auto-thinking.

The Narrative Paradigm: The extraordinary ability we have to string together a very few, loosely related data points and to fill in the gaps in our narrative to weave a compelling story. You might say that this talent is at the heart of every brilliant new scientific hypothesis and every crazy conspiracy theory.

The Confidence Paradigm: The confidence of the decision maker(s) will rarely match their ability and knowledge. They will most often be overconfident and optimistic, or they are quite often overconfident and pessimistic. Less often seen, but equally problematic, is under-confidence.

Intuition: The ability to recall and process complex data quickly and accurately in an effortless thinking mode is the payback for earlier effort invested. Of course, intuitions can be sometimes be wrong.

Once again we can map the paradigms to the activities on the DECIDE Model to provide a visual clue that can help us to find which paradigms it will be most useful to focus on at different stages in the decision process.

Part 4: A Taxonomy of Thinking Paradigms

D.E.C.I.D.E. Decision Steps	Define Objective	Establish Criteria	Consider Options	Identify Best Alternative	Develop Actions	Evaluate Outcomes	Overall Importance
Constructing Paradigms							
Framing Paradigm							
Narrative Paradigm							
Confidence Paradigm							
Intuition Paradigm							
Relative Importance							

The Constructing Paradigms have relevance right the way across the decision process, particularly in Defining Objectives and Identify the Best Alternative. This relevance naturally reduces a little in the action-oriented activities.

THE FRAMING PARADIGM

> *"Take true root by the fair weather that you make yourself; it is needful that you frame the season for your own harvest."*
> *William Shakespeare – Author*

Why did the chicken cross the road? It wanted to see how a road looked when it was angry. You might not like the joke but, unless you have heard it before, you have just had a brand new cascade of associations triggered by your imagination, conjuring up an irritated boulevard.

The Framing Paradigm can be enjoyable. This is evolution's way of encouraging us to use our powerful brains by giving us the reward of pleasure. It may be that the pleasure that we derive from the punchline to a joke is the physical pleasure of the 'synaptic jumps' we experience as a new cascade of entertaining associations break the original associations which were set up at the beginning of the joke.

Associations can also trigger disgust. The trigger of 'cupcake vomit' will have very quickly given you a negative association of unpleasant symptoms of illness connected to consuming cupcakes. My apologies if you had just settled down with a nice cup of tea and a sweet pastry to read this chapter. In that case it would have affected you even more because your frame of reference already contained cupcakes, pastries, buns, sweetness, etc. The good news is that, without reinforcement, this disgust response will quickly fade and be forgotten.

Associations can be deliberately learned and reinforced. Repeated pastry and illness jokes would eventually lock in the synaptic connections of that cascade and you would learn that cupcakes are disgusting. You can also use this trick to commit things to memory by creating memorable associations. For example, the next time I see my friend Ella I will think of an elephant, and its tusks, and then teeth, and I will remember to ask her how that dental appointment went.

This rapid and emotional response to associations, rapidly recalling many related and potentially relevant items, is a useful addition to our survival instincts. It is hard-wired into our thinking. To use a computing analogy, it is like retrieving data from the hard drive into Random Access Memory so that it is available for the next operation. Whether it is positive or negative, and whether it is instinctive or learned, the frame of associations is powerful and useful. The Framing Paradigm can also be called the Framing Paradigm, which better suggests the automatic nature of the cascade of connections. The Framing Paradigm name instead invokes the deliberate management of the cascade, as in crafting a joke, or in consciously managing Good Thinking.

Cascading Cascades

Of course it is not just words. Any stimulus to our brain triggers a cascade of electrical stimulation. This cascade connects a large number of associated concepts, emotions and memories. When you see an image of a mother you will typically think of the words baby, father, child, milk, birth, breast, etc. You will access emotions like comfort, warmth, scolding, etc. Memories of school days, birthday parties, warm baths, etc. will also be accessed ready to be used by our minds as we continue our thinking after the stimulus of that image. Had the stimulus been different, say the word 'mother', or your mother's name, the cascade would be different. A brand new stimulus, like the idea of a chicken standing beside a furious motorway, will certainly trigger a unique cascade. Every cascade is original to the individual and the moment it occurs. It is almost certainly absolutely unique as it is also created and framed by the series of associative cascades that preceded it.

You are not fully conscious of the cascade; a lot of the associations are unconscious but are still available in the frame of reference we have created to advise the next thoughts and the subsequent cascades of association. Despite scientists' best efforts, our understanding of the details of how association works is still pretty rudimentary. However, there are a lot of entertaining experiments that have been carried out which do help us to understand what conscious and unconscious associations do to our thinking, even if we don't know quite how they do it.

You've been Framed

In the famous Florida Effect experiment, young students were asked to carry out a dummy experiment while being framed with words that subtly suggested the idea of old age.[42] It was being run in the US, so the words included 'Florida, senior, mature, golden', etc. The young student subjects were then asked to walk down the hall to carry out the next stage of the dummy experiment. Those who had been framed with the words that evoked old age walked measurably more slowly than a control group who went through the same process without the trigger stimuli. The subjects were questioned and had no conscious ideas of old age in mind. This experiment demonstrates what psychologists call the Framing Effect, or 'Priming'. It shows that framing can be unconscious and that it can even cause physical effects. The same auto-suggestion works in reverse. Subjects who believed they were testing the audio quality of headphones were told either to nod or shake their heads while listening to voice recordings. Those who were nodding were more likely to agree with the statements they heard, compared to the head shakers listening to the same statements.[43]

It is a little daunting to think that we need to take account of, and to manipulate, such a deeply programmed and fundamental Thinking Paradigm in order to ensure Good Thinking and smart decisions. However, it is not as difficult as it appears, and a relatively minor but deliberate framing stimulus can be very effective, despite the cacophony of cascades in the average mind. After all, this is the normal state for all of us, all of the time. A personal favourite example of this trick is a video of an illusionist called Derren Brown who succeeded in paying for various goods in New York using plain white paper which matched the size of dollar bills. Right at the point of handing over the dummy notes, he framed the recipients by talking about 'trust' and 'accepting things' in the context of travelling by subway. Of course the video features the successful transactions and it is certainly not a controlled experiment, but it is very entertaining. He is successful in a jewellery shop buying a very expensive ring, but his frame fails with a street vendor selling hot dogs. It is a worthwhile and amusing five minutes which clearly demonstrates the power of framing and of the Framing Paradigm. Search 'Derren Brown paper money trick' on youtube.com.[44]

Anchors Away

A particular case of framing is 'Anchoring'. This is where the mind locks onto a piece of information as a datum and then uses it as the measure of related thoughts. For example, as you walk through the bazaar on your exotic holiday, a carpet seller may tell you that "this beautiful carpet costs only $500". Even if it is actually worth $100, and you buy it for $150 after a bit of haggling, you will have the idea that you got it for $350 less than the asking price. If the asking price had been $250 you would not feel quite so good about your purchase. Likewise, when a teenager asks for permission to come home at 2am and you agree midnight, they have set the anchor to frame your negotiation. The good thing about anchors is that they help us to estimate. We guess an approximate answer then apply data to move up or down from that estimate. We will see more on this technique in the Rule of Thumb Paradigm. The anchoring effect is very powerful and easily measured.[45] For Good Thinking we must resist accepting inappropriate anchors, and be careful to place the right anchors, when asking questions.

Part 4: A Taxonomy of Thinking Paradigms

> *When you have had the opportunity to study all of the Thinking Paradigms, you may decide that the Framing Paradigm is the primary paradigm, and that most of the others are simply special cases of this fundamental law of associations. You may well be right. Depending on the day you ask me, and on how well you frame the question, I would generally agree with you. However, this insight is not a very useful one. It is a little like supporting world peace, hard to argue with and not a very useful guide to your next action. An easier route to clear thinking and good decisions is to accept that the other paradigms are distinct and that we need different techniques to manage each.*

Mapped to the DECIDE Model of decision activities, the Framing Paradigm appears everywhere but is most important in: **D**efining the Required Outcome, and **C**onsidering Options activities, and **I**dentify Best Alternative activities.

D.E.C.I.D.E. Decision Steps	Define Objective	Establish Criteria	Consider Options	Identify Best Alternative	Develop Actions	Evaluate Outcomes
Constructing Paradigms						
Framing Paradigm						

This means that when ideas are being created and when choices are being made, the Framing Paradigm is influencing those choices.

Test by: Identifying the Strongest Frames

Identifying which are the strongest associations of the Thinker(s) to the issue being addressed can be done by simply paying careful attention to the words being used in their conversation. To measure more directly, a quick word association game can be enlightening. If the other person is prepared to engage in a little experiment to expose the frames in use, take one or two key terms in the description of the issue or question and ask for instant answers to the following questions:

- ✧ What emotion do you associate with <the term>? What is another word for that emotion?
- ✧ Who is the first person that you think of when you hear <the term>? What word best describes that person?
- ✧ What do you see in your mind's eye when you hear <the term>? Where in the world would you find that image?

To be effective with this technique you need to work fast and take notes. Also, it cannot be done too frequently as the responses will become more considered. Similar questions are easy to devise and variety in the questions asked is a real advantage. Questions should be designed to address verbal, emotional and visual perspectives.

After you have identified potential frames, a conversation about associations can be enlightening. It is useful to ask if the Thinker(s) believe the frame of reference being used is appropriate and relevant to the question being addressed.

The above assumes that you are examining another person's associations. It is possible to check your own unconscious associations with questions in a similar way but it is probably better to simply take some time out to reflect on the associations you have to an issue or decision.

Whether you have decided that the frame of reference is a positive or negative one, it still makes sense to utilise both the supporting and subverting techniques set out below. This will take account of the fact that many of your associations will be unconscious. The rule of thumb is to always deliberately shake up your frame of reference to encourage creativity, and then to make the effort to create a positive frame.

Support by: Creating Positive Frames

The specific techniques are:

- ✧ Deciding the kind of energy that is conducive to Good Thinking about this issue. Will a high energy environment or a calm and sedate space improve the outcome? For example, bursts of activity interspersed with periods of complete rest and distraction will help if the issue is complex and/or emotionally difficult.

- ✧ Generating optimism that good solutions are achievable can be done by sharing or reviewing success stories before or during the time spent focused on thinking through the issue. Remember, the success stories do not need to have any direct connection to the issue being addressed. They will still create a positive frame.

- ✧ Creating positive feelings about all of the stakeholders involved is generally a good thing. However, this may be counterproductive in a deliberately competitive situation, like a sport.

♦ Removing physical or mental distractions which create competing frames of reference will aid concentration. This is particularly useful for clearly defined, complex tasks where cross-pollination of ideas is not required. Think of the classic pose of a chess player, with eyes fixed on the board and hands at the side of the head, acting as blinkers.

Subvert by: Disrupting Frames of Reference

Where the Framing Paradigm is potentially delivering Bad Thinking, particularly by allowing biases to contain or contaminate thinking, some responses are:

♦ Asking people to solve the problem being addressed in a surreal context can be a simple and powerful technique. For example:

   ❖ How would you solve this problem if all the affected stakeholders were determined to get the worst outcome possible for themselves?

   ❖ Transport this issue two thousand years back in time and solve it using the technology and political structures of that time.

After a time bring the issue back to the real context and see what has changed.

♦ Deliberately moving the Thinker(s) to a new and alien environment will disrupt frames of reference. We all notice how solutions can crystallise when we are on holidays or otherwise disengaged from our normal thinking environment. At a simple level, relocating a conversation from a sedentary home or office environment to a walk-and-talk meeting will loosen up ideas.

✧ Jokes and playfulness create new and original frames of reference and can make people conscious of the frames they are using. The best way to do this is simply to encourage playfulness when it appears.

Note that the Framing Paradigm is an important component of Prospect Theory, which is addressed in the chapter on the Risk Reward Paradigm.

> *"How little do they see what really is,*
> *who frame their hasty judgment upon that*
> *which seems."*
>
> *Robert Southey – Poet*

THE NARRATIVE PARADIGM

> *"Wars produce many stories of fiction,*
> *some of which are told until*
> *they are believed to be true."*
>
> Ulysses S. Grant – U.S. General

If you visit certain beaches at certain times of the year, when the moon is full and when the tide is high, you can feast on turtle soup. If you bury some types of food in the ground, and ensure that ground stays wet through the dry season, there will be much more food of the same kind there a year later when the seeds grow. There are substantial benefits in this ability to connect apparently unrelated events to valuable outcomes. We humans, being very smart, can combine long chains of facts into narratives that can predict complex and surprising outcomes. We are so inclined to this behaviour that storytellers have long been considered valuable members of society, even in Stone Age subsistence groups, where they might have been expected to be seen as an unnecessary luxury. We even have a measurable preference for narratives that have surprising or unexpected outcomes. This is why we like a twist in the tale, and jokes. It is also why we might believe that rain dances work and why, with a little bit of hindsight and storytelling, pretty much everything that has ever happened is quite easy to explain as a coherent interconnected collection of data points.

Part 4: A Taxonomy of Thinking Paradigms

The Narrative Pigeon

Like all the Thinking Paradigms, this is innate in humans, but a simple version of the Narrative Paradigm is found even in creatures with fairly low intelligence. In an Operant Conditioning Experiment (aka a Skinner Box) the subject is rewarded for certain actions.[46] For example, pressing a lever might gain a pigeon a food reward. As in all good experiments, a control is used to establish that the outcome is not random. This is where it gets interesting. When rewards are issued randomly, with the expectation that the subject will not learn to press the lever, the subject will repeat whatever actions they were doing before the random reward. If they repeat this cycle of movements often enough it will accidentally coincide with a random reward. This encourages the subject to repeat the movements a few more times until the next random reward. Essentially, the subject, in this case a not very smart pigeon, has created a story. Hop to the right, peck to the left, flap wings, repeat a few times and somehow a food reward turns up. This pigeon is demonstrating the Narrative Paradigm in its simplest form. The fact that it appears in many animals who are less intelligent that humans shows how useful it is to survival and how deeply it is lodged in the brain.

Making up Stories

It is the Narrative Paradigm that enables us to come up with a hypothesis, set out the storyline that supports it, and look for other evidence that will fill in the gaps and prove us right. And, if we find out the hypothesis is wrong, our storytelling brain will come up with a new narrative to test. This is how all discoveries are made. From something as simple and unconscious as 'if I can make someone laugh they are more likely to find me attractive and have my babies' to hypothesising the existence of dark matter to fill the gaps discovered in the complex narrative that is Quantum Theory. All of the creativity of humankind is founded in the Narrative Paradigm.

However, while its usefulness and contribution to Good Thinking is beyond doubt, the Narrative Paradigm can also create some very Bad Thinking. You can see this in a human with Obsessive Compulsive Disorder (OCD). If an OCD sufferer *must* switch their hallway light on and off exactly twenty times before going out to ensure that nothing terrible will happen to them, the Narrative Paradigm is damaging their life. This is the extreme version of the natural superstitions we will all succumb to from time to time, when we wear our lucky shoes to the job interview for example. The strength and familiarity of the story that the Earth was the centre of the Universe because humans are the centre of creation, was what made it so difficult for Galileo to get his new heliocentric narrative accepted. This perverse effect, of the powerful familiar narrative resisting scientific advances, is discussed by Thomas Kuhn in his excellent book, *The Structure of Scientific Revolutions*.[47] Kuhn shows that the arrival of a newcomer to a scientific field, who is not locked into the accepted narrative, can come up with a new story that creates scientific breakthroughs. Of course, this new story will initially encounter fierce resistance. We also see this in the story of Wegener's Continental Drift Theory in the chapter on Emotional Thinking.

Stories about Time Travel

We can look at the Narrative Paradigm as having three modes: forward looking, backward looking and time independent. The forward looking mode is used to develop plans and anticipate outcomes. The backward mode is used to explain existing outcomes. The time independent mode is used to develop hypotheses where time is not important to the cause and effect connections being considered. A clever experiment published in 1975[48] brings the nature of the Narrative Paradigm to life by testing the forward and backward modes of the Narrative Paradigm. Participants were asked to assign probabilities to 15 possible outcomes in advance of Nixon's visits to China and Russia in 1972. Even for experts the impacts of this unprecedented event were difficult to predict, but it was possible to create a narrative based on a little knowledge that led the participants to choose a probability for various different outcomes. After Nixon's return the same participants were asked to recall their probability predictions. If the outcome in question had actually happened they exaggerated their original estimate of its likelihood. If it had not happened, they recalled giving it a lower probability. Even more interesting, they also estimated other people's prediction probabilities to be more in line with what actually happened. They were rewriting the narratives to confirm the actual outcomes. (See also the Confidence and Experience Paradigms.)

Because the Narrative Paradigm is so fundamental to our thinking, it interacts with all of the other Thinking Paradigms. As ever, these interactions can be very powerful supporters of Good Thinking but they are also capable of delivering Bad Thinking.

The risks of the Narrative Paradigm were set out very clearly by Nassim Taleb in his 2007 book, *The Black Swan*.[49] In this book he refers to the paradigm as the 'narrative fallacy' as he was focused only on the negative impacts. In particular, he pointed out the dangers of the natural human preference for simple narratives over complicated ones. However, there are two sides to that observation.

Keep it Simple, Stupid

We find uncomplicated and coherent narratives very attractive. This is because coherence and simplicity correlate strongly with truth. Therefore, a predisposition for simple stories will most often lead us to the truth, but not always. The advice given to student doctors on the art of diagnostics in the form of a simple metaphor is relevant here. When examining symptoms they are reminded, 'If you hear hoof beats in California, expect to see horses not zebras.'

Familiar and memorable stories also have an added attraction of immediacy (see the Availability Paradigm). We also very efficiently look for data points which confirm our hypothetical narrative rather than look at every single fact which may or may not be relevant (see Confirmation Bias). Coherence in the story blinds us to information gaps and leads us to assume everyone involved has the same information as us. (See the Incomplete Information (WYSIATI) and Full Knowledge (WYKEK) Paradigms.)

A Twist in the Tale

The curiosity and inventiveness of humans also lead us to prefer stories with plausible but surprising narrative links between the

Part 4: A Taxonomy of Thinking Paradigms

data points. It is easy to see how a preference for stories which are interesting in this way would help humans to make discoveries and that these discoveries could be valuable. The first human to fire pottery was putting a surprising story together, saying that wet clay can become a waterproof container by being burnt. An unexpected but very valuable twist in the tale. Unfortunately, this is also what makes a good conspiracy theory so compelling. A story that is simple, apparently coherent, and a little bit surprising is very attractive. Consider the idea that the 9/11 attacks on the World Trade Center were instigated by a criminal conspiracy in order to avoid the cost of demolishing two huge city centre buildings which were loaded with asbestos in the most litigious country in the world. Of course it is nonsense, but is there just a frisson of 'that might just make sense' when you hear it? It is also true that acts of terrorism are excluded from most insurance policies. Could that be relevant to support or disprove the idea? You can see how an interesting story draws an audience in.

Mapped to the DECIDE Model of thinking activities, the Narrative Paradigm is most important in the actions: **D**efining the required outcome, **C**onsidering Options activities and **I**dentify Best Alternative.

D.E.C.I.D.E. Decision Steps	Define Objective	Establish Criteria	Consider Options	Identify Best Alternative	Develop Actions	Evaluate Outcomes
Constructing Paradigms						
Narrative Paradigm						

This is a similar profile to the Framing Paradigm because of the connections between the two paradigms. However, unlike the

Framing Paradigm, the Narrative Paradigm refers to a chain of associations linked by a logical thread of causation. The Framing Paradigm is a semi-logical intuitive branching tree of associated ideas.

Defining the required outcome activity relies on a narrative to create a hypothesis. The more complex the decision the more data points will exist to support the required outcome. These need to be stitched together into a narrative and the pivotal connections in the narrative understood so that they can be tested to confirm that the outcome can be achieved (that it is coherent) and that it will have the expected impacts. This is usually a Time Independent Narrative.

Considering Options: This is about creating a series of alternative narratives, each with the same starting point and which may have the same or different outcomes. Generally, a Forward Looking Narrative. In the same way, the activity, Identify the Best Alternative, is comparing the outcomes of competing stories.

Test by: Mapping out the Narrative

To establish whether the Narrative Paradigm is supporting Good Thinking it is important to identify the pivotal points in the narrative and check these for factual errors, significant gaps, and hidden assumptions. The pivotal points can be identified by laying out the whole story, then omitting components one by one and asking if the story still holds. Each pivotal point in turn should be tested for veracity and the evidence supporting it cross checked. If the story stacks up under this close examination, the Narrative Paradigm is probably supporting Good Thinking.

Support by: Using Storytelling Techniques

The Narrative Paradigm is at its most useful in the creation of ideas and when persuading others of the value of one's thinking. Specific techniques are:

- ✧ Expressing a dry and uninspiring target outcome in the form of the ending scene of a narrative can increase engagement of the people involved. A common technique is to write future newspaper headlines confirming that the outcome has been achieved and suggesting the story of how that happened.

- ✧ The process of writing the story that bridges from today to that narrative outcome is a powerful way to encourage creativity in generating options and identifying pivotal data points in the story. This is particularly powerful if it is done in a group.

- ✧ Identifying the key protagonists (and antagonists) in the narrative and telling the story from their contrasting viewpoints can be very revealing and can build up the coherence of the narrative. The various points of view being considered may be those of groups as well as individuals. Even imagining the story from the point of view of inanimate objects can be useful sometimes.

Subvert by: Challenging Coherence. Creating Alternate Storylines.

Where the Narrative Paradigm is delivering Bad Thinking by

increasing the persuasiveness of wrong but coherent stories, some responses are:

- ✧ Address the pivotal points in the story and expose any gaps; find and present any data that contradicts the story.
- ✧ Develop alternative narratives using the perspective of different protagonists that rely on the same pivot points. The new protagonists may have very different views on the story's pivot points or they may see different points as being critical to the coherence of the tale.

> ***"The confidence that individuals have in their beliefs depends mostly on the quality of the story they can tell about what they see, even if they see little."***
>
> *Daniel Kahneman – Psychologist*

THE CONFIDENCE PARADIGM

"All you need in this life is ignorance and confidence; then success is sure."

Mark Twain – Author

Depending on whether they see an activity or task as easy or difficult, people will be over- or under-confident in their response. While this is a bit obvious, it is an important factor to take into account when striving for Good Thinking. People do not normally have the *right* amount of confidence for the task that they have in hand. With both hard and easy tasks they will produce a wrong answer. This mismatch leads to both recklessness and over-caution in decisions and behaviours. And both recklessness and over-caution have pros and cons.

This effect is called 'overconfidence' when it is studied by psychologists and cognitive scientists who tend to be focused on the downsides. I think that using the term 'Confidence Paradigm' better reflects the fact that it also has the potential to deliver Good Thinking and to improve decision outcomes. Also, it will manifest as positive and negative opinions which people are confident about. This paradigm is unusual in that it has two opposite aspects and we need to consider them as two sides of the same coin, rather than two distinct paradigms.

Balance is Boring

However, the answer is not simply to always be more balanced. It is important to deliberately leverage our innate overconfidence when the objective is worthwhile but the route to success is unclear or difficult. We can assume an equal number of good and bad decisions will be made in this way. If we hope that a 'natural selection' effect will kill off bad ideas quickly and keep good ideas alive in the long term, there will be a few more good than bad decisions driven by overconfidence. Nothing ventured, nothing gained.

Should under-confidence be adjusted to a balanced objective view? Here the case for remaining off balance is not strong. The fact that under-confidence is driven by a perception that the task is difficult does encourage caution, but when thinking through important decisions there is always some risk to be taken. My rule of thumb is that overconfidence has more to contribute to Good Thinking than under-confidence.

I'm better than the Average Joe

Overconfidence is well studied and very familiar. The finding that 93% of American drivers rate themselves as better than the median sums it up pretty well.[50] While overconfidence is much more common, it is worth noting the other side to the story. Work by Justin Kruger in 1999[51] showed that the overconfidence effect is limited to tasks which the subject assesses as easy. If people believe the task is difficult, the effect is reversed. People then mistakenly believe they are worse than others. Both over-

and under-confidence is caused by a focus on assessing your own skill levels and not taking proper account of the skill levels of others. This connects it to the Incomplete Information (WYKIATI) Paradigm. This link between seeing a question as easy and overconfidence also goes some way to explaining why experts reliably make more overconfidence errors than non-experts, and why non-experts, who think the question is hard, usually don't challenge them.

People are great, or they are quite positive they are. Provided, as we said earlier, they think what they are doing is not difficult or hard. It is interesting to consider how this overconfidence might deliver advantages that evolution would favour. Excessive overconfidence would encourage dangerous risk taking. On the other hand, under-confidence would result in missed opportunities, as well as disadvantaging the individual in the social hierarchy. You might expect that a genetic tendency to sober realism would be the most likely to deliver better evolutionary outcomes for the gene carrier in question. However, all the evidence says that the vast majority of people are overconfident, so it seems that a moderate amount of overconfidence is healthy. It may simply be that it translates into resilience in the face of adversity. Under-confidence when faced with a new challenge has the evolutionary advantage of avoiding risks. Both sides of the misguided confidence coin do have the merit of getting people to a decision. Perhaps avoiding prevarication, making a quick decision and getting on with it is the real evolutionary advantage of the Confidence Paradigm. It is an energy-saving paradigm which gets stuff done.

> ### Overconfident Pessimists
>
> *People can be grouped into optimistic and pessimistic types, and it is fairly well-known that dramatic changes in circumstances, like a lottery win or a life-changing injury, will shift people from their standard type for only a relatively short time.*[52] *You will guess that a tendency to pessimism will affect an individual's level of confidence, but perhaps not in the way you would expect.*
>
> *Not only are optimists overconfident, pessimists are overconfident too. Pessimists are a bit less overconfident than optimists, but they still think they know more than they do, and that they have more control over things than is really the case. Provided, like the optimists, they classify the task as easy.*[53]
>
> *I can't find any science on pessimists' confidence levels when they think the task is hard, but I'm guessing that they will be under-confident by a larger margin than their optimistic peers.*

Positivity certainly delivers advantages. Entrepreneurs are a bit more overconfident than the average person, and some of them are lucky as well. This means that, for example, the financial system, modern medicine and Google all exist because of a combination of entrepreneurial overconfidence and good luck. Famously, an average of two in three new restaurants will fail. A more reasonable view of the odds would dramatically curtail ambition and reduce restaurant openings. So a bit of positivity makes our world a better place because the best restaurant of the three survives. This contribution to greater good is not much consolation to the two wannabe restaurateurs who fail, but if they are real entrepreneurs they will try to beat the odds with a new project. You may not agree that more good restaurants is a material contribution to the greater good. However, the advantage of overconfidence is that the same effects deliver real benefits like new medicines.

Overconfidence does have some glaring disadvantages too. Wars are waged by people who truly believe they can win and gain advantage. As there are at least two sides in any war, these people are wrong at least 50% of the time. Less important, but still a profound waste of human resources, many projects which are doomed to failure continue much longer than a less self-confident team of planners would allow.

Overconfidence is manifest in three distinct ways: (1) *over-estimation* of your own performance; (2) *over-placement* of your performance compared to others; and (3) *over-precision* in estimating and forecasting.

The first two are very closely related and can be treated as one in the context of decision making. They are caused by a positive, but inaccurate, assessment of the decision maker's skills. This is generally dealt with the hard way by the experience of surprising outcomes which are worse than expected. The introduction of experts in the relevant subject can balance things. However, we do need to manage the fact that the experts suffer from the overconfidence effect in their areas of expertise even more than the average individual. Hence, it is better to introduce more than one expert with contrasting views.

Other studies on overconfidence have come up with something called the Dunning-Kruger effect in which people are asked to self-assess their abilities in humour, grammar, and logic followed by a test in those skills.

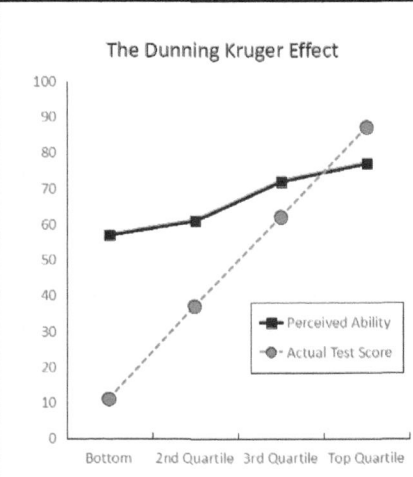

The results show that more competent people are a little more confident than novices, but everyone, whatever their level of competence, thinks their ability is in the 50th-70th percentile. So skilled individuals are relatively modest and novices are overconfident in these tasks which are not seen as difficult. Paradoxically, when training was done to improve the skills of the low-performing participants, it helped them realise the limitations of their abilities.

This chart is taken from the study.

The Future is Difficult to Forecast

The third flavour of the Confidence Paradigm, over-precision in estimating and forecasting, is worthy of special attention. The first investors in the United Kingdom's railways lost fortunes in the

1840's 'railway mania'. Only a third of the 9,500 miles (15,300km) the investors confidently predicted to be profitable were even built. The majority of the new railway companies that did succeed in running services went bust or were sold (frequently at a loss) to a few large survivors. However, the upside was that the tracks built because of their over-optimistic and inaccurate forecasts remained in place and became the infrastructure which underpinned the social and economic changes of the Industrial Revolution and the Victorian era.

This great tradition of forecasting, which is blind to the Confidence Paradigm delivering bad railway planning, continues to the present day. A study of 30 years of worldwide forecasts of passenger numbers on railway projects showed that 90% were over-estimates, and the average estimate was out by more than 100%.[54] All of these errors are public knowledge, but experts in the field have somehow failed to learn from this data. The UK's current high speed rail project 'HS2' is also based on expert forecasts of benefits to be delivered. It will be very interesting to compare the outcomes to the forecasts.

Experts are more prone to overconfidence than the average man/woman in the street. A study by the psychologist Oskamp in 1965 showed that more information increased the confidence of his experimental subjects in their predictions, but sadly not the accuracy of the predictions.[55] Two other psychologists, Raiffa & Alpert, in the early 1980s, carried out intensive studies on the question of the level of confidence people have in forecasts that they make.[56] They discovered that, in a similar way, even when participants were warned of the framing effect of any reference data they were given, their confidence in their own estimates were consistently too high. (See also the Framing Paradigm.)

Under-Confidence – It is Difficult!

So overconfidence is more common, but under-confidence can be a driver of Bad Thinking too. Again, if we think a problem is difficult for us, that we don't know enough to address it, we will be a bit too sure that we know too little, and that we know much less than others do. Under-confidence is less well studied, but referring back to Justin Kruger's work, the problem arises from our assessment of the thinking task we are addressing. The errors that this perspective produces include expecting unreasonable wide ranges in the value of projected outcomes, and predicting lower benefits values or higher risks in the matter we are addressing. At least this under-confidence will get to conclusions faster, even if they are wrong.

If we have the luxury of time and access to resources, particularly people with expertise, we can improve the thinking quality by making the task easier. We can do this by broadening and strengthening the team or by enhancing the skills of the participant Thinker(s). If we don't have this opportunity, we must simply be aware of the negative perspective that under-confidence generates and make the effort to adjust for it.

Under-confidence makes positive contributions to Good Thinking only when it prevents the Thinker(s) from taking risk actions with high impacts on the outcomes, and when it drives the Thinker(s) to include other people and information which add value.

Mapped to the DECIDE Model of thinking activities, the Confidence Paradigm affects every activity, but it peaks in Establish Criteria when forecasts must be made. This means we need to constantly be on the lookout for the potential of the Confidence Paradigm to boost or drain energy and/or to generate errors right across the decision activities.

D.E.C.I.D.E. Decision Steps	Define Objective	Establish Criteria	Consider Options	Identify Best Alternative	Develop Actions	Evaluate Outcomes
Constructing Paradigms						
Confidence Paradigm						

It is worth noting that there are strong connections between the Risk Reward Paradigm and the Confidence Paradigm. The Confidence Paradigm will affect the inputs to a risk reward assessment.

Test by: Asking if Activities/Tasks with a Critical Output are Easy or Hard

Asking yourself, or the team involved, if the task in question is easy or hard will tell you which way the Confidence Paradigm is pushing the outputs. If it is seen as being easy, or of average difficulty, watch out for overconfidence. If it is seen as hard, expect under-confidence.

If the activity outputs are critical to success, assume the Confidence Paradigm is skewing the results. An intervention can moderate over- or under-confidence towards a more reliable middle ground.

Where the activity outputs are not seen as critical to success, interventions in the decision process exploiting the Confidence Paradigm can be used to speed up or slow down the process. This counter intuitive strategy is rarely a useful intervention. However, circumstances where it can be useful to focus on affecting the decision process rather than the outcomes of an activity include:

- ✧ If the outputs of this decision activity are not critical to the decision being made, and the task is seen as easy, the positive energy of overconfidence can be a valuable boost, improving creativity, morale and self-confidence.
- ✧ Where generating some under-confidence in the decision maker(s) might be useful in making the process more considered, and encouraging people to take a wider perspective on the whole problem.

This method of harnessing of the Confidence Paradigm is risky. It should be used rarely, openly and deliberately. Used covertly it will certainly be seen as cynical manipulation and will break trust in the objectivity of the whole decision process.

We need to deal with the two uses of the Confidence Paradigm separately.

Objective One: Getting to the Best Quality Outputs

1.1. Subvert Under-confidence by: Confirming the Task is Easy

Where a perception that the task is difficult is causing under-confidence you can:

- ✧ Point out that the outcomes are less than critical, making the task lower risk and therefore easier.
- ✧ Add an expert. Re-balance the risk of under-confidence with an expert's overconfidence.

1.2 Subvert Overconfidence by: Showing the Task is Difficult and using Outside Comparisons

Where you suspect the Confidence Paradigm is delivering Bad Thinking due to overconfidence, some responses are:

- ✧ Apply the Standards of Evidence Tool (see the chapter on Certainty & Doubt) to grade the reliability of the positions being taken.
- ✧ Find data relating to similar examples outside the existing frame of reference. Other geographies, other industries, other times. For example, comparing Tulip Mania to the Dot Com Boom to Bit Coin Mania.

Objective Two: Managing the Pace of the Process:

2.1 Support Overconfidence by: Speeding Up – Confirming the Task is Easy

Where allowing a little overconfidence has more benefit than risk, specific techniques are:

- ✧ Include an expert in the team and take advantage of their (over) confidence.

◆ Set challenging deadlines for the activity to keep the auto-thinking mode in the forefront.

2.2 Support Under-confidence by: Slowing Down – Confirming the Task is Difficult

Where creating some under-confidence in the decision maker(s) might be useful:

◆ Use guest experts who can elaborate on the complexities of the matter without contributing solutions.

◆ Apply the Standards of Evidence Tool rigorously and repeatedly to the decisions being made and to the predicted outcomes.

"We must have perseverance and, above all, confidence in ourselves. We must believe that we are gifted for something, and that this thing, at whatever cost, must be attained."

Marie Curie – Scientist

THE INTUITION PARADIGM

"Intuition is nothing more and nothing less than recognition."

Hebert Simon – Psychologist

Following my gut instinct has helped me make some good decisions. In some ways this makes sense, the network of neurons in the gut is as plentiful and complex as the network of neurons in our spinal cord. What is sometimes called 'a second brain' is obviously there for a good evolutionary reason. However, it is very unlikely that it is processing information in any meaningful way. It is more likely that we experience changes in our gut's commitment of resources to digestion in response to perceived levels of stress or danger. What is true, however, is that this communication is subliminal, the first we know of our mind's concern is the sensation in our gut. So we should take those 'gut feelings' seriously.

Magical Insights

The 'magic' of intuition has long been a popular idea. Recently, the multi-million selling book *Blink*,[57] by Malcolm Gladwell, is (by those who have been too busy to read it) commonly understood to tell us that we should all trust our intuitions and rely on the phenomenal powers of our auto-thinking to give us insightful, correct answers without the trouble and time that effort-thinking costs. This is not quite true. As is explained in some detail in *Blink*, there are many situations where intuition leads to inspired Good Thinking, and many others where it is a very poor guide.

The Intuition Paradigm describes the situation where a subliminal process delivers an answer to a question based on expertise and experience which the Thinker possesses, in such a way that the Thinker cannot explain how the answer originated. Everyone has a natural capacity to use this quintessentially auto-thinking technique and it does get better with practice. Increasing the volume of experience and expertise we can gain in relation to the question as we apply our intuition is an obvious help. Less obvious is that regularly using your intuition improves your ability to use it. This was demonstrated in recent experiments where subliminal clues were given to subjects carrying out an unrelated task. Their responsiveness to intuitive clues improved with repeated exposure.[58]

We can easily see why intuition can bring great value to the Thinker relying on it. Being able to detect one hostile individual in a crowd, or unconsciously responding to a change in the forest background sounds when a predator is nearby, are ancient examples of Good Thinking based on intuition. There has been some good science done to understand this phenomenon. Gary Klein, who studies what he calls Naturalistic Decision Making, has gathered evidence of real life situations where intuition has been critically important to Good Thinking. For example, where a fire chief saved his team's lives by evacuating them just before a building collapsed because, in his words, the situation 'did not feel right'.

Three Conditions for Useful Intuitions

Whether intuition is more likely to lead to more Bad Thinking than Good was recently the subject of a scientific duel. Daniel Kahneman and Gary Klein, two leading scientists in the study of decision making and cognitive psychology were working on different sides of this debate. Kahneman was focused on the mental slips or 'fallacies' that lead to Bad Thinking and unfortunate errors. Klein, on the other hand, was studying how people could come up with inspired insights in what were often stressful situations. Klein was the one studying the fire chiefs. Fortunately, they were both smart enough to learn from each other and their joint work summed up the criteria for successful intuition.[59] Based on a surprisingly small amount of data relating to a closely defined situation, a person with expert knowledge can frequently make very high reliability decisions about how to act, particularly in relation to outcomes in the near future. There are three criteria needed to be met for successful intuition:

- ✧ Defined scope – the question needs to be clear and narrowly defined.
- ✧ Expertise – the intuitive person must have a solid base of experience related to the issue.
- ✧ Near term outcomes – immediate outcomes means that the variables will not change.

Note that the expert using intuition will have a high level of confidence in their judgement but is very unlikely to be able to explain why. Even more interesting, evidence shows that attempts to explain the rationale behind an intuitive decision typically reduce the quality of the decision.

False Intuitions

What we are talking about here is closely related to both the Confidence Paradigm and Confirmation Bias. The Intuition Paradigm is in some ways the opposite side of the coin to these. Comparing them shows very clearly that every Thinking Paradigm has both utility and risk. The combination of unjustified confidence and the tendency to select data to confirm our opening position can produce something that looks like intuition but is very likely to be Bad Thinking. The giveaway is the failure to meet the three criteria for good intuition.

Non-expert Experts

It is worth mentioning that in some situations the average person in the street can be as expert as an expert. Blind tasting experiments show that average folk can rank jams as well as trained experts. However, if they are asked to explain their choices *as they make them*, the experts will maintain their performance level while the average person's performance reverts to average. This point emphasises the importance of simply accepting intuitions if you decide to use them. Efforts to de-construct the intuition to test its quality will break the paradigm. The jam experts maintained their performance when they were broken out of the Intuition Paradigm because they could consciously deploy the same skills. The average citizens succumbed to the Confidence

Paradigm and underestimated their natural skill to identify a good flavour. Looking at the criteria for successful intuition, the expertise of sensing flavours which humans prefer was innate in the non-experts, so they did satisfy the expertise criteria.

Mapped to the DECIDE Model of thinking activities, the Intuition Paradigm is most important in Identifying the Best Alternative where it can help to make rapid selections based on expertise built up in the initial Design Activities:

D.E.C.I.D.E. Decision Steps	Define Objective	Establish Criteria	Consider Options	Identify Best Alternative	Develop Actions	Evaluate Outcomes
Constructing Paradigms						
Intuition Paradigm						

However, we need to reconsider and rework the DECIDE Model for the Intuition Paradigm.

DECIDE becomes AsTeEx

Klein's work also showed that the way experts use intuition is that they allow auto-thinking, using the Associative and Availability Paradigms, to come up with one potential solution. They quickly mentally test that solution; if it appears to work they execute on it. If it fails the mental test, they come up with an alternative and test that. Klein called this the 'Recognition Primed Decision Model'. This is essentially a very accelerated version of the DECIDE decision process. The intuitive expert carries out the first two activities, Define Objective and Establish Criteria, subliminally and solo to **As**sess the Situation. They then combine the next two activities, Consider Options and Identify Best Alternative, into one subliminal step, which we can call 'Test Option A'. If it passes that test they Execute on that basis. Because the outcomes are near term, Executing the actions and evaluating their impact can be done simultaneously. This explains why for good quality intuition you need one expert and a clearly defined problem area and immediate impacts. Their experience means that when they Assess the situation, the associations they make and the options which are most readily available to them are appropriate and relevant. In the Test stage, the mental checks they run on their intuitive 'Option A' are calibrated by extensive practical experience. The fact that their best intuitions relate to immediate or near future issues means that it is unlikely that the variables being considered will change as they Execute.

The compressed DECIDE Model using intuition looks like this:

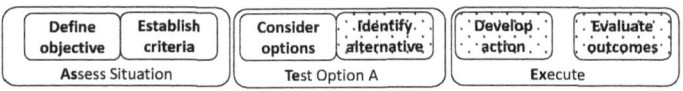

The AsTeEx Intuitive Decision Model

I find the mnemonic 'AsTeEx' useful to remember this compressed version of the process.

This compression of the DECIDE processes can also be described as a 'satisficing' strategy (accepting the first viable option), in contrast to 'optimising' or 'maximising' (comparing every alternative to choose the best).

Test by: Check for Good Intuition Criteria

If the decision being made has a defined scope; and the Thinker has the experience and expertise; and the decision relates to a near-term outcome; then the circumstances have the potential for useful intuitions. If the question being addressed is also very urgent, the Thinker(s) should be biased towards using an intuitive approach.

Support by: Using Minimum Data and not Asking for Explanations

Specific techniques to encourage intuition:

- ✧ Delegate the responsibility and accountability for producing the answer to one expert and agree to act on that advice. Intuition is typically a one-person thinking paradigm.

- ✧ Don't ask the expert to explain their decision or require them to persuade others to act. Instead, agree to act and assess the decision only in retrospect.

Subvert by: Challenging Assumptions

Where the Intuition Paradigm is delivering Bad Thinking by jumping to conclusions on inadequate data, some responses are:

- ✧ Overtly check that the three criteria for good intuition are met:
    - ✓ Confirm the scope is limited and well understood.
    - ✓ Challenge the experience and expertise of the Thinker(s).

- ✓ Check that base assumptions will not change during execution.
- ✧ Formally address each of the DECIDE activities, particularly the first three Design Activities, declaring the assumptions that are in use and checking facts.

> *"The intellect has little to do on the road to discovery. There comes a leap in consciousness, call it intuition or what you will, and the solution comes to you and you don't know how or why. All great discoveries are made in this way."*
>
> *Albert Einstein – Scientist*

4.2 REDUCING PARADIGMS

"The whole is more than the sum of its parts."

Aristotle – Philosopher

In our school days we learn to reduce all sorts of ideas, like scientific theories, mathematical problems, even works of art like books and poems, to their constituent parts. We take them apart to find out how they work, so that we can go on to analyse and even to create similar things. In science it is called 'Reductionism' and it is commonplace. It is seen in action when a four-year-old child is learning to read using phonics and when a doctorate student of engineering creates a new form of nano-engineered carbon with sticky tape and a pencil lead.[60]

This analytical thinking technique was not created by the education process. (You were right when you suspected that your teachers were really were not all that smart.) But this natural and powerful type of thinking evolved in the first humans to allow us to deconstruct things, to differentiate between the essential and the coincidental. It helped the first farmers to realise that it was the seed, the soil, the water and the light that made the crop, and that the name, or gender, or status, of the person doing the planting were not material to success.

As the name suggests, the Reducing Paradigms are most useful when there are too many options in play, or when there is spurious data obscuring the sight-lines between the Thinker and the solution being sought. Like all paradigms they can also cause Bad Thinking. In this case our laudable inclination to cut through the noise and to focus on finding answers can lead to useful or important data being missed or disregarded, metaphorically throwing babies out with the bathwater.

The Reducing Paradigms are:

Availability Paradigm: Our brain effortlessly pulls data from the vast store in our memory which is likely to be relevant to the task in hand. This highly efficient process sometimes presents the wrong data.

Incomplete Information (What You See Is All There Is): Making decisions based on the data that is available rather than wasting time searching for more data that adds little value is very efficient. Sometimes it is important to check that important data gaps have not been ignored.

Full Knowledge (What You Know Everybody Knows): The modest assumption that the data available to you is equally available to others engaged in the same decision process is generally a good one. Sometimes that assumption is wrong and this can lead people to reach different conclusions and potentially to behave in unexpected ways.

Confirmation Bias: The ability of the mind to scan large quantities of data and quickly find matching pieces is very valuable in focusing a search. However, the same focus can cause us to miss important data that does not match our search.

Ownership Paradigm: When we own something, or some idea, the value that we put on it increases, which helps us to hang onto it in the face of distractions and competition. This value can also be misplaced or exaggerated, leading to mistakes in priorities.

Visually mapping the Reducing Paradigms to the activities on the DECIDE Model, there is natural focus on the first and last activities in the decision process.

D.E.C.I.D.E. Decision Steps	Define Objective	Establish Criteria	Consider Options	Identify Best Alternative	Develop Actions	Evaluate Outcomes	Overall Importance
Reducing Paradigms							
Availability Paradigm							
Incomplete Info WYSIATI							
Full Knowledge WYKEK							
Confirmation Bias							
Ownership Paradigm							
Relative Importance							

THE AVAILABILITY PARADIGM

"To succeed, jump as quickly at opportunities as you do at conclusions."

Benjamin Franklin – Polymath

Terrorism in Western Europe is definitely a serious problem. Is it getting worse? For example, there were large-scale attacks in Madrid, Paris, Norway and London between 2004 and 2017. It does feel bad, but it is certainly not getting worse. Research by Statista[61] shows that, in Western Europe, you were roughly three times more likely to be killed in a terrorist attack in the 1970s and '80s than in the 21st Century. Right now though, if you assess the chances of an individual living in Paris or London being involved in a terrorist attack, you will almost certainly overestimate it. This is why terrorists love the Availability Paradigm. A photogenic and newsworthy atrocity gets a lot of airtime, is widely noticed and easily recalled.

This also explains why, if the assertion 'journalists create fake news', appears enough times in the media, the idea becomes much easier to believe. On a more positive note it also means that as an invented term like 'Universal Human Rights' becomes established by frequent use, it is easier for people to see it as a reasonable and natural expectation. The easier something is to recall, the more likely we are to accept it is true and meaningful. The current favourite guru of branding, Professor Byron Sharp, shows through his extensive research on the emotional drivers of purchasing that maintaining the 'mental availability' of a brand is the only worthwhile objective of advertising.[62]

Availability Confirms Value

What is the first thing that comes to mind? It is not surprising that we humans are inclined to use the most easily available information when we address a question. After all, data from recent memory, or which is frequently used, is more likely to be relevant than memories which are years old or rarely accessed. The usefulness of this effect is very obvious when we are studying for an exam, deliberately making the relevant material available by cramming in the days before. It is also a side-effect of our natural preference for the ease of auto-thinking over the difficulty of effort-thinking.

This is a paradigm that is easily explained, readily understood, and quickly accepted as something that all of us are frequently affected by. When the question is, 'Where shall we go to for lunch?' the usual places come to mind immediately. Most of us can readily recall other practical examples of the Availability Paradigm which have affected them directly. See what we did there? However, its very ubiquity sometimes makes it very hard to consciously detect it, and it has the power to exaggerate the effects of other paradigms for better and for worse.

Making sure that Thinkers are 'up to speed' by enabling the Availability Paradigm can greatly accelerate the thinking process. This in turn will inject energy into the thinking process and get to decisions faster. Making the right data available can be done by including people in the team who have relevant data 'at their fingertips' and/or preparing advance briefing materials. This is true whether you are a one person thinking team or the thinking is being done by a group. Exploiting availability in this way makes sense, particularly when the issue being considered is well defined and a range of effective solutions are available to choose from, for example, when developing a plan for a project very similar to previous ones. Of course this does pander to the Confirmation Bias so, when new thinking and an original solution is required, a less prepared and less expert Thinker can actually be at an advantage.

Engagement Changes the Measure of Availability

The level of engagement of the Thinker with the issue can change the way the Availability Paradigm works. In general, the measure of availability is: how easy it is to come up with an adequate volume of evidence to support the hypothesis? A combination of ease of access and volume of evidence translates into confidence in the conclusion reached. However, an engaged Thinker will pay much less attention to the *ease of recall*. Instead, they will use the *volume of evidence* found to determine the validity of the hypothesis.

This was demonstrated in 1998 by Rotliman and Schwartz at UCLA.[63] They used the presence or absence of a family history of cardiac disease to select two sets of student subjects who would show different levels of engagement in questions designed to establish their personal risk of cardiac disease. The two groups were asked to list examples of their behaviours that would increase their risks of cardiac disease. Some were asked to generate three examples, which made availability easy. The others were given the more difficult task to come up with eight, giving them the sense that availability was low. Of the students given the difficult task of coming up with eight examples, the 'casual students' considered themselves to be low risk, the 'engaged students' considered this as evidence that they were at risk. The casual students had treated the *difficulty of finding examples* as being key, considering the number of examples unimportant. The engaged students treated *the number of examples found* as being the key data. When students had the easy task of finding only three examples of risky behaviour, the casual students translated the easy availability as showing that they were at risk, whereas the engaged students thought that the low number of examples showed they were not at risk.

Repeating the experiment with a reverse framing, looking for examples of behaviours that would reduce the risk of disease gave exactly the same results.

So what does this mean for Good Thinking? Objectively, a larger volume of evidence is more meaningful than a little evidence, regardless of how easily it is accessed. If the Thinker(s) are not personally engaged with the question, they will consider a ready availability of a little evidence as supporting the hypothesis they are testing. If the Thinker(s) are engaged with the question being addressed we can expect they will disregard ease of access and focus on the volume of evidence they can access. Therefore, if the answer to the question is important you want Thinker(s) with skin in the game. On the other hand, if you want speed and energy to be applied to less important questions, you can exploit the bias towards easy availability by making sure the Thinkers are not too engaged in the outcome.

> *The Availability Paradigm can sometimes act as a special case of the Substitution Paradigm. The question, 'Does the evidence support the hypothesis?' is being substituted with the question, 'Is relevant evidence readily available?' It is a special case because the substitution question here has more relevance to the original question than is typical.*

Mapped to the DECIDE Model of thinking activities, the Availability Paradigm is most important in: **D**efining the required outcome and **C**onsidering Options activities.

However, it is a constant companion when we are thinking and it is particularly prone to exaggerate the positive and negative effects of other paradigms.

D.E.C.I.D.E. Decision Steps	Define Objective	Establish Criteria	Consider Options	Identify Best Alternative	Develop Actions	Evaluate Outcomes
Reducing Paradigms						
Availability Paradigm						

Test by: Measuring Engagement of the Thinker(s).

If the level of engagement of the Thinker(s) is matched to the importance of the outcomes, the Availability Paradigm will probably be driving Good Thinking. Either a low engagement to low importance or a high-to-high match is good. Any mismatch will drive Bad Thinking. Engagement is best measured by asking the Thinker(s) to rate the importance of these outcomes relative to others in the decision process and by asking how they will be personally affected by these outcomes.

Support by: Enhancing Availability

If the engagement and importance of outcomes is matched, improving access to relevant data will accelerate decisions.

Specific techniques to achieve this include:

- ✧ Adding Experts. By definition, experts will have a head full of readily accessed relevant information. Experts can be included in the thinking team or available on demand.
- ✧ Briefing and teaching the Thinker(s) in advance will naturally improve the availability of relevant data.

Subvert by: Changing the Engagement Level

If there is a risk that a mismatch of engagement and the importance of outcomes is in place, once you understand the real importance of the outcomes, adjust the level of engagement to match the importance of the outcomes.

To reduce the engagement level:

- ✧ Highlight the fact that these outcomes are relatively less important than other outcomes in the decision process and will have little impact on the Thinker(s).

✧ Declare deadlines to encourage the Thinker(s) to deliver these outcomes quickly and move on to more important questions.

To increase the engagement level:

✧ Require the Thinker(s) to formally analyse the data discovered, perhaps presenting it in the form of a report or a graphic. Or ask them to present it to another interested party.

✧ Highlight the importance of the outcomes of the question to the overall decision process.

✧ Re-frame the question to make them more personally relevant to the Thinker. (See also the Framing Paradigm.)

"He who hesitates is sometimes wise."

Malcolm Forbes – Author

Part 4: A Taxonomy of Thinking Paradigms

INCOMPLETE INFORMATION (WYSIATI)

> *"There are also unknown unknowns,
> the ones we don't know we don't know…
> it is the latter category that tend to be the
> difficult ones."*

Donald Rumsfeld – Politician

Here is a true story. At Sandown Racecourse on a cold afternoon in February, Kadisha bet £4,000 on a horse, called Moon over Miami, to win against four others in the Henry the Eighth Novice Chase. She had borrowed £1,000 from her dad and another £3,000 from a high interest lender to make this bet. She knew nothing about horse racing and was just following a tip. You might say that this was reckless behaviour. On the contrary. Her tipster had given her only five tips before this one and he had picked the winner every single time. She had made substantial returns by betting on these earlier tips and she knew that this was going to be the last tip. This was her last chance to win big.

What she did not know was that her tipster, Derren Brown the famous illusionist, had sent out thousands of tips, tipping every horse in the first race to win. He then sent tips for every horse to win in the second race, but only to people who have received a winning tip in the first race. And so on, until, after five races, a small number of people had received only winning tips. This small group, including Kadisha, were then told they would get a final tip so they had a last chance to win big. Kadisha took her chance and placed her big bet, watched by Derren Brown and his TV cameras. She then watched the green and white checks of her jockey on Moon over Miami come in a very disappointing fourth. She had lost £4,000 that she could certainly not afford to lose. She swore and fought back tears. It was great TV! You can watch it on youtube.com. Search for 'Derren Brown The System'.[64]

This is a classic example of the Incomplete Information Paradigm at work. The evidence she had access to looked good, and Kadisha had assumed that What You See Is All There Is (WYSIATI). This happens a lot when in auto-thinking mode, but it will also easily and frequently happen with effort-thinking.

Not Completely Bad

It is quite easy to see that the Incomplete Information Paradigm has its down sides. It can be dangerous to make decisions based on incomplete information. Of course, it has its upside too. You can never have *all* of the information that might apply to the question you are addressing. A lot of that information will be pretty much irrelevant, and there is a limit to the volume of information that you can process. If you are constantly concerned that there is information missing, you will always be unsure of your decision. In the worst case you may not be able to make an important decision because you are too concerned about missing data. A mildly misguided confidence that you have considered all the facts can be really useful.

On Balance, Avoid Asymmetry

There can be a temptation to withhold information deliberately from stakeholders involved in a decision in order to encourage speed and manage outcomes. This is unwise in most circumstances. Information asymmetry is commonly a factor in commercial trading. If one party has information the other cannot see, they may identify a difference between the asking price and the true value of a good or service. In the long term this 'arbitrage' reason for price differences has a negative effect on markets. *The Market for Lemons*, by the economist George Akerlof, uses the example of the second-hand car market to explain how information asymmetry leads to a market stocked with dud cars, known as 'lemons'.[65] As buyers insist on paying low prices to allow for the risk that any car may be a 'lemon', sellers of good cars are driven from the market. This suggests that, in decision making, the use of deliberate information asymmetry between stakeholders will have negative effects over the long term. Participants will hold back to allow for the risk that there is other relevant information which they have not yet seen.

Focus is Everything

When Kadisha was making the decision to place that enormous bet at Sandown her attention was focused. It was the most important thing in her life at that moment, and she expected that, win or lose, it would have a dramatic effect on her life. She was not aware of it but she was exaggerating. She was experiencing what science has dubbed the 'focusing illusion'. Nothing in life is as important as you think it is when you have your full attention focused on it.

Psychological studies on questions as banal as whether Californians have a better life because of the weather, to questions as profound as whether someone who is paraplegic following an accident can ever be as happy as they were before their misfortune, the science shows that when we focus on the subject we give it too much weight.[66] We ignore other information which is material to the wider context. The same is true of good events like winning the lottery. How happy winners expect to be, or outside observers expect them to be, tends to be exaggerated.

As ever, this particular example of the WYSIATI Paradigm has its uses. It is what we normally call concentration. Humans have bandwidth limits when we are effort-thinking. The feeling that what we are focusing on is vitally important stops us from getting distracted and helps us to get results. We should take full advantage of the focusing illusion when we need to concentrate, like just before an exam. However, if the effect of that concentration is to increase stress to counterproductive levels, remember that it is definitely not as important as you believe it is.

A Happy Ending

By the way, you will probably be relieved to hear that Derren Brown does have a conscience and that Kadisha was ok in the end. She left the Sandown race course with the £13,000 she would have won had she placed her bet on the horse that actually won. She was up by £9,000. For her, a huge amount. She was very lucky after all. Lucky that paying her the hoped for winnings was a trivial cost in the context of a prime-time TV budget.

Mapped to the DECIDE Model of thinking activities, the Incomplete Information Paradigm is most important in the first three design activities, particularly in the Establishing Criteria and Considering Options activities. It also impacts the final activity, Evaluate Outcomes because unintended consequences can not be included unless they are observed.

D.E.C.I.D.E. Decision Steps	Define Objective	Establish Criteria	Consider Options	Identify Best Alternative	Develop Actions	Evaluate Outcomes
Reducing Paradigms						
Incomplete Info WYSIATI						

Test by: Measuring Importance and Urgency

How do you know whether to look for potentially important missing information? Do this when: i) you have an important question to answer; and ii) when you have time, in that order. With an important but genuinely urgent decision, it is better to allow the paradigm to do its thing and engender confidence and speed of action. If it is less urgent you need to make a judgement on its importance. We talk about ranking big decisions in the chapter on Triage Thinking. For smaller decisions, often nested at lower levels inside the decision process, the importance of the decision is based on your best opinion on how much it will impact the bigger decision. If you decide the question is important, then you must ask yourself how much time you can afford to invest in information gathering before this cost to the decision process becomes excessive. Whatever you decide, time limiting any search for new information is always a good policy.

When a search is underway there are two types of additional information that will be identified:

'New Knowns' – new facts and data which can usefully guide your thinking.

'Known Unknowns' – where relevant questions are discovered where the answers will affect outcomes. It may make sense to try to answer these questions, but they can also be incorporated without answers, using risk management techniques.

You will be pleased to hear that the notorious 'Unknown Unknowns' (the important questions that we cannot even identify) can safely be ignored in the context of the Incomplete Information Paradigm. (Refer also to Risk Management in the section on Decision Tools.)

Support by: Maintaining Pace

Where the Incomplete Information Paradigm is proving a useful effect by speeding up small unimportant decisions in the larger thinking challenge, or where speed is more important than accuracy. Specific techniques to support it are:

- ✧ Establish the minimum 'need to know' data points first. Limit research to these points which are necessary to support the decision. Time limit the research.

- ✧ Decide which questions should be biased towards speed rather than completeness, because they are less important. Establish deadlines to deliver answers, and stick to them.

- ⬥ Delegate less important questions to individuals or small sub-groups with full authority to answer them and simply inform the wider team of the answers.

Subvert by: Broaden Perspectives

The Incomplete Information Paradigm can deliver Bad Thinking by coming up with inadequate answers to important questions that require new perspectives. In this situation encourage the Thinker(s) to look at the problem from new angles. For example:

- ⬥ Slow down the process to allow the Framing Paradigm and some brainstorming to do their work, allowing the Thinker(s) to make links to other resources and data points.

- ⬥ List all the stakeholders who have an interest in the answer and ask what data would those stakeholders use to address the question.

- ⬥ Examine the question from the viewpoint of random alternate skill-sets or professions. Ask how a scientist, a teacher, a footballer, a banker, etc., would tackle this question.

- ⬥ Do some research to locate new expertise relevant to the question being addressed and include it by bringing an expert into the process or by getting the Thinker(s) to educate themselves a little in this skill-set and viewpoint.

"What's good about the digital revolution,
is it makes information asymmetry
much harder to maintain."

S J Dubner – Author

FULL KNOWLEDGE (WYKEK)

> *"A man is never astonished that he doesn't know what another does, but he is surprised at the gross ignorance of the other in not knowing what he does."*
>
> *Thomas C Haliburton – Author*

Understanding what another person knows, and does not know, is essentially about empathy. We are not quite born with this skill. Experiments by Wimmer & Permer in the 1970s show that this develops from about the age of four years.[67] They staged a scene where a concealed object was secretly relocated. They then asked children where the person who had originally concealed it would look for it when they returned. Up to the age of four they thought the original concealer of the item would look in the new location even though they were not present when the object was moved. They were thinking, 'What You Know Everyone Knows' (WYKEK). As they got older they correctly selected the original location as the target for the search, recognising that another person did not have information that they held.

Loose Lips Can Avoid Sinking Ships

When it comes to hidden toys in staged scenarios most of us are pretty good at understanding that we might have access to information that others don't. In more complex situations it can be harder. Some historians argue that the First World War was largely the result of a set of secret alliances in which countries contracted to defend an ally if attacked. Potential attackers were assumed to be aware of the alliances and hence of the hidden strength of their enemies. Also, some alliances were then secretly upgraded to offensive alliances, so an attacker would be automatically supported by allies. This made them more inclined to be confrontational. The other side, who could not see all of that extra power behind the pre-combat sabre rattling, were less likely to back down. For example, in the Bosnian Crisis of 1908, Germany was supporting Austria, while Russia was on Serbia's side, turning a small quarrel between two countries into a much larger conflict involving four countries. All four countries expected the others to know what they knew. A dangerous assumption which laid the foundations of the First World War. It is good to know that our modern era of openly visible alliances like NATO is a better way to ensure everybody knows what risks they are taking if they threaten hostilities.

In the smaller scale of domestic warfare, most of us have heard the phrase 'he/she must have known that all I really wanted was xyz, I don't know why they overreacted'. The issue is not that he/she did not know something they should have known, but that the aggrieved party assumed a common knowledge or understanding. This is quite likely to be also true on the other side of the argument.

The Full Knowledge Paradigm is particularly important when considering how to keep all the members of a thinking team 'in the loop'. However, it is equally important to consider its impact on people outside the thinking process who need to understand, accept, and support the decision being made. For example, if the management team decide to cancel the annual bonus, do the staff affected realise that this decision means that redundancies have been avoided? When in doubt, and the knowledge might increase support, take the small risk of re-stating the obvious.

The downsides of the WYKEK Paradigm are quite clear. Effective communication and alignment are unlikely if full information is assumed when important knowledge is not available to all the affected parties. The contributions that the Full Knowledge Paradigm makes to Good Thinking are not quite so obvious, but one of these is speed. Group thinking maintains its pace by assuming everybody is on the same page. Often, if the gaps are small, they don't affect the outcomes and people can fill them in as they go. No time is wasted ensuring everybody has a full set of the same data. Another slightly counter-intuitive advantage is that an assumption that others know what you know encourages open communication. If you believe others know what you know, you will not try to withhold information in a discussion.

Mapped to the DECIDE Model of thinking activities, the Full Knowledge Paradigm is most important at the beginning of both the Design activities and the Execution activities. These activities, **D**efining the required outcome and **I**dentifying the Best Alternative, are places where a common understanding of the context is key to success.

D.E.C.I.D.E. Decision Steps	Define Objective	Establish Criteria	Consider Options	Identify Best Alternative	Develop Actions	Evaluate Outcomes
Reducing Paradigms						
Full Knowledge WYKEK	■			■		

Test by: Looking for Incomprehension

The best sign that there are problems arising from the Full Knowledge Paradigm is where people can't understand why another party is proposing a solution which 'obviously' cannot work and the proposing party cannot understand why they are objecting. A more subtle sign is when one or both parties cannot believe how easy it was to agree on a decision. In such a case there is an excellent chance that both sides have a different view of the relevant facts of the case.

Rapidly reaching agreement in an open and frank engagement with feelings on both sides that 'finally we all understand each other' suggests that the Full Knowledge effect is a positive one.

Support by: Confirming the Relevant Facts after the Decisions are Made

When there is a good flow of communications and good progress is being made, maintain it until an outcome or decision is clear. Then decide what facts should be confirmed or need to be validated to support the decision. Relevant Techniques are:

- ◆ Decide in advance to keep a note of data points to be validated which arise in the thinking process, but to put them aside until an outcome is reached. This is sometimes called 'car-parking' the questions.

- ◆ Pre-brief and educate the Thinker(s) before the thinking process starts.

Subvert by: Focusing on Context and Key Data Points

Where the Full Knowledge Paradigm is likely to deliver Bad Thinking, slowing the thinking process to validate data points and confirm understanding is a worthwhile cost if the decisions being made are important.

Useful approaches include:

- ✧ Plan a series of thinking sessions with breaks for research and background work.
- ✧ In a group of Thinkers, ask participants to begin the thinking process by saying what they guess the others will consider to be important context or data points to be used in DECIDE activity one, **D**efine the objective.
- ✧ For an individual Thinker, ask stakeholders with an interest in the outcomes what they believe it is important to know before reaching a conclusion.

"Life is the art of drawing sufficient conclusions from insufficient premises."

Samuel Butler – Writer

CONFIRMATION BIAS

> *"What human beings are best at doing is interpreting all new information so that their prior conclusions remain intact."*
>
> Warren Buffet – Investor

This is probably the best know of the Reducing Paradigms and generally considered to be only a thinking fallacy, a commonplace cognitive error, with no upsides. This is an unfair assessment. When you are searching for edible plants in a forest full of other green things which might have zero food value, or even be poisonous, it is very useful to be acutely tuned into the various characteristics of your target lunch. That example was more relevant in the bad old days. In a modern environment, spotting another person who might help to advance your career in a conference hall full of less useful types is a real advantage. Confirmation Bias is also very useful when sifting a large set of CVs for potential candidates. However, it is also true that, when we are looking for evidence to back up our suspicion that our spouse does not respect our opinions, we will miss all the little bits of evidence that contradict our pet theory and pounce on every hint that backs it up. This highly selective data can then be delivered in a rant which leaves our opposite number bemused. It might add evidence to their (biased) view that we are a little unbalanced and unreasonable. Yes, there are downsides to the Confirmation Bias.

The workings of the Confirmation Bias Paradigm are well

understood and have been the subject of quite a few classic experiments. The original experiment is still the best example, which establishes how even well-educated people can get stuck in a Confirmation Bias.

In 1960, Peter Watson coined the term and defined Confirmation Bias with an experiment carried out on a set of university graduates.[68] He showed them a number sequence and asked them to work out the rule that determined the following numbers. They were allowed to suggest as many numbers as they liked and the experimenter would confirm whether or not they fit the rule. However, they could then guess what the rule was only once. If they were wrong they were disqualified. The sequence used was 2, 4, 6. You probably already have a theory. The numbers 8, 10, 12 do fit the rule, but the rule is not 'add 2' – disqualified! You might test a more subtle rule, such as 'the middle number is the average of the first and last' by offering the numbers 8, 11, 16. These numbers do fit the mysterious rule, but this rule is not correct. Disqualified! The numbers 7, 2986, 9999999 also fit the rule. But what is the rule?

The people who get the rule right are generally people who ask for feedback on numbers that *do not* fit the rule. 6, 4, 2 does not fit. -8, -10, -12 does not fit. The rule is 'the following number is larger'. The experiment showed that the experimental subjects would come up with a hypothesis and then diligently look for confirmation that it worked. Don't be too hard on them; further experiments have confirmed that is how the majority of humans work.

I Believe

The attempt to confirm a hypothesis is the natural, auto-thinking response that we humans have built in. This is because the action of hearing or formulating a hypothesis leads to trying to believe it. This is the first test we apply. We ask ourselves is this believable? If it is, we are then primed and ready to find evidence to support this belief. The psychologist Daniel Gilbert, in 1991, demonstrated that the effort-thinking of disbelieving is a much higher cost than the auto-thinking of believing.[69] Therefore, we default to the more efficient approach of 'if I believe it is possible, then it feels true, so let's find some evidence to back that up'. This approach makes sense if the hypothesis is unimportant. For example, whether or not 'Luigi cooks the best pasta in town', the question is not worthy of much mental effort. On the other hand, the idea that 'Luigi is a member of a criminal gang and his restaurant is a front for money laundering', is worthy of a bit more effort to validate. The trick is to focus on any hypothesis which has important, high impact outcomes and to look for evidence to refute it.

It is useful to relate this Paradigm to Karl Popper's 'falsifiable statement' test for truth we mentioned in the chapter on Certainty and Doubt. Looking for contradictory evidence is the essence of the scientific method.

I Want to Believe

It is worth noting that Confirmation Bias is measurably stronger for views that have a strong emotional effect on the 'believer' and on views that have been held for an extended period of time. This is the effect of the combination of the Availability Paradigm with Confirmation Bias in such cases. A person brought up in a culture that believes foreigners represent a threat to their family's well-being will readily identify lots of evidence to support this view.

> ### Distracting to Conform
>
> *The fact that since 2007 more than 40% of board members in Norwegian listed companies are women is evidence that the Norwegian business community is naturally less sexist than that in other European countries. Elsewhere the numbers only passed 20% in 2012 and female board members are still below 30% in the UK.*
>
> *It sounds convincing, and the Nordic countries do have an egalitarian brand.*
>
> *The quota was introduced in Norway first (in 2006). Norway raced ahead of other European countries, who introduced quotas a bit later. However, a study in Norway found the quotas had no effect on the representation of women in senior management in the firms where it applied. So the evidence better supports the simpler hypothesis; that quota's work!*[70]

Resisting the Confirmation Bias requires effort-thinking. This means that the bias has a much more powerful effect if the subject is either tired or distracted. A useful device to exploit this effect and embed an idea by enabling the Confirmation Bias is to present the idea in combination with a mild intellectual challenge. It is even more effective if that mild challenge is also a piece of confirming evidence. The classic example of how to make this happen is to provide some attention engaging statistic with the hypothesis. (See the box above.)

The use of a combined 'assertion with evidence' pitch to encourage Confirmation Bias in the audience may be either accidental or deliberate. If it is deliberate, it might be well-intentioned or malicious. It is very popular with demagogues. Wherever it comes from, being alert to its effects is a useful guard against Bad Thinking.

Mapped to the DECIDE Model of thinking activities, the Confirmation Bias Paradigm is most important in the activities:

Define the required Outcome and **E**valuate Outcomes.

D.E.C.I.D.E. Decision Steps	Define Objective	Establish Criteria	Consider Options	Identify Best Alternative	Develop Actions	Evaluate Outcomes
Reducing Paradigms						
Confirmation Bias	■					■

Test by: Assessing the Characteristics of the Thinking Being Done

An activity which challenges us to identify the valuable needles in a metaphorical haystack of varied and irrelevant data is one where the Confirmation Bias can be a useful accelerator. On the other hand, where new thinking and fresh perspectives are needed, Confirmation Bias is generally a threat to Good Thinking.

Where the implications of a hypothesis are significant to the decisions being made, Confirmation Bias is more likely to be a negative influence.

Support by: Encouraging Speed

Specific techniques are:

- ✧ Maintain Speed – Auto-thinking supports the bias effect.
- ✧ Agree and prioritise the key characteristics of data matches being sought.
- ✧ Design 'rules of thumb' to speed assessment against agreed criteria.

Subvert by: Opposing Views

Where Confirmation Bias is likely to deliver Bad Thinking, some responses are:

- ✧ Actively identify the Confirmation Bias matches on a first pass of the data. Put these matches aside. Then review the data again, looking for any other relevant data.
- ✧ Flip the bias. Reframe the question or data search as an attempt to contradict the defined hypothesis and search for the evidence to back up that contradiction.

> *"Facts do not cease to exist because they are ignored."*
>
> *Aldous Huxley – Writer*

THE OWNERSHIP PARADIGM

"Attachment is the root of suffering."

Buddha – Philosopher

Everybody puts a value on what they own. That value is set at a premium over the value for the same item set by someone who does not own it. That premium has even been measured. One experiment exploring this ownership premium showed an average difference of 130% in the price of a mug, depending on whether you own it or want to acquire it.[71] In the experiment to measure this 'endowment effect' (run by Richard Thaler at Cornell University), the 50% of students who were given a free coffee mug said they would be prepared sell it for an average of $5.25. The other 50% of students were, on average, not prepared to pay more than $2.25 to buy it. The 130% difference in this value perception does not apply to everything that is owned. After all, people selling their house tend to overvalue it at first, but they do sell it eventually, and not at a more than 50% discount to that first price. Where things have an easily measured market value the difference is much smaller, but the premium of the Ownership Paradigm does still persist.

Two Sides to Ownership

Ideas, concepts and perspectives have no measurable market value but they are very much owned. It can be hard to let them go or to exchange them for alternative ideas. The value of putting value on your opinions is clear. Whether you have acquired them through effort or adopted them through habit, being steadfast makes for stability in behaviour both of the individual and of the social group. We refer to this also in the chapters on 'Social Thinking' and on 'The Narrative Paradigm'. A familiar example is Galileo's ownership of the idea of heliocentrism in the face of strong criticism. Of course, challenges to his theory came from a very similar ownership of the idea that the Sun rotated around the Earth, which his critics sincerely believed.

The Ownership Paradigm is one of the most balanced in terms of its pros and cons for Good Thinking. It can make ideas robust and resistant to change, sometimes much more than they deserve to be. The artificial premium placed on ideas by their owners needs to be understood so that we can exploit it both to promote Good Thinking and to avoid Bad.

The concept of 'Sunk Cost' is a particularly important manifestation of the Ownership Paradigm. A good example is a theatre ticket that you can no longer use. Let's say that you have managed to get non-refundable and non-transferable tickets to a 'must-see' show a few months in advance. When the day arrives you are ill and you know that you will be miserable sitting in the theatre when you really should be at home in bed. When deciding whether or not to go the decision feels like throwing away the money and effort that you invested to get the booking. However, you cannot recover this cost, whether or not you attend, so therefore it should be ignored. The decision is just 'will I have a good time if I go?' Notice that there are two sides of the Ownership Paradigm in play here. Because you have looked forward to attending the show, you feel that you already own this experience. You also feel that you still own the sunk cost of the effort and money invested in getting the booking. Neither of those perceptions is true. In the same way, when there has been substantial investment made to develop an idea, abandoning that idea seems like losing that investment. However, if the investment has already been made, if it represents a sunk cost, then it should be ignored when deciding whether or not the idea is worth continuing with.

Work by Lita Furby[72] identified that Psychological Ownership has three sources which may act separately or in combination:

Control – anything in your control becomes in some way a part of yourself. This is how a free mug gains value through ownership.

Intimate knowledge – the more we know about something the more likely we are to feel ownership. This can be the result of study or assimilation like cultural norms. The Availability Paradigm also reinforces this effect.

Self-investment – expending energy and time in something creates a sense of ownership. If that investment is made as a team it is also enhanced by the common in-group effect described in the chapter 'Social Thinking'.

Being aware of these drivers of ownership and how they can combine enables us to spot where Ownership Paradigm is likely to occur and where it will drive Good Thinking, and Bad. It also allows us to actively create a sense of ownership of ideas where that might be useful.

Mapped to the DECIDE Model of thinking activities, the

Ownership Paradigm has more influence in the Execution Activities, particularly in Identifying the Best Alternative, and in Evaluating Outcomes. These are activities where ownership can cause bias towards options where we have made substantial investments and which are familiar.

D.E.C.I.D.E. Decision Steps	Define Objective	Establish Criteria	Consider Options	Identify Best Alternative	Develop Actions	Evaluate Outcomes
Reducing Paradigms						
Ownership Paradigm						

Test by: Taking the Balanced View

We should always assume that the Ownership Paradigm is in force. The challenge is to establish whether it is driving Good or Bad Thinking. It may be doing both simultaneously, but for different sides in the argument. Checking for the combination of reasonable and rational thinking used to support the idea will help. (Refer to the chapter on Rational and Reasonable Thinking.) Unreasonable + Irrational arguments are a sign of negative impacts of ownership. Reasonable + Rational positions will always appear with positive ownership. With the other combinations (Rational + Unreasonable and Irrational + Reasonable) the effect of ownership might be positive or negative. However, identifying the combination of 'R&R' thinking being used will help to expose the Ownership Paradigm at work and identify its effects.

Support by: Investing in Ownership

Where ownership will create support for useful new positions and ideas, the psychological ownership drivers can be deployed to create it.

Specific techniques are:

- ⬥ Control – Give the Thinker(s) responsibility and authority for the idea. This might be by asking them to formally record it and/or asking them to communicate it to others in a way they think is appropriate.

- ⬥ Intimate Knowledge and Self-Investment – Provide the Thinker(s) with the time, information or training they need to deeply understand, and to build on, the idea.

Subvert by: Creating Distance

Where the Ownership Paradigm is delivering Bad Thinking by causing resistance to change, solutions include:

- ⬥ Ask the Thinker(s) to take the opposite side to the one they are owning, as they would in a formal debate. Creating arguments for this new position will challenge the assumptions that have been hidden due to the Ownership Paradigm. Also, the self-investment and improved knowledge will create ownership of the new position.

- ⬥ Carry out a Sunk Cost Analysis on important ideas or positions. Clarifying which efforts and investments can no longer be recovered will reduce the sense of ownership.

> *"When a team takes ownership of its problems,*
> *the problem gets solved.*
> *It is true on the battlefield, it is true in*
> *business, and it is true in life."*
>
> *Jocko Willink – US Navy Commander*

4.3 HEURISTIC PARADIGMS

> *"Setting an example is not the main means of influencing another, it is the only means."*
>
> *Albert Einstein – Scientist*

A heuristic is an approach to problem solving that uses a practical method which is not guaranteed to be optimal or perfect, but which is sufficient for the immediate goals. Heuristics remind us of the value of accuracy over precision. It is always better to be roughly right rather than precisely wrong. They also rely on the law of diminishing returns. When an answer is correct to plus-or-minus 10%, the cost of improving that margin of error to plus-or-minus 5% is not worth the effort, unless it will change the decision to be made because of that extra detail.

To deliver Good Thinking we need to distinguish between three types of heuristic paradigms: unconsciously created substitutions, consciously designed simple rules of thumb, and the more complex maps and models.

Maps and Models are usually seen as the domain of geographers, architects and engineers but we all use them all of the time. The most commonly used model is the metaphor. We have all heard that Internet e-commerce can be described as a retail store with 'infinite aisles', or a refugee arriving in a new environment as a 'fish out of water', or DNA as the 'software of life'. Models are heavily used in science. Famous examples are Heisenberg's Uncertainty Principle, which put Schrödinger's metaphorical cat into a life-threatening situation in a dangerous box and Einstein's tram ride at the speed of light through Zurich. Models are a powerful technique to simplify complex concepts and to bring an idea to life. We can find them inspiring or even fun, as when a poet or songwriter crafts a powerful metaphor, or when a teacher creates that 'aha moment', making a complex and difficult concept snap into focus by explaining a clever model.

Intensity Matching

We create and use models both consciously and unconsciously. They are far more often unconscious. Both conscious and unconscious models will often exploit what psychologists call 'intensity matching'.[73] This is the effect, for example, where the sympathy you feel for a worthy cause can be matched to the amount of money you feel is appropriate to donate to it. The monetary donation you make does not really have a logical or exactly measurable link to the sympathy the cause inspires, but you feel very comfortable making that translation. In fact, if your attention is drawn to this subconscious intensity matching it can even be a bit disconcerting. We will see this intensity matching effect working through all of the Heuristic Paradigms.

Models are never a full refection of reality. They are generally summaries of big complicated things from a focused, narrow, perspective. This is often the very reason that they are useful. They can capture the insight and learning of one individual or group into a powerful summary and make that information available to many others. A good heuristic both captures and enables Good Thinking. You might even say that a model can be seen as a powerful artefact of pure thinking. The process of consciously making a model, choosing the right perspective, and finding a useful way to capture and communicate an idea, is a useful process. It will always enhance the understanding the modellers have of whatever it is that is being modelled.

However, when one is using a model it can sometimes take on a semblance of reality. It can then become confused with what it intended to represent. We will see that when the Substitution Paradigm allows this switch to happen unconsciously it very often leads to Bad Thinking.

Cognitive Models

For clarification we need to state we are not talking here about models as 'Mental Models' in the sense that cognitive scientists use it. The theory of Mental Models is used to explain how decisions are made, the very act of thinking. The theory says that we unconsciously create constructs to allow us to get our brains around reality. The theory of Mental Models, which originated in the 1990s, has its fans who are currently experimenting to develop the theory. Other psychologists who disagree prefer a Rules of Inference model. It is a hot topic and it is complicated. Mental Models theory is a meta-model; a model used for modelling models. We will avoid this fascinating rabbit hole by staying out of the cognitive

> *psychologists' backyard of how low level, unconsciously generated, models actually work. We will simply accept that Mental Models Theory is correct when we look at the Substitution Paradigm. In the other Heuristic Paradigms we will focus on higher level models, created consciously.*

The Heuristic Paradigms are:

Substitution Paradigm: Unconsciously replacing complex questions, which we may not have the data or time to answer, with easier questions which are broadly comparable can save a lot of effort. When the question is a critical one it is important to test to see if any substitution is in play, and to check that it is a useful one.

Rules of Thumb: A conscious distillation of a complex decision or analysis process into a simple method which gives a good approximate result is obviously a very useful thinking technique. The risks are using an inappropriate rule, or forgetting that the answer is only approximately right.

Models, Maps & Metaphors: A deliberate replacement of a complex, multi-dimensional, or even intimidating idea with a simple, compelling one can help analysis and focus efforts. However, a misjudged map design can have unfortunate and far-reaching consequences. And we must always remember that the map is not the territory.

The Heuristic Paradigms are relatively equally important right across the decision process. This is reflected in the DECIDE mapping diagram. Substitution and Rules of Thumb are the most important of the Paradigms in this class.

D.E.C.I.D.E. Decision Steps	Define Objective	Establish Criteria	Consider Options	Identify Best Alternative	Develop Actions	Evaluate Outcomes	Overall Importance
Heuristic Paradigms							
Substitution Paradigm	■					■	■
Rules of Thumb		■	■		■	■	■
Models, Maps, & Metaphors	■			■			
Relative Importance	■	■		■	■	■	

Part 4: A Taxonomy of Thinking Paradigms

THE SUBSTITUTION PARADIGM

> *"I wish I had an answer to that because I'm tired of answering that question."*
>
> *Lawrence Peter 'Yogi' Berra – Sports Coach*

Never mind what the advertisement claims, is the model in the advertisement attractive? If the answer to this easier question is 'yes', then we usually believe the claim in the ad is true. In the Introduction to this book we briefly mentioned the Substitution Paradigm in its most common manifestation, in advertising. It is quite easy to spot a substitution in this context but still very difficult to resist. Substitution is another example of our natural bias to low energy, auto-thinking. In advertising there is also a strong complementary effect with the Availability Paradigm. The logo for the product may be a familiar one. If so, we readily substitute questions like, 'Do I trust this supplier? with 'Am I familiar with this logo?' These substitution devices have been used for selling and persuasion for a very long time. Since long before any scientist tried to measure the effect. But in the last twenty years there has been a lot of work done to understand how and why the Substitution Paradigm works.

The technical description of the Substitution Paradigm is: If the 'target question' does not present an easy answer in auto-thinking mode, rather than switch to effort-thinking, we will first try to find a replacement, 'heuristic question', which can be answered in automatic mode. If an easy heuristic question is available, we unconsciously attach this answer to the target question. The

Framing Paradigm and the Availability Paradigm quickly kick in to support this substitution process. We can test the heuristic question's validity as a substitution using effort-thinking, provided we are aware of the substitution happening.

It is easier for a substitution to be unconsciously accepted if it is closely related to the target question. The heuristic questions that we choose are driven mainly by the Framing Paradigm. The target question and the context in which it is asked trigger a cascade of related items in our minds to ensure that our substitution is relevant. Then the Availability Paradigm encourages us to choose easily retrieved data for the substitution. It is important to note that the target question context might have very little to do with the question but it still triggers associations which can influence the substitution we make. In a job interview for the role of a computer programmer, the fact that the applicant has a squint has no bearing on their ability to do the job. However, it might prompt the substitution question: 'Do I feel comfortable around people who don't maintain normal eye contact?' In an advert where the target question is: 'Is this vacuum cleaner good value for money?' the fun young couple appearing in the advert can prompt the substitution question, 'Do this couple look happy together?' and you have a lot more information available to answer that much easier question. In an election campaign, the real question, 'Are these policy proposals realistic?' can become 'Does this candidate look mature and competent?'

Swapping Dates

An experiment[74] which clearly shows substitution (and how it is combined with availability) asked randomly selected students two questions in a different order. The questions were:

How many dates did you go on last month?

How happy are you these days?

Asked in this order, dates first, happiness second, there is a very strong correlation between the answers to the two questions. Not surprisingly, more dates equalled more students reporting themselves as happy. However, asking the question in the opposite order, happiness first, dates second, produced results with no correlation between the two answers. What was happening here? The students who were encouraged to think about their dating success first used this easier question as a substitute for the happiness question. The students who came across the complicated happiness question first substituted other heuristic questions for this question and came up with a wide range of different answers. (See also the Framing Paradigm.)

Of course, this habit of substitution is not all bad. The benefits of the Substitution Paradigm are that it acts like an unconscious version of the Rules of Thumb Paradigm (described in another chapter). Replacing complex questions with related simple ones saves energy and time. Deciding if a complex economic strategy being proposed by a political figure is valid can be usefully, and safely, substituted with the question: 'Is this an intelligent and trustworthy person?' A confident 'yes' to the heuristic question allows you to delegate thinking about the more complex question to the person proposing it and to their team of experts. In an unfamiliar situation where time is of the essence, substitution might even save a life. For example: In a war zone the simple question, 'Are elderly women likely to be armed and dangerous?' might be a useful substitution for the more complicated target question of 'Which of the warring factions is this person aligned with?'

Mapped to the DECIDE Model of thinking activities, the Substitution Paradigm is most important at the start and the end when **D**efining the required outcome and **E**valuating Outcomes. It may also have an impact when **I**dentifying the Best Alternative. All of these activities are focused on answering questions.

D.E.C.I.D.E. Decision Steps	Define Objective	Establish Criteria	Consider Options	Identify Best Alternative	Develop Actions	Evaluate Outcomes
Heuristic Paradigms						
Substition Paradigm	■			■		■

Test by: Focus on the Questions

It is a good idea to assume that the Substitution Paradigm is always going to be working unconsciously any time you are thinking. Much of the time it will be bringing you to perfectly good answers faster than if it was not there. If the issue being addressed is significant then take the Thinker(s) out of the substitution zone by engaging them in effort-thinking. This will validate the quality of the answers and tell us if the Substitution Paradigm is a benign influence.

Support by: Minimising Distractions

The way to get good unconscious substitutions going is to keep the context congruent with the subject. For example:

- ✧ Work in an environment that the thinking efforts are addressing.
- ✧ To encourage rational thinking, discuss the idea of rational and reasonable thinking before addressing the issue. For emotional thinking, present the Thinker(s) with images of people and places associated with the issue.

Note that the deliberate and conscious substitution of difficult questions with easier ones is addressed in the chapter on Models, Maps and Metaphors.

Subvert by: Waking up the Thinker(s)

Where the Substitution Paradigm is delivering wrong answers, the best subversion is a switch to effort-thinking. Some ways to do this are:

- ✧ Slow down and repeat the question. Take a pause to clear the mind then come back to the start of the question again.
- ✧ Be explicit about what the target question is and how well the answer fits it. This is especially important in a group setting where a number of different substitutions can happen simultaneously to different members of the thinking team. Encourage the Thinker(s) to capture the question in words and to rephrase it from different perspectives.

> *"It is not every question that deserves an answer."*
>
> *Publilius Syrus –Writer*

RULES OF THUMB

> *"You are remembered for the rules that you break."*
>
> Douglas MacArthur – Military General

It is possible to make the case that because the whole of civilisation is based on the sharing of knowledge, civilisation is simply an enormous collection of Rules of Thumb masquerading as education and culture. Let's see if I can persuade you.

We all have Rules of Thumb that we use in day to day life. For example: Being less than 5 minutes late for a 45-minute face to face meeting is embarrassing, but just about ok. However, if you are 5 minutes late for a 15-minute telephone conference, that is rude. Rules of Thumb can be personal, or be shared by a social group where they are sometimes referred to as the 'culture' of the group. Another example: Based on their accent, dress sense, and the fact that they are at the same event as me, I will probably be comfortable chatting to this person. In these cases they are the rules that promote social cohesion and determine 'the way we do things around here'.

Business Rules

A business acquaintance of mine recently asked me how much it would cost to build a block of 12 small apartments in an average London suburb. He asked me this because many years ago I trained as an architect and I still dabble in property. After a few moments thought, and a quick reference to my mobile phone calculator, I told him that "£1.2m would be the building costs and that a site for 12 apartments would be about £2.25m with planning permissions." I could be confident of my estimate because I used the following London specific simplifications: Build cost = £1k/m², Average gross apartment size = 100m² (inc. common circulation space), Target margin for a simple development = 25%, average cost of apartments = £350k. His response was: "About £3.5m, so roughly £300k per apartment?" I had taken a very complex question and answered it based on a few Rules of Thumb. He then took the information in the answer and created a new Rule of Thumb. This is a great way to quickly get fairly accurate, approximate answers to complicated questions. It is very like the Substitution Paradigm we looked at in the previous chapter, but it begins as a conscious, deliberate substitution.

Making Rules of Thumb Respectable

We might think of Rules of Thumb as somehow inferior to a direct and detailed approach to a problem. However, the use of Rules of Thumb is a very respectable approach to formally addressing difficult technical problems. A Hungarian called George Pólya is perhaps the greatest populariser of using Rules of Thumb in mathematics and other sciences. His book on the subject formalised techniques for approximation and sold more than a million copies. This is pretty impressive for a book called *How to Solve It, Mathematics and Plausible Reasoning* by a professor of mathematics.[75] He does refer to his Rules of Thumb as 'heuristics' despite the fact that he omitted the unconscious Suggestion Paradigm and he did not formally include Models, Maps and Metaphors. However, we must forgive him this slip of the pen as he certainly did give Rules of Thumb a solid scientific credibility.

Rules of Thumb for when to use Rules of Thumb

Using a Rule of Thumb is always a good response when a question is characterised by both complexity and repetition. In an example like the one given earlier about the cost of building apartments, a 'rough cut' rule which can sort out the irrelevant potential sites from the opportunities worth more consideration is very valuable when assessing many potential projects.

Where we have complexity without repetition, the value of using a Rule of Thumb is driven by the law of diminishing returns. Precision and its cost often have a logarithmic relationship. It can cost twice as much effort and resources to get from an answer which is correct to plus-or-minus 10%, to an answer improving that margin of error to plus-or-minus 5%, and ten times as much to get to plus-or-minus 1%. This extra cost is not worth it unless that increase in precision in the answer is very likely to change the decision to be made. For example, if you know that 70% (+/- 10%) of your customers have a bad experience with your customer services team, you don't need to invest the effort to establish that the more precise number is 65% (+/- 5%). You already know that you need to take action to fix customer services.

The Pros – It is Easier

The value of the Rule of Thumb Paradigm is pretty obvious. For the individual Thinker it moves thinking from the resource hungry effort-thinking to a nearly auto-thinking mode. It avoids the repetition of addressing the same question in detail again. Also, when shared in a group, Rules of Thumb act as a division of labour for thinking. When a particular question has been answered, sharing the resulting rules means others reusing them can focus their efforts on new thinking challenges.

The Cons – It is Too Easy

What are the downsides of the Rule of Thumb Paradigm? The big risk comes from the fact that deploying Rules of Thumb is auto-thinking or close to it. Because it is conscious auto-thinking it feels like considered thinking, a bit like effort-thinking. This inspires confidence in the Thinker. However, the Thinker is relying on the unconscious assumption they are making that the rule is reliable. This may not be a safe assumption. This is particularly true with the widely accepted Rules of Thumb that make up the culture of a group or organisation. Just because the general rule is that the best chess players are skinny nerdy guys doesn't mean that the drop dead gorgeous girl in the chess club can't be the one with real championship potential. Unless, of course, this is Hollywood. Then the scriptwriters' Rule of Thumb says she will certainly win.

I'm Biased against Prejudice

Rules of Thumb are what underlie bias and prejudice. The word 'bias' gets bad press; it is actually a neutral thing and very often delivers good outcomes. Bias is an opinion based on a Rule of Thumb which is either built on personal experience or absorbed from the surrounding group. I'm biased against stealing. You probably are too. That is mostly a Rule of Thumb that I have picked up from other people. I do have a little personal experience to support this view, and it may also be supported by some built-in, evolved social instincts, but it is a good and useful bias.

Prejudice is a special example of bias that is based on bad data, whatever its origin. It can be unreasonable and/or irrational in origin. Let's say you don't like Ethiopian food. If you have tried a few Ethiopian restaurants and have not enjoyed the food, you have a reasonable and rational bias against it. If you have never tried it, and the Framing Paradigm has reminded you that Ethiopia suffered many famines, and then the Substitution Paradigm has suggested the alternative question, 'Do people suffering famine tend to eat well?' and you think, 'Well, it can't be good food'. Then that is an irrational prejudice. It is a Bad Thinking bias.

Mapped to the DECIDE Model of thinking activities, the Rules of Thumb Paradigm is most important in the **E**stablish Criteria and **D**evelop Actions activities. Here they accelerate the whole decision process as discoveries and observations made in the **D**efine Objectives and **I**dentify Best Alternative activities become Rules of Thumb which are specific to this problem.

D.E.C.I.D.E. Decision Steps	Define Objective	Establish Criteria	Consider Options	Identify Best Alternative	Develop Actions	Evaluate Outcomes
Heuristic Paradigms						
Rules of Thumb						

Test by: Identify the Rules of Thumb that are used in Key Outcomes

We can rely on the rule of thumb that Rules of Thumb will always be in use in the thinking process. We can't unpick them all without destroying their value as accelerators, so we need to focus on points where they may be acting as unhelpful prejudices rather than useful biases. If experts are consciously and fluently using Rules of Thumb which other experts understand and agree with, it is likely that Rules of Thumb are adding value in the process. It is worth noting in passing that some prejudices may be benign or irrelevant to the question being addressed. Don't waste the Thinker(s) time on these. When important outcomes are at the point of being finalised in the decision process, ask the question: 'What assumptions and Rules of Thumb have been used to support this answer or output?'

Support by: Taking a Positive Attitude to Rules of Thumb

If new Rules of Thumb are being agreed to be deployed later in the decision process, these should be highlighted and noted. If existing Rules of Thumb are in use, these should be accepted and noted without debate. Specific techniques are:

- ⬥ Experts are defined by being repositories of relevant and useful Rules of Thumb. Use them.

✧ Target and reward the creation of new Rules of Thumb as successes in the process, particularly for repetitive thinking tasks.

Subvert by: Unpicking Prejudices

Where the Rules of Thumb are actually prejudices and are therefore delivering Bad Thinking by limiting options, some responses are:

✧ De-construct these rules into their component assumptions and data points to be tested and validated for relevance and accuracy.

✧ Reverse the Rules of Thumb to test the impact on decisions if they were to say the opposite of what they do. For example, 'women don't like to study economics, therefore…' becomes 'women love to study economics, therefore…'

"If you can't solve a problem, then there is an easier problem you can solve. Find it."

George Pólya – Mathematician

MODELS, MAPS & METAPHORS

"The map is not the territory."

Alfred Korzybski – Scientist & Philosopher

Maps can be very valuable. Petrus Plancius made a map in 1593 that was kept top secret for 20 years. It also made his fortune; he was a founder of the Dutch East India Company and his maps showing routes to the Spice Islands in the Indian Ocean were the key to enormous wealth.

Models are Looking Good

Models too can create real value. The structure of DNA that James Watson & Francis Crick came up with in 1953 in a one page scientific paper was a breakthrough which crystallised a huge amount of research and theory. This 'aha moment' opened the floodgates of applied genetic research. The model integrated insights from genetics, biochemistry, chemistry, physical chemistry, and X-ray crystallography to show that DNA had a structure both complex enough to hold enormous amounts of data and yet elegantly simple enough to reliably code life itself.

An example of a powerful metaphor from the author's personal experience is a Chief Information Officer (CIO) comparing the replacement of a company IT infrastructure to a mayor building a subway in a busy city. The CIO's challenge was that his project was dull, uninteresting, and very aggravating to the other executives on the board. The story of how the expensive disruption of removing old computers to replace them with new, more flexible machines so that the company could arrive at the point where they could do exactly the same things, but just a little better, was not compelling. Using his metaphor of the new subway, the CIO explained how the mayor of an imaginary city was deeply unpopular when the streets were being torn up and the citizens could not see the expensive tunnelling work happening underground as a new metro system was built. The mayor's unpopularity meant that he risked his re-election and was only vindicated once the streets were back to normal and transport was much easier than before. This story was much more engaging than the actual IT project. The sympathy for the mayor doing the right thing against strong resistance was transferred to support for the CIO from the board.

Models, Maps and Metaphors are essentially the same thing from the point of view of the Thinker. They are a representation of something we need to think about which are designed to make Good Thinking easier. They are also very useful when communicating our thoughts. To an architect or engineer, a model suggests a three-dimensional representation of a physical thing. It might have a physical reality or a digital one. To a financier or economist, a model is generally a mathematical construct (often in the form of a spreadsheet) which can be used to explore the financial impacts of various strategies. To scientists, a model might be a drug pathway or a mathematical formula representing an astronomical event, things which they will never see in real life.

Any of these could just as easily be called a Map or a Metaphor. For convenience I will use the terms interchangeably.

Metaphor Machines

We all understand that metaphors help with new perspectives. Corts & Pollio carried out research in 1999[76] leading to the observation that university lecturers delivered bursts of metaphors when they introduced new subjects, or attempted to throw new light on familiar facts in their lectures. Earlier work by Pollio suggests that we typically use six metaphors a minute; combining four 'frozen' (non-original) with two novel metaphors.

That the use of abstract models is so commonplace in human communications is actually quite surprising. I'm not aware of any direct evidence that other creatures can use models the way humans can. It is likely that the smartest ones do to some extent, but it is without doubt a higher order thinking ability. It is also a fundamental ability of humans. We can unconsciously deploy immensely complex models. Think of the grammar that underpins language in a way that is not yet fully understood by science. The linguists, psychologists and neurologists between them still haven't decided if use of the grammar model is learned or innate. Thinking in abstractions is a very impressive bit of evolution.

The evolution from the conscious to the unconscious use of abstract models is equally fascinating. The psychologists Gentner & Stevens pulled together an impressive overview of current thinking on consciously deployed mental models.[77] They have gathered evidence that shows that using different models can have substantial impacts on people's speed and depth of understanding of ideas. They look at the way models, which have developed to address the same concepts at different times and simultaneously in different cultures, have impacted the degree of understanding of the concepts. It is worth noting that their focus is on consciously developed abstract models. They include models which, after being consciously created, have become an accepted perspective. These are models which people rely on without being fully aware of them.

Does Modelling Fit the Paradigm Model?

We are treating modelling as a Thinking Paradigm, rather than simply taking note of it as a one of the underlying cognitive processes which we look at in the Thinking about Thinking part of this book. Why does this make sense? The answer is in its extraordinary effectiveness in decision making and problem solving. It is most important in the initial activity of Defining Objectives in the DECIDE decision process. Creating or choosing the right map, metaphor, or model at the start of the decision process can have a more positive influence than any other paradigm we deploy, consciously or unconsciously. Compelling models are very 'sticky' and will frame thinking throughout the decision process. When they are good they are great. However, if they happen to be inadequate or misleading they can have powerful Bad Thinking effects.

Where a model is very convincing or attractive it can become seductively lifelike. This particular example of the Substitution

Paradigm relating to models was christened the 'Ludic Fallacy' by Nassim Taleb in his book *The Black Swan*. The origin of the word 'Ludic' is a game, as the problem is where the Thinker(s) confuse the game for the reality it was designed to represent.[78] An amusing example of this effect is in the book *Catch 22*. A line on a map showing the position of ground forces is moved beyond the besieged town of Bologna even though the situation on the ground is unchanged. The position of the line is then used to justify a decision that the pilots are not required to fly an air-raid over the very dangerous anti-aircraft batteries there.

So models are important. How do we go about creating a good one? Modelling is a broad and complex subject in its own right but the headline characteristics of a good model are:

The appropriate level of detail. Maps and models need to have just enough detail to be useful, any more than that is a waste of effort in creation and a distraction in use.

Include all the key dimensions. The model needs to address the most important dimensions of the problem. For example, in a project the usual suspects are time, cost and quality.

Simple is better. A good model is one that is used, by as many people as possible, with a minimum of training. Also, if a model is simple it is less likely to become a black box which generates answers that are not understood. Generally, models can handle higher levels of complexity. Maps take the middle ground. Metaphors, on the other hand, need to be very simple to be effective.

These three headline rules are explained in more detail in the section on Decision Tools.

Mapped to the DECIDE Model of thinking activities, Models, Maps & Metaphors are most important when **D**efining the required outcome.

D.E.C.I.D.E. Decision Steps	Define Objective	Establish Criteria	Consider Options	Identify Best Alternative	Develop Actions	Evaluate Outcomes
Heuristic Paradigms						
Models, Maps, & Metaphors						

Test by: Looking at Model Dominance

Where models are promoting Good Thinking there will be general agreement which models are relevant, and frequent use of these models to support discussions. Agreed models evolving as the decision process unfolds are a very good sign that the model is both robust and appropriate.

A sign that models are less useful is where there are competing models being used to support competing views. Asking the Thinker(s) to explain how the models they are using work, and how they map to the problem being addressed, is an excellent way to check their understanding. This will also validate the relevance and usability of the models in play.

Support by: Building Models

The primary support mechanism to improve the influence of the Models, Maps, and Metaphors Paradigm is to focus the Thinker(s) attention on the models in use. Specific techniques are:

✧ Carry out an exercise to identify and develop a model that can explain the problem and/or the solution to all of the stakeholders involved. If useful maps and models are in place ask the Thinker(s) to come up with compelling metaphors. Even if there is an existing model, teasing out the relevant dimensions of the issue and identifying the key stakeholders' reactions are valuable.

✧ Training in model design and use is very valuable. Particularly where mathematical models are used, agreeing which assumptions are most relevant and what ranges they should allow will highlight the sensitivities in the problem in a concrete way. Also, a common understanding of good practice in model design and testing has valuable communications impacts. (See also the section on Decision Tools.)

Subvert by: De-constructing Models

The use of models can deliver Bad Thinking, either by the Thinker(s) substituting managing the model for managing reality (Ludic Fallacy), or when models artificially limit the Thinker(s) perspective on the issue. Some responses are:

✧ Bullet-proof the models. Ask the Thinker(s) to identify scenarios where the model(s) will fail. Then assess whether these failure scenarios are likely. If there are competing models, bullet-proofing should be done on each of them individually. A competition or comparison is not the objective. If competing models are being promoted it suggests that both are flawed.

✧ Develop models of alternative types. If a metaphor is the common model, try to build a map or an alternative model to deliver a different perspective on the issue. This may enable the Thinker(s) to present the issue more persuasively to different audiences or stakeholders.

> *"[It is] impossible to map the world –*
> *we select and make graphics*
> *so that we can understand it"*
>
> Roger Tomlinson – Geographer

4.4 EXPERIENCE PARADIGMS

> *"Experience is not what happens to a person.*
> *It is what a person does with*
> *what happens to them."*
>
> *Aldous Huxley – Author*

Francis Ysidro Edgeworth was a brilliant (if frequently incomprehensible) philosopher and economist. In 1881, he came up with a clever conceptual machine, the hedonimeter. This imaginary machine would constantly and accurately measure an individual's level of pleasure and pain. This theoretical measure of the quality of experience, combined with some experimental observations, later inspired Daniel Kahneman to carry out formal experiments to measure the pleasure or pain an individual experienced. His scientific approach broke experience into three parts. What the individual: i) expects to experience; ii) actually experiences; and iii) remembers experiencing, related to a single event. He proved that these three measures are substantially different for a single subject looking at one experience. Kahneman come up with the terms 'decision utility', 'experienced utility', and 'remembered utility' to distinguish between these three perspectives on experience.[79] This is important because utility (pleasure or pain), whether it is psychological or physical, is the most powerful driver of human behaviour. Because our perception of utility changes with our time perspective on our experience, our behaviour is directly affected by this highly subjective measure.

At the boundary of cognitive science and behavioural psychology our experience becomes the critical factor affecting the quality of our thinking. The emotional or instinctive response we have to the thinking that we do will affect the conclusions we draw and the choices that we make. Like all of the other Thinking Paradigms, these responses are both useful for Good Thinking and have the potential to lead to Bad Thinking. Because these Experience Paradigms are by definition informed by quick auto-thinking and have a large emotional component, it is difficult to be self-aware of their presence, and to be objective about their influence.

The Experience Paradigms are:

Risk Reward Paradigm: (Decision Utility). As we reach extremes of risk, our behaviour becomes more extreme. Also, whether a possible outcome is framed negatively or positively strongly affects our perception of the level of risk associated with it. For good evolutionary reasons, our fear of negative outcomes is much stronger that our attraction to positive outcomes.

Creative Memory Paradigm: (Remembered Utility). False memories are the norm. We can trust that our memory will be effective most of the time. However, we should be aware that our memories, and other people's memories, should be treated as only broadly correct.

Experienced Utility, the feelings that we have 'in the moment' are not considered as a separate paradigm. This is because this kind of experience can only be mentally processed in the form of Decision

Utility or Experienced Utility. We influence Experienced Utility through other paradigms like the Framing and Substitution Paradigms.

Experience Paradigms have influence throughout the decision-making process and we are frequently completely unaware of them or their impacts. They are most often expressed in our perception of risk and reward. This includes the way our creative memory contributes to framing risks and rewards. They are personal paradigms. It is the risk to us, the rewards we expect, and our personal experience in memories. Outcomes for others are much less affected by the Experience Paradigms; we are better at being objective when we don't have skin in the game. It is important to be alert to these paradigms at the many points in our thinking when decisions are driven by our prediction of outcomes affecting us directly, and/or based on our personal recollection of previous experiences.

The Experience Paradigms are most important in the Execution Activities in the DECIDE decision process. They are also important when Defining Objectives. This reflects the point that the Experience Paradigms are more about how we expect to feel when we *do* things, rather than our emotions when we are designing and planning things.

We can see this in the visual mapping below.

D.E.C.I.D.E. Decision Steps	Define Objective	Establish Criteria	Consider Options	Identify Best Alternative	Develop Actions	Evaluate Outcomes	Overall Importance
Experiencing Paradigms							
Risk Reward Paradigm							
Creative Memory							
Relative Importance							

RISK REWARD PARADIGM

"Nothing will ever be attempted, if all possible objections must be first overcome."

Samuel Johnson – Writer

I bet on the Lottery. I know that it is not a good use of my money. In the UK the odds of winning the first prize is 1 in 14,000,000. So I am basically giving the money away each week. I am not behaving with rational utility in the eyes of an economist. However, quite a lot of people who understand economics play the lottery and, just like the lottery players who don't understand economics, they are proving that Prospect Theory works.

Amos Tversky and Daniel Kahneman in their seminal 1974 paper set out the principles of Prospect Theory.[80] It is a descriptive model of the real-life choices that people make when making decisions involving risk, where the probabilities of all potential outcomes are known to them. The theory says that individuals will typically make choices based on the potential value of *immediate* gains (or losses) rather than the final outcome, and that they do *not* evaluate these choices rationally. Hence the popularity of lotteries. The theory is a little complicated and has had quite a lot written about it. I have put a summary explanation of Prospect Theory in the Appendix. Here we will focus just on its implications for Good Thinking, and Bad. If the theory is new to you, it is worth having a look at the Appendix. However, it is not essential to look at that detail before you read this chapter.

What Prospect Theory says in practice is that there are four levers that will make a human become irrational about risk:

- **Certainty** – We like it, and we will pay a premium to get it.

- **Small probabilities** – We don't intuitively understand them, so we tend to 'round' them to 0% or 100%. i.e. treat them as certainties.

- **Loss aversion** – Potential losses are much more powerful than potential gains as motivators.[81]

- **Relative Benefit** – Benefits are always relative (above the level of basic needs).[82] If you are considering yourself, £100 is a lot to gain if your weekly income is £200. It is not so important if you earn £5,000 per week. However, relative to others, £100 for you and £0 for him is worth much more than £1,100 for you and £1,000 for him.[83]

As any combination of these levers impinges on our risk reward analysis, we may make extreme and irrational decisions. They are, however, also quite reasonable decisions, or they look reasonable from the perspective of another normal human.

This idea of extreme choices when the person making the decision is 'close to the edge' is reflected in this graphical model of Prospect Theory.[84]

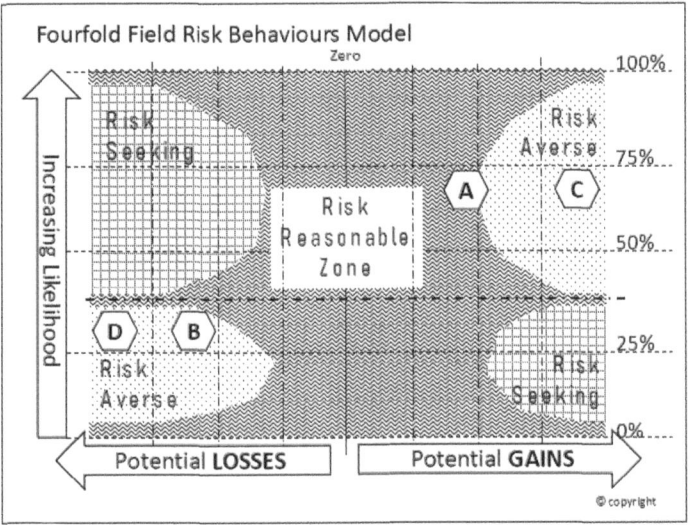

Looking at the four levers as they affect the diagram.

- ✧ **Certainty** only appears at the top and bottom edges of the plane.

- ✧ **Small probabilities** (close to 0% and 100%) occur at the top and bottom of the diagram.

- ✧ **Relative benefit** has more impact as we move left or right from the centre. It is extreme on the left and the right of the diagram, as the value of losses and gains increases.

- ✧ **Loss-aversion:** The risk-reasonable area is asymmetrical around the vertical zero axis. This is because expected losses have more impact than gains; the risk-rational area is smaller on the losses side of the picture, the left-hand side.

When I 'invest' in a lottery ticket, framing it as a potential gain, with very high gains and low probability, it is in the bottom right risk-seeking area. On the other hand, framing it as a loss it has a very high probability and low value. It is mapped high and just to the left of the zero loss/gain line. So I am being risk-rational in my purchase. From both perspectives it is an understandable decision.

An alternative example is a patient being told that an operation has a 70% chance of a cure. Their position is likely to remain in the risk-rational zone [A], whereas a patient told that they have a 30% chance of no improvement to their health after the operation may end up in the risk-averse zone [B]. This is despite the fact that the impacts described (cure or no-cure) are equal, and the 70% cure versus 30% no-cure are also equal. The asymmetry of loss aversion creates a different response to the same risk when framed differently.

If the stakes are raised and the patient is told the possible outcomes are 70% for survival [C] versus a 30% risk of *death* [D], both the gain and the loss frames will probably put the patient into the risk-averse area. If the probability is revised to be closer to the extreme (98% survival or 2% death) the patient will simply round that to a certainty and behave as if the outcome is guaranteed survival.

It is important to note that two individuals mapping the same issue onto the map from their own perspective will usually end up in different places. If it is a zero sum game, one will be positioned on the losses side, the other will be on the gains side. If the outcome impacts are not the same for each of them, they will be relatively different distances from the zero impact vertical line in the centre. Also, if they have different views on the probability of the outcome we will see them at different heights on the vertical probability scale. If they end up in different risk-behaviour zones, then communications between the two parties will be strongly affected. Perhaps one is in a risk-reasonable mode while another is risk-seeking. Misunderstandings are likely, particularly if the Full Knowledge Paradigm (WIKEK) comes into play.

Like all the Thinking Paradigms, the tendencies which contribute to the Risk Reward Paradigm and our irrational response to risk and reward have pros as well as cons for the Thinker. We can compare these for each of the four risk/reward levers.

Risk/Reward Lever	Advantages	Disadvantages
Certainty	*A bias to certainty encourages us to answer questions and supports definite decisions.*	*Accepting and dealing with ambiguity is key to getting from the hypothesis to the proof on any new idea.*
Small Probabilities	*Rounding small probabilities to a definite 'Yes' or 'No' simplifies and speeds thinking.*	*This trait blinds us to high impact, rare events. The so called 'black swans' that can have significant impact.*

Relative Benefit	Seeking advantage relative to others and to our current circumstances means we are focused on what delivers competitive advantage and maximum benefits.	This can translate into chronic dissatisfaction which can cause unnecessary stress, after our real needs are already met.
Loss Aversion	A human strongly driven by loss aversion will prioritise avoiding risks and dangers and stay alive longer.	Real opportunities can be overlooked because a material reward will be overshadowed by the minor risk.

Whether the Risk Reward Paradigm is supporting Good or Bad Thinking is very much a matter of context and the perspectives of different stakeholders as they are affected by the outcomes of the decision process. Being aware of its influence is the key.

Mapped to the DECIDE Model of thinking activities, the Risk Reward Paradigm has most impact when choices are being made, i.e. in the activities: **D**efining Objective, **I**dentifying the Best Alternative, and **D**eveloping Actions.

D.E.C.I.D.E. Decision Steps	Define Objective	Establish Criteria	Consider Options	Identify Best Alternative	Develop Actions	Evaluate Outcomes
Experiencing Paradigms						
Risk Reward Paradigm	■■■			■■■	■■■	

Test by: Mapping Stakeholders and Looking for Dissonance

Mapping the position of various stakeholders with an interest in the outcomes of the decision process to the Fourfold Field Risk Behaviours Model and assessing if they are out of the Risk-Rational area, and/or out of synch with each other is the first step. Next try to assess if the behaviours driven by their position in the map are helpful or not. For example, realising that a stakeholder has been pushed into a risk-seeking zone might be useful if they need to come up with new ideas, or counter-productive if the risk impacts are severe.

Support and Subvert by: Moving People's Position on the Map

In the case of the Risk Reward Paradigm, supporting or subverting the paradigm are both done by moving the stakeholder(s) and the Thinker(s) position in the Risk Reward Map. These moves are made by adjusting some or all of the four risk reward levers.

- ⬥ **Certainty** – To get people out of the risk-seeking or risk-averse zones to provide certainty. Remember that people will pay a premium to get certainty, so it may be possible to trade it for concessions of some kind. Likewise, deliberately removing certainty can be an effective, if risky, way to get Good Thinking, and Bad started if the Thinker(s) are too complacent.

- ✧ **Small probabilities** – Formal Risk Management techniques which identify and record low probability possibilities that have high impacts (positive or negative) are useful. This will stop these outcomes from being rounded to a certainty. It will also allow low probability and low impact possibilities to be assessed, and perhaps safely ignored.

- ✧ **Loss aversion** – Accept the fact that losses are much stronger than gains as motivators, and educate the Thinker(s) to be aware of this. Re-frame impacts as losses to increase energy levels in the decision process. Or, re-frame potential losses as gains to reduce the intensity. Identify common, objective, and neutral measures of outcomes – like financial impacts or numbers of people affected to make the comparison of negative and positive outcomes as objective as possible.

- ✧ **Relative Benefit** – Take advantage of this lever by expressing target and actual outcomes in relative terms. Choosing the frame by which relativity is measured will avoid unhelpful alternatives coming into force. Identify unconscious measures of relativity and bring these to the Thinker(s) attention if it is helpful.

> *"Risk it; go for it. Life always gives you another chance, another go at it.*
> *It's very important to take enormous risks."*
>
> *Mary Quant – Designer*

CREATIVE MEMORY PARADIGM

> *"The difference between false memories and true ones is the same as for jewels: it is always the false ones that look the most real, the most brilliant."*
>
> *Salvadore Dali – Artist*

In 1906 in Chicago, a farmer's son was hung when he confessed to a murder, despite the fact that he had a credible alibi which was recognised by the police. The Harvard psychologist who reported the detail of the case, Hugo Munsterburg, described how the accused willingly produced more elaborate and detailed confessions in repeated interviews. In the end his false memories overwhelmed the alibi evidence and it cost him his life.

Poor on Precision but Broadly Accurate

George Markus carried out a fascinating experiment over a ten-year period. He asked 3,000 people for their views on contentious issues like the legislation of drugs, and then ten years later he asked them again. In the second round he asked them their recollection of their position ten years earlier and what their positions were now. He found very little difference between the remembered and current positions. People felt sure that their opinions had not changed much in the ten years. However, he found much larger differences in the actual views from ten years ago compared to the updated views. It seems that our memories are not as accurate as we like to think.

Other experiments have shown that very detailed, multi-sensory, false memories of being involved in a crime can be created in 70% of subjects with suggestive interviewing techniques.[85] The cause appears to be related to the Framing and Availability Paradigms. These work in the same way as subjects who confidently remember additional words which did not appear on a list of words presented to them previously. Brain scanning evidence shows that they are engaging the frontoparietal region of their brains, the area associated with 'a sense of familiarity'.[86]

So if the science says that we can't trust our memories, and thinking relies on memory, how do we trust our thinking? Every moment of thinking involves retrieving memories of facts and concepts as the raw materials for thought. On a more positive note, if human memory was constantly unreliable the world would be a very chaotic place. It is obviously not as much of a problem as we might think. For Good Thinking we just need to be aware of the risk of memory errors and what might cause them, particularly when our memories are a critical input.

Getting the Gist of it

We humans have two types of memory: 'verbatim' and 'gist'. Verbatim as the name suggests is an accurate and exact recall. Gist (defined as the general meaning, or essence, of something) is a more sophisticated type of memory that takes advantage of mental associations for speed, and possibly supports broader creativity. As we grow from childhood to adulthood we rely more on gist. In extremis, if brain damage or old age damages our memory we will rely more on gist to close the gaps. The 'gist' model of memory is a part of the, very scientific sounding, 'Fuzzy Trace Theory' of memory, which has been experimentally confirmed many times since it was created by V.F. Reyna and C.J. Brainerd in the mid-1990s.[87] The understanding is emerging that the verbatim and gist memories are parallel and separate cognitive processes. If one is interrupted the other is not directly affected. Our memories as we recall and express them are a synthesis of the two systems.

Right Most of the Time

An interesting question to ask is: 'What are the evolutionary advantages of having a memory which is sporadically unreliable but does not reduce our confidence in what we believe we can remember?' One example is that amnesia in relation to the extreme stress of childbirth would be useful for survival by encouraging repeat performances. Less obvious but also useful is the effect of this confidence in our memories that helps us to make solid decisions based on information that is broadly correct. Other clear advantages are: the speed and efficiency of recall that 'gist' memory provides, and the link between memories and the mental associations delivering creative capabilities. On balance, confidence in our memory will be more conducive to Good Thinking than it will be a risk factor for Bad Thinking.

We need to give memories the benefit of the doubt. Because the recollection process is unconscious and out of our control, memories are driven by our best intentions and in the honest belief that they are true. If two people naturally come up with alternative memories of the same event, most likely neither is lying or trying to deceive the other. We need to accept this fact when our memories are challenged, despite our natural confidence in them, and despite the way that the Narrative Paradigm will fill in the blanks to ensure that they are coherent and credible. We also need to give the alternative memory presented as a challenge the benefit of the doubt. If the two memories are broadly aligned there is little value in challenging the details. For example, if we both remember that we had a great time on our honeymoon, it doesn't matter whether or not that really was the first time we tried Thai food.

Mapped to the DECIDE Model of thinking activities, the Creative Memory Paradigm is most important in **D**efining the required outcome and **E**valuating the Outcomes activities.

D.E.C.I.D.E. Decision Steps	Define Objective	Establish Criteria	Consider Options	Identify Best Alternative	Develop Actions	Evaluate Outcomes
Experiencing Paradigms						
Creative Memory Paradigm	■					■

These are the activities where previous experiences are key to the quality of the thinking.

Test by: Knowing the Main Tricks that Memory Plays

If the memories of one or more individual are critical to the quality of the decision process outcomes, then the memories should be assumed to be broadly correct and only the important details need to be challenged. If disagreements on the shared 'history' between the thinkers and/or stakeholders are causing tensions, there is a good chance that the Creative Memory Paradigm is causing Bad Thinking.

Some useful pointers to common memory distortions are:

Peak Experience: The highest intensity experiences, positive or negative, are highly available to our recall. For better or worse they are a disproportionately powerful influence on our judgement. Manage this distortion by asking the Thinker(s) to take the time and invest the effort to also actively recall the low intensity experiences.

Duration Negligence: We tend to distort time and our measure of the sum of positive or negative impacts in retrospect. This can lead to errors of judgement when comparing experiences. Objectively comparable summaries will help to avoid this. Compare actual durations, as well as measures of the highs, lows and averages of the experiences being compared.

Support by: Quickly Capture Broad Implications

Where the Creative Memory Paradigm is delivering Good Thinking by encouraging speed and creative cross-fertilisation. Maintain that momentum by:

- ✧ Accepting approximations and discouraging in-depth recollections by maintaining the speed of thinking.

Subvert by: Encourage Verbatim Memory of Key Facts

An emphasis on verbatim memory is less creative and more reliable. Specific techniques to encourage verbatim memory use:

- ◆ **Focus on evidence.** Maintain records of important events and inputs in an accessible and searchable format. For groups of Thinkers working together over a long period a shared repository of data, communications and records of the decisions they have made is very valuable.

- ◆ **Agree which are reliable data sources.** The Thinker(s) should invest energy is validating sources before beginning the initial Design solutions activity in the DECIDE process. Memory sources should also be validated as they are added during the decision process.

> *"Memory presents to us not what we choose, but what it pleases."*
>
> *Michel de Montagine – Philosopher*

CONCLUSIONS

"The empires of the future are the empires of the mind"

Winston Churchill – UK Prime Minister

I am passionately interested in the science of Good Thinking, and Bad. I am not a scientist, but I do hope that by organising the information collected here in a coherent and logical way it will make the powerful scientific insights of the last few decades accessible to more people.

As well as the new taxonomy of Thinking Paradigms that the book is based on, I have also set out two original syntheses of existing thinking in the book. These are the three-dimensional Empathy_IRM Model and the Four Field Risk Behaviours Model. I do hope that these might pique the interest of some scientists who are experts in those areas.

I hope too that some of my enthusiasm for cognitive science makes it from this book into the education system, perhaps by inspiring some students and some educators. I believe that there are good reasons to include some of the contents of this book into the study of subjects like psychology, or economics, or even philosophy as these are taught in second level schools and colleges.

I was also inspired by the ambition of Daniel Kahneman. In the introduction to his seminal and inspiring book, *Thinking, Fast and Slow*, he said that he hoped the ideas in that book would become 'water-cooler material'. He imagined that people would begin to use cognitive science concepts in everyday office chatter. This would be real evidence that the concepts are accepted and more widely understood. I think that the water cooler test is an excellent measure of success for any book about thinking. I sincerely hope that this book passes that test.

As I said in the Introduction, the virtuous circle is very powerful; better thinking about thinking improves the way we do our thinking, and so on. I hope that I have injected a little bit of energy into that virtuous vortex.

The Downside of Cognitive Science

Discussions with reviewers of the early drafts of this book raised an interesting observation. It is that a detailed understanding of the practical applications of the Thinking Paradigms and the other principles described in this book would be very useful to 'the bad guys'. That they might educate and inspire a con-artist, a would-be dictator, or anyone else with malign intentions. This is undoubtedly true. Any tool can be put to use to inflict harm. On the other hand, my view is that the vast majority of people are well intentioned. For this reason I am sure that, whatever impact it does have, it will do more good than harm.

In that spirit there are two areas I want to focus on in this conclusion:

- ✧ What future we might expect to see in cognitive science and the tools of Good Thinking; and
- ✧ The power of teaching to spread ideas, and to consolidate learning.

Conclusions

THINKING ABOUT THE FUTURE

"It's not a human move. I've never seen a human play this move. So beautiful."

Fan Hui – Professional Go Player

In this age of AI (Artificial Intelligence) we cannot look to the future without considering the impact of computers on Good Thinking, and Bad.

Go is a game that has been played for 2,500 years and which is exponentially more complicated than chess. Unlike chess it has no defined winning end state; it is known as a game of intuition as much as strategy. In March 2016 an AI programme called AlphaGo, built by a Google subsidiary called Deep Thought, beat Lee Sedol five times. Lee, the world champion at Go, said that he was at first surprised, then overawed by Deep Thought's capabilities. Before the five game match started he expected to win the series. Then he kept playing because he hoped to win at least one of the games. This first version of AlphaGo had been trained by being fed the moves and outcomes of thousands of professional games to find patterns that won. It took some time but this machine learning approach worked. The second version, called AlphaGo Zero, was not given access to the data on previous games. Instead it started from scratch, playing games against itself. In 40 days it was much better than the first version. It was creating strategies that humans had not come up with in 2,500 years of playing. It was "no longer constrained by the limits of human knowledge," said Demis Hassabis the CEO of Deep Thought. Amazing, and just a bit scary.

OK Computer

Is this the end of civilisation as we know it? Is this the 'singularity'; the frequently discussed 'inflection point' where AI becomes smarter than humans. Are we carbon-based life forms about to be out-gunned by the silicon-based ones? The short answer is not yet, and not for some time. AlphaGo does not know it is playing a game; it has no concept of beating another player. It has neither the interest nor the capacity to understand the reactions of its competitor. It is an Expert AI System, very good at doing just one thing. It is not evidence that General AI is close. (General AI is defined as the intelligence of a machine that could successfully perform any intellectual task that a human being can.)

To illustrate this point we can look at AI attempting to do something that humans don't like doing. A recent experiment set two one-armed industrial robots the challenge of assembling flat-pack IKEA furniture.[88] The results were pretty impressive. Following a set-up stage using simple instructions analogous to the printed instructions, they spent 11 minutes scanning and planning, then 9 minutes to assemble a chair frame, which had 19 components. The large components were scattered about at random in reach of the robots' arms but the more fiddly fixings were organised in a dispenser. It is not 2,500 years of gaming strategy, but it is a pretty practical use of technology. It is another high potential application for Expert AI System, but not yet quite capable of ending of the nightmare of assembling flat-pack furniture. AI has some way to go before it becomes humanity's saviour or its nemesis.

Out of the Box Thinking

One matter which will need some careful thought now and in the future is the 'black box' effect of AI. While it is true that every AI is designed by humans, that does not mean that there is always an individual or group of individuals that understand exactly how it works. Layers of programming and components are built up to create an AI capability. It is literally not possible to track the exact steps that are taken to deliver each AI output. But we don't need to panic. We accept the outputs of black boxes all the time. If you have booked a flight based on what a comparison site told you, you have spent your hard earned cash on the advice of an AI black box. This is analogous to trusting your auto-thinking unconscious (your biological black box) to help you to do Good Thinking. On the other hand, if that AI is controlling a vehicle and an error that it makes might hurt a human, or worse, if it is guiding a weapon which can kill people, that black box effect raises profound moral and legal questions. Even an AI HR Assistant filtering resumes for a job application might filter based on race or gender because previous data shows few black women are successful in the target role. If the reason for that fact is that very few black women have had the opportunity to do the role, then the AI has a built-in prejudice, rather than a useful bias. The fascinating risks of unintended prejudice in sophisticated AI solutions are outside of our scope here. However, it is worth remembering this: If Thinkers don't understand how a tool supporting their decision works, it is by definition a black box. No matter how complex or simple it is, blindly accepting the output of a black box is not Good Thinking. At the very least we need to be aware of it, and to have conscious and logical reasons why we choose to rely on its outputs.

Please don't misunderstand me. I am not suggesting for a moment that the current AI breakthroughs are not worth the risks. The future is bright. Humans, expertly assisted by AI, are already beginning to make extraordinary advances in medicine and science. AI will help us to make giant leaps in the most difficult challenges we face, including a big cognition science question, 'How do our brains work?' Perhaps these future AI-assisted breakthroughs will take us closer to a true General AI. If and when they do, they will probably be based on a new generation of quantum computing rather than our old-fashioned digital technology.

These are exciting times, but we will not be delegating the job of Good Thinking to the AI machines for some time yet. When might we finally develop a machine that passes as human in Alan Turing's famous test? When will an AI be able to make a suspicious human judge believe that it is human, while carrying out a range of different tasks on demand? All the evidence says that this is still a very long way into the future. In any case, all of these advances are just another step on a long road. AI-assisted thinking has been with us for millennia already. Despite the fact that it has been based on relatively limited technology, it has had a huge and positive influence.

AI is an Old Story

Recollection is a critical component of thinking. As we have seen in the chapter on the Creative Memory Paradigm our memory has two parallel processes, verbatim and gist. We have been supporting the verbatim component for as long as we have been telling stories in the form of ballads. The meter and rhyme provides a structure to the data that helps with recollection. The clay tablets and cuneiform writing invented by the Sumerians in Mesopotamia around 3,500 BCE enabled perfect verbatim recollection of trading transactions. This was an early AI, a technology-assisted memory.

A major improvement in this assisted memory technology was the printing press. Invented first in China about 600AD it was dramatically improved by the addition of moveable type by Gutenberg in Germany about 1,000 years later. We mention the abacus in the chapter on Decision Tools. This is another simple AI technology which has been extending human thinking capabilities for about 3,000 years. AI is already old. We are getting rapidly better at it and there is lots of good stuff around right now that just about anyone can use. When we are thinking, it makes very good sense to be familiar with the commonplace and cheap calculating and memory enhancement tools that are available to all of us right now: spreadsheets to calculate with and searchable electronic notes and databases to super-power our memory, including the extraordinary searchable memory of almost our whole species available via the Internet.

What is Next?

The latest state-of-the-art, technology-assisted Expert AI Systems will certainly have profound and positive impacts in Cognitive Research. There will be hardware developments too which will catapult us forwards in our understanding both of how the brain works and of how we think. The wearable brain scanner developed in the UK by UCL and the University of Nottingham, announced in March 2018, is a good example.[89] It will allow the working of our brains to be observed in action in normal active situations, rather than while lying prone in a traditional magnetoencephalography (MEG) scanner. When you consider that we will also be applying the new machine learning techniques (that we developed so AI could do stuff like play Go) to the data captured by such a device, we can expect powerful insights to come very quickly.

We can also expect that the cognitive psychologists doing experiments on human behaviour will also make great strides in the near future. This is a very young area of scientific research with only a few decades of thinking and experimenting carried out so far. As these new insights make their way into our public awareness, the human race will keep on getting better at thinking. We still have lots of potential to learn and to behave as an even smarter version of the multi-headed human organism that inhabits the earth.

We have already come a long way by doing some very good quality thinking about thinking. There is a lot to look forward to.

LEARNING BY TEACHING

> *"The most effective teacher will always be biased, for the chief force in teaching is confidence and enthusiasm."*
>
> Joyce Carey - Author

There is a common saying which originally appears in a play by George Bernard Shaw:

"Those who can, do. Those who can't, teach."

I would counter that cynicism with this alternative;

"Those who do, will teach by example.
Those who can't are likely to be poor teachers."

I was flying from Sydney to London in the early 1990s and I found myself sitting beside an interesting character. While my wife was very sensibly sleeping, he and I got into a long conversation about a book that he had just read called *The Seven Habits of Highly Effective People* by Steven Covey. He was very enthusiastic about how useful the book was and, as I showed some interest, he took the opportunity to talk me through all of the seven habits. His passion to communicate the content persuaded me to buy the book. I have found it useful ever since.

If you know the book you will know that the last of the seven habits is called 'Sharpening the Saw'. It explains how teaching others is an excellent way to confirm your own understanding and to strengthen your commitment to what you have learned. This explains my fellow traveller's enthusiasm. There are a lot of good ideas in that book. One of the best ideas, in my practical experience, is that idea of consolidating your learning by teaching.

Teaching is Stressful

Evidence suggests that mild stress enables memory consolidation and retention. This is of course very useful in that strong memories of stressful situations help us to avoid them in the future. However, stress and emotional intensity are two sides of the same coin. There is good scientific evidence that strong emotions enhance memory consolidation and recall. [90] Teaching someone is always more engaging emotionally that studying alone. It requires attention to the student. Their physical response and body language are unconsciously monitored by the teacher to assess their interest. Their questions are a challenge to explain further, and to provide better examples and metaphors to get concepts across. This emotional intensity will always enhance the teacher's learning consolidation. In addition, students can present new perspectives on ideas which will improve the teacher's understanding.

As I wrote this book, I imagined that I was teaching these concepts to an audience that was not present and who I had not met. I learned a great deal. My thinking about thinking evolved. For example, the Taxonomy of Thinking Paradigms is the skeleton on which this book relies for structure. This taxonomy evolved substantially from the initial concept through the various drafts.

Conclusions

Attempting to summarise and explain the many concepts that I believed I already understood was hard. Choosing what to omit, and what to emphasise, gave me a better insight into what I thought I already knew. This was also very much the case when I got feedback from early reviewers and editors, to whom I am greatly indebted.

You have made it this far. First let me say thanks. I hope that means you both enjoyed the book and that you learned some stuff that you believe might be valuable to you. Second, let me recommend that you try to share the ideas you do like with others. I am sure that you will find it as entertaining as I do to hear other people's reactions, positive or negative. I am also very sure that you will learn a lot in your efforts to teach your selected students.

> *"No one learns as much about a subject as one who is forced to teach it."*
>
> Peter F. Drucker – Author

APPENDICES

THINKING PARADIGMS QUICK REFERENCE

I dog-ear books. I turn down the corners of pages to help me to locate parts that I find interesting and that I might refer back to. Perhaps you do too. Maybe you have dog-eared a few pages in this book? I hope so. For me, the number of dog-eared pages is a measure of how good a book is. In addition to dog-ears, summaries can be very useful. In some ways this Quick Reference chapter is the reason I set out to write this book. I wanted to create an accessible, well-structured reference of tools and tips that anybody can use to improve their thinking. Then I discovered that I needed to write the book before I could create the summaries.

This section contains a high level summary of each Thinking Paradigm. These can be used as a prompt to memory. You might use this section to quickly explore which paradigm might be encouraging Bad Thinking, making a decision activity difficult, or to look for ways to plan for Good Thinking in the decision process. They are divided into our four classes of:

- ⬥ **Constructing Paradigms** – used in the creation of thoughts and ideas.

- ⬥ **Reducing Paradigms** – used in analytic and critical thinking.

- ⬥ **Modelling Paradigms** – used to simplify complex questions to facilitate creative and analytical thinking

⬥ **Experience Paradigms** – influencing our reactions to, and our risk perceptions of, ideas.

The paradigms are mapped to the activities in the DECIDE decision process. The maps take advantage of 'equivalent intensity' showing the important intersections in a darker colour. The diagrams also exploit our capability to process graphical information to find patterns. The maps are structured as hierarchical levels. I find it very useful, I hope you will too. On the other hand, if this is not how you like to think and these pictures don't help you, you can safely ignore them. There is no extra information in the maps; they are simply a different view on the same data set out in the book.

The top level map (Level 0) shows that Creating Paradigms and Experience Paradigms have the most influence on both Good Thinking, and Bad.

Level 0

D.E.C.I.D.E. Decision Steps	Design Activities	Execution Activities
Creating Paradigms	■	
Reducing Paradigms		
Heuristic Paradigms		
Experience Paradigms	■	■

Notes on the Map Structure:

The Thinking Paradigms are ranked individually at Level 2.

Levels 0 and 1 are an average of Level 2 Rankings.

Relevance Rankings at Level 2 are $1 = Low$, $2 = Medium$, $3 = High$.

Appendices

At this level we can also see that, as you might expect, the Design Activities have a little more influence on decision quality than the Execution Activities.

Drilling down to Level 1, we look at the relationship of the four sets of Thinking Paradigms to the DECIDE activities. We can see that Identifying the Best Alternative involves the majority of the Thinking Paradigms.

Level 1	DESIGN ACTIVITIES			EXECUTION ACTIVITIES			
D.E.C.I.D.E. Decision Steps	Define Objective	Establish Criteria	Consider Options	Identify Best Alternative	Develop Actions	Evaluate Outcomes	Overall Importance
Creating Paradigms							
Reducing Paradigms							
Hueristic Paradigms							
Experience Paradigms							
Relative Importance							

At the lowest level (Level 2) the paradigms are mapped individually. Once again they are grouped into the four classes.

Level 2							
D.E.C.I.D.E. Decision Steps	Define Objective	Establish Criteria	Consider Options	Identify Best Alternative	Develop Actions	Evaluate Outcomes	Overall Importance
Constructing Paradigms							
Framing Paradigm							
Narrative Paradigm							
Confidence Paradigm							
Intuition Paradigm							

Good Thinking, and Bad

Level 2							
D.E.C.I.D.E. Decision Steps	Define Objective	Establish Criteria	Consider Options	Identify Best Alternative	Develop Actions	Evaluate Outcomes	*Overall Importance*
Reducing Paradigms							
Availability Paradigm							
Incomplete Info WYSIATI							
Full Knowledge WYKEK							
Confirmation Bias							
Ownership Paradigm							

Level 2							
D.E.C.I.D.E. Decision Steps	Define Objective	Establish Criteria	Consider Options	Identify Best Alternative	Develop Actions	Evaluate Outcomes	*Overall Importance*
Heuristic Paradigms							
Substitution Paradigm							
Rules of Thumb							
Models, Maps, & Metaphors							

Level 2							
D.E.C.I.D.E. Decision Steps	Define Objective	Establish Criteria	Consider Options	Identify Best Alternative	Develop Actions	Evaluate Outcomes	*Overall Importance*
Experiencing Paradigms							
Risk Reward Paradigm							
Creative Memory Paradigm							

I imagine people using this summary to identify which paradigms are the 'likely suspects'. First they will identify the decision activity where they want to ensure Good Thinking or where they have experienced difficulties. Then they check which Thinking Paradigms are the most influential in that activity in the DECIDE process. Once they have identified which paradigms are of interest they can use the summaries in the following pages to refresh their memory on how to use the paradigms to promote Good Thinking. There is also the option to delve a little deeper by going back to the chapter that gives a more detailed description of the specific paradigm.

Appendices

Constructing: THE FRAMING PARADIGM

The cascade of associated concepts that is triggered by any stimulus will prime our minds to create a frame of reference. This 'framing' will make large volumes of related information readily accessible, both consciously and unconsciously, for the next action or thought.

Test if it is supporting Good or Bad Thinking by:

Identifying the frame of reference created by observing what is being associated by the Thinker(s) to the issue being addressed. Asking if the frame of reference is appropriate and relevant to the question being addressed.

Mapped to the decision activities model: **D** E **C** I D E

Defining the required outcome
Considering Options activities

D.E.C.I.D.E. Decision Steps	Define Objective	Establish Criteria	Consider Options	Identify Best Alternative	Develop Actions	Evaluate Outcomes
Constructing Paradigms						
Framing Paradigm						

Pros: The Framing Paradigm is at the heart of the efficiency and creativity of the human mind.

To Support: Use carefully chosen framing stimuli to initiate a focused thinking process. Remove distractions which trigger irrelevant frames.

Cons: The alternative word for a frame of reference is a bias. Conscious or unconscious bias narrows creativity and reduces objectivity.

To Subvert: Deliberately reframe the thinking process by challenging the Thinker(s) to take a radically different (even playful) perspective on the issue. Relocate the Thinker(s) to an unfamiliar environment and ask them to do their thinking there. Tell jokes.

Interacts with the following paradigms:

- Narrative
- Confidence
- Availability
- Substitution
- Intuition
- Rules of Thumb

See also the chapters:

- Rational and Reasonable
- Auto-thinking vs Effort-thinking
- Emotional Thinking

Constructing: THE NARRATIVE PARADIGM

The human mind can link together almost any collection of facts to create a credible storyline. This storyline will imply clear cause and effect and will skip over, or automatically fill in, any missing sections in order to maintain coherence.

Test if it is supporting Good or Bad Thinking by:

Identifying the pivotal points in the narrative (the key points that provide continuity and coherence). Check for hidden assumptions and data errors at the pivotal points.

Mapped to the decision activities model: **D** E **C I** D E

Defining the required outcome
Considering Options
Identify Best Alternative activities

D.E.C.I.D.E. Decision Steps	Define Objective	Establish Criteria	Consider Options	Identify Best Alternative	Develop Actions	Evaluate Outcomes
Constructing Paradigms						
Narrative Paradigm	■		■	■	■	

Pros: The creation of a storyline can produce 'aha' moments as insights are gained, explaining how things are connected. A strong storyline will help greatly with the listener's understanding, support, and retention. The credibility of the story and of the storyteller is enhanced by a good story.

To Support: Use metaphors and storytelling techniques.

Cons: The coherence of a false story can be so compelling that the story may even survive the discovery of facts that contradict it.

To Subvert: Challenge coherence. Create credible alternate storylines.

Interacts with the following paradigms:

    Framing
    Ownership
    Availability
    Incomplete Information (WYSIATI)
    Full Knowledge (WIKEK)
    Confirmation Bias

See also the chapters:

    Auto-thinking vs Effort-thinking
    Emotional Thinking
    Probably Just Lucky

Appendices

Constructing: THE CONFIDENCE PARADIGM

The confidence of decision makers will rarely match their ability and knowledge. Both overconfidence and under-confidence are caused by a focus on your own skills and disregarding the skills of others. The effects are strongest in forecasting and prediction.

Test if it is supporting Good or Bad Thinking by:

If the decision makers believe the task/decision is easy, assume overconfidence. If they see it as difficult, assume under-confidence. Anything in between suggests that the Confidence Paradigm is not making a negative impact.

Mapped to the decision activities model: D **E** C I D E

The Confidence Paradigm is unusual in that its positive and negative effects are quite evenly distributed across the decision process. There is a focus in **E**stablish Criteria activity.

D.E.C.I.D.E. Decision Steps	Define Objective	Establish Criteria	Consider Options	Identify Best Alternative	Develop Actions	Evaluate Outcomes
Constructing Paradigms						
Confidence Paradigm		■				

Pros: The Confidence Paradigm can either inject energy or encourage reserve. Provided the outcomes of the decision activity are not critical we can take advantage of these effects and ignore the natural errors in outputs it will cause.

To Support: Maintain speed on non-critical tasks/decisions. Slow down and focus on the complexity of important elements of the decision.

Cons: The Confidence Paradigm means that forecasts and opinions are rarely right. They are either above or below what is correct. If the outputs are important to the decision this must be corrected. It can also drain energy through under-confidence or encourage undue haste by overconfidence.

To Subvert: Point out the complexity in what appears easy and provide the expertise to simplify what looks difficult. Use the Standards of Evidence tool (see Certainty and Doubt) to measure the degree of truth in positions taken.

Interacts with the following paradigms:

Intuition
Incomplete Information (WYKIATI)
Full Knowledge (WYKEK)
Rules of Thumb
Creative Memory

See also the chapters:

Certainty and Doubt
Auto-thinking vs Effort-thinking
Social Thinking

Constructing: THE INTUITION PARADIGM

Intuition occurs when a subliminal process delivers an answer based on expertise and experience which the Thinker possesses. Typically, the Thinker cannot explain how the answer originated.

Test if it is supporting Good or Bad Thinking by:

Check that conditions for useful intuition are present: 1) The Thinker is an expert; 2) The Scope is defined and narrow; and 3) The Outcome is immediate or near term.

Mapped to the decision activities model: D E C **I** D E

The Intuition Paradigm is most important in **I**dentifying the Best Alternative where it can help to make rapid selections based on expertise built up in the initial design activities.

D.E.C.I.D.E. Decision Steps	Define Objective	Establish Criteria	Consider Options	Identify Best Alternative	Develop Actions	Evaluate Outcomes
Constructing Paradigms						
Intuition Paradigm						

Note that DECIDE becomes AsTeEx in the Intuition process.

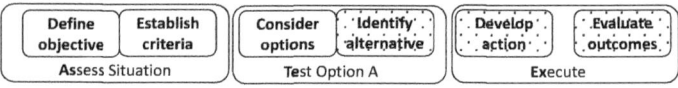

The AsTeEx Intuitive Decision Model

Pros: In the right conditions, especially in urgent situations, intuition can efficiently deliver better solutions than more detailed approaches to decision making.

To Support: Focus the decision on one expert. Agree to act on that expert's decision rather than debate.

Cons: Where expertise is weak, the scope of the issue is wide, or the question being addressed in new, intuitive answers are likely to be wrong despite the confidence of the decision maker.

To Subvert: Carefully follow the DECIDE activities. Agree to decide as a group. Ask for explanations of the origins and logic of proposed solutions.

Interacts with the following paradigms:

   Framing
   Confidence
   Confirmation Bias
   Incomplete Information (WYSIATI)
   Rules of Thumb

See also the chapters:

   Auto-thinking vs Effort-thinking
   Emotional Thinking
   Default Thinking Style

Appendices

Reducing: THE AVAILABILITY PARADIGM

The tendency of thinkers to be most influenced by information that is readily recalled. Also, the tendency we all have to confuse the easy availability of ideas with their validity and importance.

Test if it is supporting Good or Bad Thinking by:

Matching the level of the Thinker's engagement to the importance of the outcomes. Low-to-low and high-to-high matches mean that the Availability Paradigm is a benign influence. A mismatch of engagement and importance suggests there will be problems.

Mapped to the decision activities model: **D** E **C** I D E

Defining the required outcome
Considering Options activities

D.E.C.I.D.E. Decision Steps	Define Objective	Establish Criteria	Consider Options	Identify Best Alternative	Develop Actions	Evaluate Outcomes
Reducing Paradigms						
Availability Paradigm						

Pros: Availability means fluency and brings energy and speed to decision activities.

To Support: Introduce expertise. Educate and pre-brief the Thinker(s).

Cons: Readily available information gets too much weight in decisions. Availability can block out important new data. Availability of data can become a proxy for validity.

To Subvert: Ensure that the Thinker(s) are engaged emotionally and intellectually in the question by requiring formal analysis of data.

Interacts with the following paradigms:

Substitution
Associative
Incomplete Information (WYSIATI)
Peak Experience

See also the chapters:

Auto-thinking vs Effort-thinking
Emotional Thinking
Default Thinking Style

Appendices

Reducing: INCOMPLETE INFORMATION (WYSIATI)

It is easy and natural to believe that the information you hold is a complete set (What You See Is All There Is). This very often happens in automatic-thinking mode but is also quite common in effort-thinking mode.

Test if it is supporting Good or Bad Thinking by:

If the question being considered is important but is not urgent then the Incomplete Information Paradigm will probably have a negative effect. For less important and for urgent questions it is more likely to have a useful effect.

Mapped to the decision activities model: D **E C** I D **E**

Establishing Criteria
Considering Options
Evaluate Outcomes

D.E.C.I.D.E. Decision Steps	Define Objective	Establish Criteria	Consider Options	Identify Best Alternative	Develop Actions	Evaluate Outcomes
Reducing Paradigms						
Incomplete Info WYSIATI						

Pros: Confidence in the completeness of the Thinker's data encourages speed and decisiveness. Useful for both less important and urgent questions.

To Support: Maintain and drive thinking speed.

Cons: Where the outcomes of decisions are important a full review of all the data for completeness is essential.

To Subvert: Slow down. Broaden perspectives. Bring in new expertise

---

Interacts with the following paradigms:

Narrative,
Full Knowledge (WYKEK)
Confirmation Bias
Creative Memory

See also the chapters:

Auto-thinking vs Effort-thinking
Probably Just Lucky
Social Thinking

Appendices

Reducing: FULL KNOWLEDGE (WYKEK)

The assumption that others have access to the same information that you have (What You Know Everybody Knows).

Test if it is supporting Good or Bad Thinking by looking for incomprehension:

If opposite sides are surprised at how difficult, or easy, it is to get to a decision there is a good chance that one or both are wrongly assuming the other side share full knowledge. On the other hand, a positive sense that both sides 'get it' is a sign of a positive WYKEK impact.

Mapped to the decision activities model: **D** E C **I** D E

Defining Objectives
Identifying the Best Alternative

D.E.C.I.D.E. Decision Steps	Define Objective	Establish Criteria	Consider Options	Identify Best Alternative	Develop Actions	Evaluate Outcomes
Reducing Paradigms						
Full Knowledge WYKEK	■			■		

Pros: The WYKEK assumption delivers speed in thinking and encourages openness in communications.

To Support: Agree on which data points are relevant only after a decision is proposed.

Cons: Not realising that others are missing key information may lead to an impression that they are intransigent or stupid. This will seriously interfere with Good Thinking.

To Subvert: Declare and agree key assumptions and data points in advance of working out solutions and taking decisions.

Interacts with the following paradigms:

    Incomplete Information (WYSIATI)
    Confirmation Bias
    Risk vs Reward

See also the chapters:

    Auto-thinking vs Effort-thinking
    Emotional Thinking
    Social Thinking
    Default Thinking Style
    Creativity

Reducing: CONFIRMATION BIAS

The tendency to seek for, and to easily find, evidence in support of a hypothesis which you believe to be correct.

Test if it is supporting Good or Bad Thinking by:

Consider the impact of the hypothesis being considered. High impact, important matters should have effort-thinking applied in a search for contradictory evidence. Low impact outcomes are good with an auto-thinking, Confirmation Biased approach.

Mapped to the decision activities model: **D** E C I D **E**

Defining the required outcome
Evaluating Outcomes

D.E.C.I.D.E. Decision Steps	Define Objective	Establish Criteria	Consider Options	Identify Best Alternative	Develop Actions	Evaluate Outcomes
Reducing Paradigms						
Confirmation Bias	■					■

Pros: An efficient auto-thinking device. Good for scanning large volumes of data.

To Support: Maintain speed and agree specific search criteria.

Cons: Can deliver evidence which appears to prove and embed false hypotheses.

To Subvert: Reverse the hypothesis and look for evidence that supports the contradiction.

Interacts with the following paradigms:

- Framing
- Availability
- Narrative
- Incomplete Information (WISIATI)
- Substitution
- Creative Memory

See also the chapters:

- Certainty and Doubt
- Rational and Reasonable
- Auto-thinking vs Effort-thinking
- Emotional Thinking
- Social Thinking
- Default Thinking Style

Reducing: THE OWNERSHIP PARADIGM

Ownership of ideas and solutions is a natural result of time and energy invested by the Thinker(s). It is a great motivator for Thinkers to invest energy in the decision process. However, it can equally cause resistance to change by putting a false value premium on 'owned ideas'.

Test if it is supporting Good or Bad Thinking by:

Check the combination of thinking modes being used to support the ideas under debate. Rational + Reasonable => positive ownership effects. Irrational + Unreasonable => negative ownership effects. The other combinations (Rational + Unreasonable or Irrational + Reasonable) could be either positive or negative but the discovery process will help to make clear which it is.

Mapped to the decision activities model: D E C **I** D **E**

Identifying the Best Alternative
Evaluating Outcomes

D.E.C.I.D.E. Decision Steps	Define Objective	Establish Criteria	Consider Options	Identify Best Alternative	Develop Actions	Evaluate Outcomes
Reducing Paradigms						
Ownership Paradigm						

Pros: Ownership promotes determination to get through the decision process, even against resistance.

To Support: Invest in creating ideas. Grant a right of control over outcomes.

Cons: Ownership can overvalue ideas and positions leading to resistance to Good Thinking.

To Subvert: Step back and use debating rules to change ownership for a defined period.

Interacts with the following paradigms:

Framing
Narrative
Availability
Incomplete Information (WYSIATI)
Confirmation Bias
Creative Memory

See also the chapters:

Rational and Reasonable
Default Thinking Style

Heuristic: THE SUBSTITUTION PARADIGM

Unconsciously substituting an easy (and potentially irrelevant) 'heuristic' question for a difficult 'target' question and then accepting this easy answer as being the answer to the tough question

---

Test if it is supporting Good or Bad Thinking by:

Tease out a clear definition of the target questions and validate the answers by explaining how each answer was arrived at.

Mapped to the decision activities model: **D** E C **I** D **E**

    Defining the required outcome
    Identify Best Alternative
    Evaluating Outcomes

D.E.C.I.D.E. Decision Steps	Define Objective	Establish Criteria	Consider Options	Identify Best Alternative	Develop Actions	Evaluate Outcomes
Heuristic Paradigms						
Substition Paradigm	■			■		■

Pros: The unconscious swapping of easy for hard questions speeds up thinking and may give equally good answers.

To Support: Minimise distractions which can generate less relevant substitutions.

Cons: The process of substitution is unconscious and may give the Thinker(s) high confidence in wrong answers.

To Subvert: Focus on the questions and deliberately engage in effort-thinking.

Interacts with the following paradigms:

    Framing

    Intuition

    Availability

    Rules of Thumb

See also chapters:

    Certainty and Doubt

    Auto-thinking vs Effort-thinking

Appendices

Heuristic: RULE OF THUMB

A conscious distillation of a complex decision or analysis process into a simple method which gives a good approximate result. Existing Rules of Thumb include the culture of 'the way we do things here'. Useful new Rules of Thumb can be generated in the decision process.

Test if it is supporting Good or Bad Thinking by:

Assume they are always in use and generally helpful. Check which Rules of Thumb underpin key outcomes and validate them.

Mapped to the decision activities model: D **E** C I **D** E

   Establish Criteria
   Develop Actions

Discoveries and observations in the Define Objectives and Identify Best Alternative activities become Rules of Thumb specific to the problem being addressed.

D.E.C.I.D.E. Decision Steps	Define Objective	Establish Criteria	Consider Options	Identify Best Alternative	Develop Actions	Evaluate Outcomes
Heuristic Paradigms						
Rules of Thumb						

Pros: Experts bring specific rules of thumb to accelerate the decision process. General Rules of Thumb support speed and social coherence in thinking teams.

To Support: Recognise the value of Rules of Thumb. Recruit experts. Take note of new rules as they are developed.

Cons: Bad Thinking can come from using an inappropriate rule, accepting an irrational prejudice as a reasonable bias, or forgetting that the answer is only approximately right.

To Subvert: Identify where important outcomes rely on Rules of Thumb. Test the assumptions inherent to the rules.

Interacts with the following paradigms:

Intuition
Availability
Confirmation Bias
Substitution

See also the chapter:

Auto-thinking vs Effort-thinking

Appendices

Heuristic: MODELS, MAPS & METAPHORS

The deliberate use of a simple, compelling model to substitute for a complex, multi-dimensional, or intimidating idea can help with analysis and focus efforts. However, a misjudged model design can have unfortunate and far-reaching consequences.

Test if it is supporting Good or Bad Thinking by:

If a model is widely accepted and encouraging discussions, it is probably promoting Good Thinking. If the model supports rational but unreasonable answers, it is probably flawed. If debates about the validity of alternate models are common and long lasting, assume that models are channelling Bad Thinking.

Mapped to the decision activities model: **D** E C I D E

Defining the required outcome

D.E.C.I.D.E. Decision Steps	Define Objective	Establish Criteria	Consider Options	Identify Best Alternative	Develop Actions	Evaluate Outcomes
Heuristic Paradigms						
Models, Maps, & Metaphors	■■■					

Pros: Models can make complex ideas comprehensible, engaging, and emotionally satisfying. Developing models can in itself encourage objective analysis and create insights.

To Support: Build models and maps. Create metaphors which can persuade interested parties on the importance of questions and the validity of answers.

Cons: The model can be confused for the issue. Poorly designed models can either over-simplify or over-complicate the questions being addressed.

To Subvert: Subject models to bullet-proofing – look for scenarios which will break the model.

Connected to the following paradigms:

Framing
Narrative
Substitution
Availability
Confirmation Bias

See also the chapters:

Emotional Thinking
Creativity

Experiencing: THE RISK REWARD PARADIGM

The human response to risk and reward becomes irrational at the boundaries. If an outcome is high or low probability and/or high or low impact it will strongly affect our response to risk and reward. We measure impact relatively and from a personal perspective.

Test if it is supporting Good or Bad Thinking by:

Mapping the Thinker(s) and other stakeholders on the Fourfold Risk-Response Field. A mismatch in expected behaviour between two parties is a good predictor of Bad Thinking.

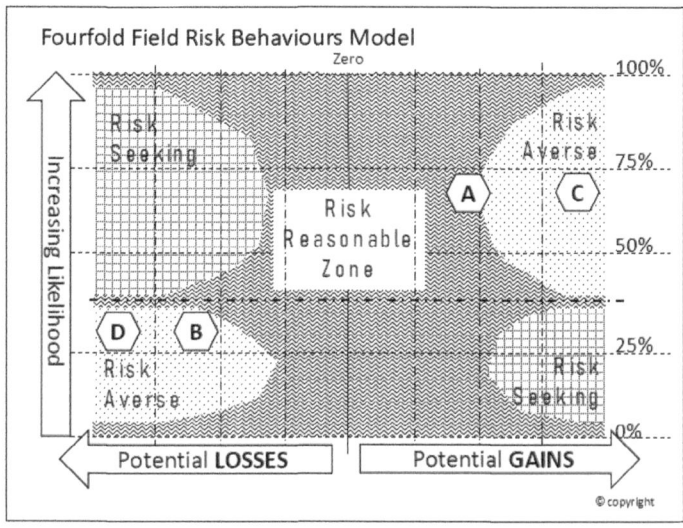

Mapped to the **D** E C **I D** E Model of thinking activities, the Risk Reward Paradigm has most impact when choices are being made:

Defining Objective
Identifying the Best Alternative
Developing Actions

D.E.C.I.D.E. Decision Steps	Define Objective	Establish Criteria	Consider Options	Identify Best Alternative	Develop Actions	Evaluate Outcomes
Experiencing Paradigms						
Risk Reward Paradigm	■			■	■	

Support and *Subvert* when required by shifting the Thinker(s) and stakeholders on the risk-reward field. This can be done by changing perceptions: Make or remove certainties. Re-frame losses as gains and vice versa. Choose the measures of impacts to frame them relative to the Thinker'(s) and stakeholders' positions, to achieve strong or weak impact assessments as required.

Interacts with the following paradigms:

Availability
Full Knowledge (WYKEK)
Ownership
Substitution

See also the chapters:

Rational and Reasonable
Probably Just Luck

Experiencing: CREATIVE MEMORY PARADIGM

False memories are the norm. We naturally combine the outputs of verbatim and gist memory systems. We must trust that our memory will be effective most of the time but be aware that all memories should be treated as only broadly correct.

Test if it is supporting Good or Bad Thinking by:

Assessing which memories are key inputs affecting decision outcomes. Look out for Duration Neglect and Peak Experience affecting our assessments of past events.

Mapped to the decision activities model: **D** E C I D **E**

Defining Objectives
Evaluating Outcomes

D.E.C.I.D.E. Decision Steps	Define Objective	Establish Criteria	Consider Options	Identify Best Alternative	Develop Actions	Evaluate Outcomes
Experiencing Paradigms						
Creative Memory Paradigm	■					■

Pros: Our creative memory is quick and efficient and promotes the cross-fertilisation of ideas.

To Support: Accept approximations in memories. Get the gist of the memory and keep going.

Cons: We can have false confidence in the details of memories which are only broadly correct. We can also (rarely) have clear memories that are completely wrong.

To Subvert: Focus on the evidence. Compare different people's memories. Check facts and agree on reliable information sources.

Connected to the following paradigms:

Framing
Narrative
Availability
Substitution

See also the chapters:

Certainty and Doubt
Social Thinking

TOOLS FOR THINKING

*"You cannot mandate productivity,
you must provide the tools to
let people become their best."*

Steve Jobs – Entrepreneur

The abacus is underrated. It has been around in various forms for centuries, since long before the adoption of the Hindu-Arabic Numeral System that we use today. It contributed to the creation of that system, and it still provides a very practical and valuable calculator for anyone who is sight impaired. The Chinese version, called the 'suanpan', incorporates techniques to do multiplication, division, addition, subtraction, square root and even cube root operations at speeds that can compete with a user of an electronic calculator.[91] Can we describe the abacus as a decision support tool? In common with its more sophisticated descendants, the calculator and the spreadsheet, it enables you to process numerical data to generate answers. Answers generated by calculators can support decisions from the trivial: 'Can I afford that holiday?' to the profound: 'Can I afford to bail out that bank before it brings down the entire global financial system?' I think this proves that counting and calculating devices qualify as decision support tools, though they do have other uses. We have been using a variety of decision tools since we started thinking.

The field of decision support tools is a very wide one. Dedicated decision tools range from what are frankly fiendishly complicated things like Monte Carlo Simulations, to the deceptively simple two-by-two priority matrix (sometimes nicknamed the consultograph). Decision tools and the closely related subject of Game Theory are fruitful areas to explore if you are often involved in very complex decisions. However, most of the time we end up dealing with low complexity decisions where the real difficulty comes from choosing between closely balanced options and then persuading non-expert stakeholders of the merits of the recommended decision. For that situation, simple tools that everyone understands are more useful. We will focus on a few simple tools here.

The criteria I have used in choosing the tools detailed below are:

- ✧ Simplicity: Is it likely the majority of people will understand it and be able to use it?
- ✧ Accessibility: Ideally these tools can be deployed with no more than a pencil and paper. At the worst they are accessible by a competent user of a standard PC or Smartphone.

The tools covered in this section are:

Managing Options

Most Good Thinking involves similar steps. We generate options to consider, reduce these options to a short-list of preferred options, then choose a best option. I have collected a set of simple and familiar techniques to enable Thinkers to generate and test options.

Prioritisation Tools

Very often there are many valid options in which we need to identify the best. I have picked out two easy to use, intuitive, tools which are orientated towards giving answers by establishing priorities.

Guidelines for Maps, Models and Metaphors

The most powerful and intuitive tools for Good Thinking are Maps, Models and Metaphors. In this section we look at some basic guidelines for creating and using models. See also the chapter on the Maps, Models and Metaphors Paradigm.

Risk Management Tools

Difficult decisions usually address risks. For large, complex decisions, formal risk management is a good discipline. For smaller problems it is enough to understand the principles of risk management.

Truth: Standard of Evidence

Knowing the validity of the facts that we rely on to support our thinking is important. I have included a summary of the Standards of Evidence tool referred to in the chapter on Certainty and Doubt for convenience.

Creativity: Dogs and Catz

Creative thinking is a valuable part of Good Thinking. This tool, which is introduced in the chapter on Creativity, is powerful and easy to use.

You will not be surprised to see that I have already used all of the selected tools in this book in the expectation that they are easily understood, even at first glance.

MANAGING OPTIONS

"The first step is to establish that something is possible; then probability will occur."

Elon Musk – Entrepreneur

Can't decide? Just flip a coin. However, this only works when you have reduced the range of options to two, with roughly equal outcomes. Being between a rock and a hard place is always tough but in many ways it is easier than having too many choices. Reducing options and imposing tight constraints make decisions easier. However, when you do this it is important to:

- be aware of the limits you choose to impose, versus the real constraints on a decision;

- have tools available to open up new options when neither the rock nor the hard place is an acceptable answer.

In the chapter describing the DECIDE decision process we explain where divergent and convergent thinking naturally occur in the thinking process, but the ability to increase and reduce options are important skills to apply at any time. The vast majority of education systems will teach constructive criticism as a quick route to get to the bottom of things. This deductive reasoning is very useful to narrow options and make a quick decision. This thinking technique is so common that we don't hear much about the opposite, and equally important, initial step of generating options.

Elementary My Dear

The archetype of this reductive technique is Sherlock Holmes with his famous 'deductive reasoning'. However, this is an inaccurate description of his technique, and a real oversell of the value of converging to a solution. Sir Arthur Conan Doyle does not only use deductive reasoning to craft the plot in Sherlock's various adventures. This reduction can only be applied once a set of premises are established which are true. These premises are initially generated as a series of speculative hypotheses which are tested to establish their validity. Sherlock's fictional brilliance is based on a combination of his brilliantly imaginative hypotheses and his encyclopaedic memory (which is deployed to establish that the premise is true). Only then does his rigorous deductive logic crack the case. A good example appears in *The Adventure of the Bruce-Partington Plans*. Sherlock has the brilliant idea that a body by a railway track might have been placed on the roof of the train. The more obvious premise, that the victim was pushed from or fell from a train, was disproved by a lack of blood. However, the key to Mr Holmes' brilliant deduction is not that logical critique of the obvious hypothesis. Instead, he comes up with the creative idea that the body might have travelled some distance on the roof before falling to the tracks. For Good Thinking, generating numerous 'out of the box' options is as important, not more or less, than reducing these options to a set of valid premises, and finding the solution by deductive testing.

In this chapter we will focus on some practical techniques to quickly generate, and to reduce, possibilities. In the chapter on

Certainty & Doubt we look at Karl Popper's falsability approach to science which is key to validating hypotheses. There is detail on how to resist the seductive power of compelling stories in the chapter on the Narrative Paradigm, which warns about the importance of deploying logic to test assumptions.

Divergent Thinking – Expanding Your Options

This is what puts the creative into 'creative problem solving'. Deep expertise can make it particularly difficult to expand the potential solutions or options in a field where the teams or individuals doing the thinking are very familiar with the majority of existing solutions. It makes sense that existing proven solutions should only be abandoned where changes in context mean they have become inadequate. When this happens we need an approach to address the situation where reusing an existing solution will not work. Taking new non-expert perspectives on the problem, and brainstorming are two techniques that will help, especially in combination.

Smart Non-expert Perspectives

The reader may be familiar with Thomas Kuhn's discovery that cross-fertilisations of disciplines are responsible for many creative breakthroughs.[92] A good way to exploit this observation is to get one or more very smart people, who are novices in relation to the problem being addressed, involved in the thinking. However, you cannot always do this, perhaps because you are working alone, or you have significant time constraints. An alternative way to spark new ideas is to deliberately apply solutions for different problems in other fields to the issue being addressed. The thought experiment of force-fitting an unrelated solution to a problem is a good mental work-out. For example, Spotify's idea to rent access to their music catalogue rather than sell individual tracks is a bit like selling a season ticket to Disneyland. Exploiting entertainment assets without transferring ownership created new value in music, and it has the bonus of maximising customer choice.

Whether it is generated by a smart non-expert or a thought experiment, the transferred solution more often than not will simply not work. This is OK. It is the exercise of trying to get it to work that can generate new ideas. The trick is to push through the initial feeling that 'this is stupid and obviously can't work' to a 'I know this will not work but let's play with it for a while' attitude. In other words you need to become the smart non-expert for a while.

If you are lucky enough to be able to persuade a smart outsider to help, the real challenge is how to get them engaged, and to make sure that you actually listen to them. Yours and the thinking team's expert reflex will be to critique each idea they come up with and demonstrate with your expertise how little they know. This is not only ineffective but it is also a very rude way to treat someone who is stepping out of their comfort zone to offer ideas and to help. This is where a *real* brainstorming activity can help.

Brainstorming – Back in Fashion

Brainstorming was a victim of its own success. These days, pretty much anyone who gets a whiteboard pen in their hands and says,

"Let's get some ideas down," thinks that they are facilitating a brainstorming session. In truth, it is a hard thing to do well and the few rules, which are simple, require real discipline to stick to.

There are three rules to Brainstorming.

1) **Don't judge, build:** Use prompting phrases like, "And it would be even better if…" to extend and expand the conversation. If anyone passes judgement in this creative stage you must call them out on it, and loudly. Anyone slipping up by judging in this creation phase needs to be embarrassed enough to feel that it is better to come up with daft ideas than to judge.

2) **Encourage random ideas:** Force new perspectives by asking people for ideas if the solution needs to work, for example, in the 25th Century, in a world where everyone is blind, in a dictatorship, in a submarine situation, etc. Force the pace. Speed impairs judgement, and this is what you want. Capture every idea proposed, without editing, and as fast as possible.

3) **Stop Brainstorming (eventually):** Be explicit from the start that the ideas generated will be processed at the end, by the same team. Include enough time to carry out the process of picking the gems out of the cornucopia of entertaining rubbish that you have deliberately created. A time split of 75% Idea Generation to 25% Assessment is usually about right. A brief break between the two parts is very useful to re-frame the participants' mode of thinking.

> The assessment stage should deliver actions to validate, to explore interesting ideas, gather relevant data, test new ideas on specific stakeholders, etc.

To pick out the usable ideas, to separate the gold from the ore, we need to be able to make some choices.

Convergent Thinking – Making Choices

Removing alternative ideas which can be invalidated by logic is not an issue. The problem situation is where many options are at least possible solutions and there is either not enough time and/or not enough evidence available to rule any out. This is generally the case with a list of alternative plans. Even with the resources and time to invest, it can be impossible to logically reduce the list of options which might work to one. After all, the future is notoriously difficult to predict. Some other 'quick and dirty' methods must be deployed to prune the decision tree.

First-cut choices to generate a shortlist need to be quick and efficient. Some example techniques:

Top and Bottom Sorting

Whether on your own or in a group, you may be faced with a long list of options which must be reduced to a shortlist. This is best done by sorting them quickly into two halves of top or bottom ideas. Start with the bottom. Quickly choose an idea which is a candidate for worst idea then switch to the top, looking for a candidate for best idea. No comparison between the ideas is required as you are just choosing candidates. When the long list has to be split into top and bottom, discard the bottom half. Take the top half list and run the exercise again. Stop when the unranked 'top list' is short enough to be put through a more rigorous analysis. For a useful shortlist, three is better than five. More than five almost always costs too many resources to compare in detail.

Democratic Sorting

This should only to be used with large numbers, a minimum of 10 people. With large numbers this is more efficient than a debating approach. Depending on the number of participants and number of options the voting approach will change. Approaches include: rank all the options, pick your top three, or each individual does a Top & Bottom Sorting exercise on the list, so that a consensus can be reached. The approach of each person simply choosing one favourite option is generally a bad idea because the Ownership Paradigm encourages irrational support for these 'owned' ideas (see the chapter of the same name). Taking the top three options to a stage of further analysis based on the vote is a good idea. Use single transferable votes to keep everyone on side. Secret ballots can be useful for sensitive matters, provided there are enough people and a reliable and efficient process.

> ### Technology Enabled Sorting
>
> *Electronic voting systems which take advantage of mobile phones are fun and efficient for large numbers whether co-located or in distributed groups. Be very careful that the result of the vote is used, and seen to be used, to inform the decision. This means that the options voted on must be simple to understand, and the opinion of the voters needs to be valid.*
>
> *Tools like Voxvote.com or Doodle.com are readily available for this type of selection.*
>
> *Please note: This is very rarely a useful contribution to good decision making. It is far more likely to be a fun tool to use in stakeholder management to agree criteria or to establish ownership of decisions already made.*

To pick the final single option from a shortlist needs a more considered approach. Techniques include:

Decision Matrix: Very useful for comparing a shortlist of options in a complex decision. The key success criteria for the decision are selected. Each of the options is placed in a matrix against the key success criteria and an estimate of the outcome at each intersect is agreed. The intersects are then assessed on the extent to which they deliver the best outcomes. This is described in more detail in the section on Prioritisation Tools.

Bullet-proofing: This is a resource hungry and potentially disruptive approach. It will normally be used only on the final proposed solution and where the decision is important.

Also called 'Black Hat' thinking because you become the bad guy, the technique is simply to look for possible failures in the solution by considering everything that might go wrong. This exploits the valuable critical skills of the people addressing the problem. However, there is the very real risk that this technique will kill support for a perfectly good option. To avoid this unintended outcome, the potential causes of failure need to be treated as risks, and both their likelihood and impact need to be assessed separately. (See the section on Risk Management.)

Scanning for unintended consequences is another useful bullet-proofing technique. This is best done by looking at the solution from the perspective of different stakeholders. These should also be assessed as risks with estimates for likelihood and impact.

To protect a good solution from negative effects, the bullet-proofing process should be time limited. It should also be made very clear that it is designed to create and examine a set of unrealistic, worst possible, scenarios.

Finally, the bullet-proofing process may, of course, kill the solution because it is not viable. This should only happen when it identifies a real potential for failure. The good news is that this will prevent a lot of wasted effort and identifying the failure will have identified previously hidden essential success criteria.

Meeting these new criteria will contribute to creating a new and better solution that can work. The first step would be to examine the other shortlisted solutions to see if they can successfully address these new criteria.

The prudent reader will be thinking, 'That sounds like a lot of work, I can't possibly invest that much energy in every decision I make'. That is absolutely correct. Have a look at the chapter on Triage Thinking to see how issues can be prioritised and always ask the question: 'Can the overall solution survive if this particular sub-decision turns out to be wrong?' If the answer is 'yes', do not waste time reviewing the sub-decision in detail. Move on.

> *"I doubt, therefore I think,*
> *therefore I am."*
>
> *Antoine Léonard Thomas – Poet*
> *(after Rene Decartes)*

PRIORITISATION TOOLS

These simple analytical tools are helpful in unpicking complex information to make it easier to understand and to discuss. They are mainly used to compare options and make choices.

The Two-by-Two Priority Matrix

We used the Two-by-Two Priority Matrix in the chapter on Triage Thinking, comparing the two primary axes of Value and Urgency, and overlaying a third dimension of Complexity. The picture is reproduced below.

This tool is useful when there is a long list of items to be considered. In this example, it is which problems should be addressed, but it could be anything; which people to influence, which songs to include in a concert etc.

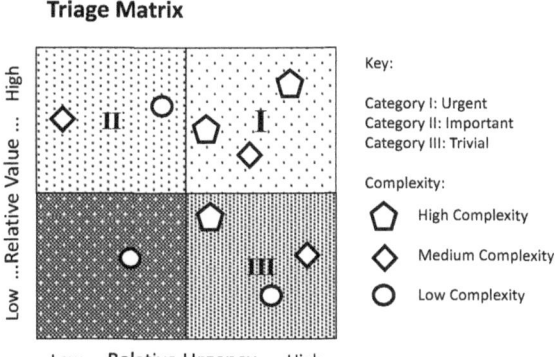

You can consider a minimum of two or a maximum of three criteria in a two-by-two matrix. One criterion is shown on each axis and a third is indicated by the graphic you choose to represent each point. Generally, the least important criterion will be the graphic overlay. Much of the value in this tool is in the process of using it. Agreeing which criteria are relevant and considering each point's relative place in the matrix is what gets the thinking and the discussion working. Using a binary high vs low scale is useful to push decisions away from indecisive neutrality. However, a three-by-three matrix (high - med - low) may be useful with long lists. Taking this to the next level of detail by using numbers on each axis can sometimes be useful. With numbered axes, a forced ranking of the items under consideration against each criterion can be mapped onto the matrix. Finally, the points on the matrix can be annotated to reflect their value on a third dimension.

Probably the best known example of this 'fully detailed' Two-by-Two Priority Matrix is the 'Product Portfolio Matrix' created by Boston Consulting Group founder Bruce Doolin Henderson in the 1960s and also called the Boston Matrix.[93]

This matrix made the Two-by-Two Priority Matrix a consulting staple for decades. In this famous example, the quadrants are given names: Stars, Cash Cows, Dogs and Question Marks. These names exploit the 'Intensity Matching' effect that was mentioned in the section on Heuristic Paradigms. The size of the points show a third dimension of product value.

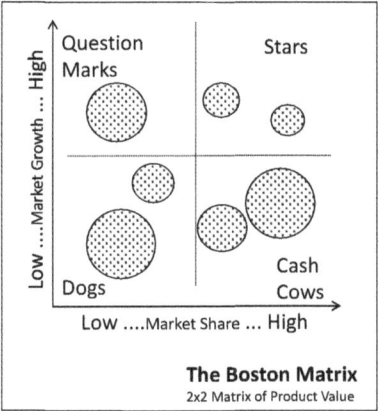

The Boston Matrix
2x2 Matrix of Product Value

A good rule of thumb is: the simplest low vs high, 'relative values', version of this tool is usually the best. It will be easily understood and can be easily and intuitively manipulated by the Thinker(s). Don't add complexity unless you have a good reason to.

The Decision Matrix

When we are dealing with a large number of options and a lot of criteria, a Decision Matrix is a good solution. Generally, any more than three options compared against three or more criteria is a lot for a typical human brain to manage without a map of some kind.

A Decision Matrix enables this comparison of a number of options against a number of different criteria in the form of a table. Whether you put the options on the vertical or horizontal does not matter. Whatever looks better and fits on the page is right.

In the Managing Options chapter in the section on Outcomes

Analysis we used a Decision Matrix to compare optional holiday destinations against the success criteria of different family members.

	Cost	6 Year Old Pool & Kidsclub	16 Year Old Peers & Cool factor	Mum Culture & History	Dad Outdoors & Exercise
A] Florida	Cheap	Perfect. Disney is possible	Very uncool but lots of peers	Non existent	Great - Gym & Golf in Hotel
B] Ibiza	Moderate	OK - caters well for families	Cool & Lots of Peers	Not Bad, some old towns	Some outdoor activities
C] Easter Island	Very Epensive	Not good - no family hotels	Fairly cool - but no Peers	Perfect	Interesting activities

As you can see, it is comprehensive and captures all the comparison data testing options against criteria in one place. This makes sure that each option is checked against every criterion. However, in this example, comparing 'Not Bad, some old towns' to 'Cool and lots of peers' is not that easy. So it can make sense to give the assessments a value, like 'Good - OK - Bad' or even to use numbers to facilitate the comparisons, like this:

	Cost	6 Year Old Pool & Kidsclub	16 Year Old Peers & Cool factor	Mum Culture & History	Dad Outdoors & Exercise	Total
A] Florida	Cheap	Perfect. Disney is possible	Very uncool but lots of peers	Non existent	Great - Gym & Golf in Hotel	
Score	2	2	1	-2	2	5
B] Ibiza	Moderate	OK - caters well for families	Cool & Lots of Peers	Not Bad, some old towns	Some outdoor activities	
Score	1	1	2	1	1	6
C] Easter Island	Very Epensive	Not good - no family hotels	Fairly cool - but no Peers	Perfect	Interesting activities	
Score	-2	-2	-1	2	2	-1

Here, minus numbers are used for negative assessments. We can sum the scores for each option and decide that Ibiza wins by a small margin. Of course, this raw score might not reflect the relative importance of some criteria. Perhaps the cost, or maybe the six-year old's preferences, should be given a higher priority.

To address this problem we add a weighting overlay to the criteria to help with the choice. With the weighting added Florida is a clear winner.

	Cost	6 Year Old	16 Year Old	Mum	Dad	Total	Weighted Total
		Pool & Kidsclub	Peers & Cool factor	Culture & History	Outdoors & Exercise		
Weighting x	10	5	1	1	1	-	
A] Florida	Cheap	Perfect. Disney is possible	Very uncool but lots of peers	Non existent	Great - Gym & Golf in Hotel		
Score	2	2	1	-2	2	5	
Weighted score	20	10	1	-2	2		31
B] Ibiza	Moderate	OK - caters well for families	Cool & Lots of Peers	Not Bad, some old towns	Some outdoor activities		
Score	1	1	2	1	1	6	
Weighted score	10	5	2	1	1		19
C] Easter Island	Very Epensive	Not good - no family hotels	Fairly cool - but no Peers	Perfect	Interesting activities		
Score	-2	-2	-1	2	2	-1	
Weighted score	-20	-10	-1	2	2		-27

The value in this tool is in the act of creating and using the table which is specific to the decision being addressed. Whether working solo or in a group of Thinkers it is the analysis activity that holds the value. The shortlisting of the options to consider, the agreement of the criteria the options should be measured against, the weighting of the criteria, and the assessment at each intersect, are all important enablers of the Good Thinking that this tool encourages. Finally, breaking the analysis into a series of focused questions allows each to be addressed separately and quite objectively. If everyone agrees that the holiday cost criterion really is the most important one, then everyone can accept that Ibiza deserves a '2' for cool factor.

There are many other decision tools available, including some which are software based. We mentioned electronic voting tools in the section on Managing Options. Choose wisely, based on the people doing the thinking. An important point to remember is that even the simplest tool becomes a 'black box' if the Thinker(s) don't understand how it works. Accepting the answers that come out of a black box is not generally conducive to Good Thinking.

CHARACTERISTICS OF A GOOD MODEL

A guide to designing and choosing Maps, Models and Metaphors. There are three rules to follow:

1) The minimum level of detail

Lewis Carrol and George Luis Borges both wrote parodies at different times about a kingdom which decided to create the ultimate map, showing every detail of their land. This amazing document was expected to have a myriad of uses in commerce and governance. Once completed, however, it was never unfolded as the resulting full-scale map would have covered the whole country. It was not only useless, but it was a hindrance rather than a help. It was quickly abandoned and ignored until only a few scraps of paper were left blowing about in the desert. Maps and models need to have just enough level of detail to be useful, any more than that is a waste of effort in creation and a distraction in use.

2) Include all the key dimensions

To be useful a model must include all of the important aspects or dimensions of the idea or question that it represents. The Stakeholder Map that we used in the chapter on Intelligence is a useful example. The dimensions of the matrix are 'relative support' and 'relative impact'. This is enough structure to show which groups and individuals will be responsive to change, but a choice of which stakeholders to focus on based only on these two dimensions is not enough. A third dimension is added to the diagram, indicating the relative influence of the stakeholders involved. If two stakeholders are roughly equal in their support and impact position on the map, we can choose the more influential one to focus our communications efforts on.

Stakeholder Map
Example Outsourcing Project

Support for Change (Low...... High) vs Impact of Change (Low...... High)

- High Support / Low Impact: ■ *Shareholders*, □Senior Exec Team
- High Support / High Impact: □Project Manager, □ Outsourced Management
- Low Support / High Impact: ❖ Outsourced Staff, ■ *Redundant Staff*, □Outsourced Executives
- Low Support / Low Impact: ■ *Retained Staff*

Key
□ HIGH Influence
❖ MEDIUM Influence
■ *Low Influence*

If the Thinker(s) decide that influence is a more important dimension than impact, the map could be redrawn with 'relative influence' on one axis and with 'relative impact' described by graphic symbols.

3) Simple is (always) better

A good model is one that is used by as many people as possible, with a minimum of training. A simple model is less likely to become a black box which generates answers that are not understood. The Collateralised Debt Obligations (CDOs), which were behind the 2008 financial crash were 'complex derivatives modelling the behaviour of multiple mortgages'. One factor leading to the crash was that these models were complex and opaque even to their creators.

Using the standard two-by-two matrix example again, the third dimension is normally represented by different shapes. We could instead make the model three dimensional in space. This might make it more subtle in the way that it represents information but would make it much harder to use. It would move outside the average person's ability to manage and would require exotic tools to represent it visually.

A good rule of thumb is that, after the most important two or three dimensions are represented in the model, including any further dimensions can be counterproductive. It has a high cost in complexity compared to the information it will provide. Of course, many professional analysts will use models with much higher complexity levels, but the point is that this is what they do for a living. In a thinking team, the best model is the one that everyone understands without training.

These three headline rules demonstrated using the Two-by-Two Matrix Model will apply equally to any Model, Map or Metaphor you create. Generally, models can handle higher levels of complexity. Metaphors, on the other hand, need to be very simple to be effective. A metaphor is like a street sign compared to a model, which is like your Sat Nav.

> *"The mechanic that would perfect his work must first sharpen his tools."*
>
> *Confucious – Philosopher*

RISK MANAGEMENT

"To be alive at all involves some risk."

Harold MacMillian – Politician

The International Organisation for Standardization (ISO) says that a decision process must include risk management to be fit for purpose. I don't want to take the risk of disagreeing with them.

Managing risk is important. There is a hint in the name. Risks are scary, but we shouldn't just ignore them. From the perspective of Good Thinking, the biggest problem with risks is that we don't usually remain logical when we are managing them. This is especially true if the risk impacts are personal. (See the chapter on the Risk vs Reward Paradigm.) One thing that can help us all to be logical when we look at risks is to have a disciplined approach. Much has been written about the subject. There is a Global Institute of Risk Management. You can even study for a Master's Degree in it. Fortunately, the fundamentals are not that complicated.

Likely Impacts

There are two factors you really need to understand about a risk to get a handle on it. These are the aspects of a risk which will tell you its priority relative to the other risks that your thinking project might face. They are:

✧ **Impact:** If it does happen, what will the consequences be?

⬥ **Likelihood:** How likely is it to graduate from a possibility to a reality, becoming an issue not just a risk?

We tend to intuitively judge that the likelihood is the more important of the two factors. The word 'risk' is a synonym for 'likelihood' and immediately brings to mind the idea of a probability. But when you think about it, the impact is much more important. Low impact risks are not very interesting no matter how likely they are to materialise. High impact + low likelihood (Taleb's now notorious *Black Swans*) are worth our attention to consider how we might mitigate them by reducing the potential impacts.[94] A double high (high impact + high likelihood) should get all of our attention until and unless we can implement some mitigation to shift one or both of these to an acceptable level.

To manage risks (formally) these are the steps:

1. **Identify Threats and Opportunities:** Scan the context to see what might go wrong – or right. Upside risks are important too. Consider framing threats as opportunities.

2. **Expose Vulnerabilities:** Work out how these events might have effects on the situation that concerns you. What are the chains or webs of cause and effect?

3. **Assess Impacts:** Measure the size of the effects. Whether this is a hard measure (e.g. financial cost) or a soft measure (e.g. morale of the team), at the very least get a measure relative to other risks in your analysis.

4. **Estimate Likelihood:** Estimate the probability of the potential risk becoming a real issue.

5. **Design and Cost Mitigations:** What can you do to reduce the negative impacts and/or the likelihood? Is the mitigation cost less than the impact costs, after being factored by the likelihood? For upside risks, mitigation is designed to maximise impacts and increase likelihood. The cost question becomes: 'Will the investment deliver a worthwhile potential return?'

6. **Implement Mitigations:** Do what is prudent.

7. **Monitor for Changes:** Regular reviews over time to spot changes.

To effectively monitor for changes we need a Risk Register. It should look something like this:

Risk	Risk Description	Likely	Impact	£k Impact	Risk Mitigation	Impact Mitigation
1	No Risk analysis is carried out	H	H	£0	Include Risk analysis in project commencment workshop	N/A
2	Risk Reviews are not carried out	M	M	N/A	Include Risk Reviews in agenda of regular Project Meetings	N/A
3	Project Manager leaves Project	L	L	£0	Schedule a regular PM Perf Review with Project Sponsor	Appoint Deputy PM. Ensure Project progress records are up to date.
4						

Note that the risk to be managed is *everything* on the row, not just the likelihood of that risk. All of the columns are important. Strangely, a common error is to omit one or both of the mitigation columns. The only reason we identify risks is so that we can mitigate them.

Risky Bullet-proofing

Bullet-proofing a solution to test it is essentially running a new and focused risk management process late in the decision process. It can be dangerous in that it can cause a loss of confidence in a perfectly adequate solution. (See also the Bullet-proofing section in Tools for Managing Options.)

High Impact risks are one problem.

> If a risk identified in bullet-proofing has a very high impact but this is balanced by an extremely low likelihood of it happening, then it should not be allowed to undermine the solution. On the other hand, a medium impact + high likelihood risk should be seriously considered and a mitigation plan might be necessary. Mitigation actions can change the profile of a risk. For example, buying insurance against weather destroying a crop can take impact from high to low.

The volume of identified risks can also be disconcerting. The Availability Paradigm can exaggerate the emotional impact of a long list of risks. If the list is too long, cut the risks to be monitored to a minimum and overtly discard the remainder.

- ✧ All low impact risks can be discarded regardless of likelihood.
- ✧ Medium impact + low likelihood risks can be discarded.
- ✧ Medium impact + high likelihood risks can be flagged as 'to be monitored'.

✧ High impact + high likelihood risk must be addressed.

> ***"The desire for safety stands against every great and noble enterprise."***
>
> *Tacitus – Roman Senator*

STANDARDS OF EVIDENCE TOOL

Use: To discuss and to understand the reliability of facts supporting the decision-making process.

See also the chapter: Certainty and Doubt.

This is a variation of the legal concept of degrees of certainty.

The Standards of Evidence, from less certain to more certain, are set out below:

Legal Standard	Common Term	Notes
no credible evidence	Guess	*No attempt has been made to test veracity. If it is an attractive guess which might lead to clarity, begin to test it.*
some credible evidence	Idea	*Enough evidence is readily available to make it worth examining and refining.*
a preponderance of evidence	Hypothesis	*Enough evidence pro and con has been reviewed to suggest this may be true. Use with caution in your thinking process.*

clear and convincing evidence	**Theory**	*An evidence-based assumption which is coherent and reasonable. Use as it is, but keep an open mind.*
beyond reasonable doubt	**Truth**	*Treat this as true. Searching for contradictory evidence is no longer useful. Ideally, it will be represented as a falsifiable statement.* *Accept that it might some day be disproved.*
beyond any shadow of a doubt	**Belief**	*i.e. undoubtable – recognised as an impossible standard to meet – this is used only as a device to terminate the legal Standards of Evidence list.* *Take anything represented this way as suspect. If it is an important component of the thought process, test the impact of the opposite belief.*

Use of the Standards of Evidence challenges Thinkers to assess the level of confidence they should have in different facts which they are relying on to support their decisions.

Agreeing on a common language in a group of Thinkers is an equally important benefit of using this tool.

ADAPTER DOGS AND INNOVATOR CATZ TOOL

Use: To encourage and enable conversations between the two different types of creative thinkers.

See also the chapter: Creativity.

The Dogs and Catz framework below is a light-hearted description highlighting the differences between the rule-breaking Innovators and the rule-bending Adapters described by the Kirton Adapter Innovator (KAI) Model. Most people are a mix of the two styles with a bias to Innovator or Adapter.

It is a quick self-assessment to get an understanding of your personal preferred creative style. It should also encourage some respect between the Dogs and Catz as they use their different styles of creativity. Both styles are equally valuable, it just depends on the context. Most people have an illogical bias in favour of innovator Catz due to their higher visibility and potential to come up with entertaining ideas. Remember also that intelligence is *not* related to creative style.

Appendices

Are you happier with the Adapter Dogs or the Innovator Catz?
What is your default creative style? How do you prefer to address a problem?

D Defined Scope – focuses the effort   **C** Creative Licence – provides freedom

O Organised – first step, a pragmatic plan   **A** Anarchy – that is what creativity needs

G Grounded – it is all about the facts   **T** Theoretical – it is all about ideas

S Straight to results – waste no time   **Z** Zig zag – best route to the solution

What criticism of your thinking style do you normally hear?

Dogmatic – unimaginative, boring to work with   *Chaotic – Unfocused, trusting to luck, frustrating to work with*

Method:

Give each statement a mark out of 4.

1 = Disagree, 2 = Somewhat Disagree,

3 = Somewhat Agree, 4 = Totally Agree.

Total each column. The larger number identifies your Creative Type.

A score of Dog: 10 to 12 = Strong Adapter. A score of Cat: 10 to 12 = Strong innovator.

A score of Dog: 7 to 9 = Adapter. A score of Cat: 7 to 9 = Innovator.

Now subtract the smaller number from the larger.

A difference in scores of between 0 and 4 means that you have a flexible style.

A flexible style in an individual and a mix of creative styles in a team are valuable in general problem solving.

- ✧ When negotiating in a complex environment you may not have the time, or any good reason, to disrupt it. That is when getting a bit of ingenious Adapter thinking by the Dogs is going to find the best path through to the right response.
- ✧ When problems seem intractable, a burst of Innovator thinking from the Catz can break out of assumptions and norms that might be unimportant but stifling.

When working alone, the trick is to switch your own thinking mode deliberately for a while to gain a different perspective.

PROSPECT THEORY

Prospect Theory: A Summary and an Extension

Amos Tversky and Daniel Kahneman in their seminal 1974 paper set out the principles of Prospect Theory.[95] It is a descriptive model of the real-life choices that people make when making decisions involving risk, where the probabilities of all prospective outcomes are known to them. These are the 'prospects' that the theory addresses. The theory shows that behaviours are consistently irrational, but predictably so. This is an important idea and a very powerful one. It earned Kahneman a Nobel Prize. Tversky would have shared the prize but unfortunately, and to Kahenman's lasting regret, he did not live long enough to receive the honour.

I have set out a simple summary of the theory here.[96] I have also described how the theory supports a new model synthesised from the two scientists' work. This extension to the theory is based entirely on their work. It is only new in the way that it presents their conclusions. I believe it is helpful when looking at the practical implications of the theory in various situations.

Prospect Theory says that individuals:

✧ will typically make choices based on the potential value of *immediate* gains (or losses) rather than the final outcome; and that

✧ they do *not* evaluate these choices rationally.

The theory suggests that people's evaluation of risk and behaviours are characterised by the following four tendencies:

✧ Certainty

People have a strong preference for certainty and are willing to sacrifice potential benefits to achieve it. For example, in one study conducted by Tversky and Kahneman, people were almost four times more likely to choose a sure gain of $30 over an 80% chance possibility of winning $45 (worth a theoretical $36). In other words, people are typically risk averse.

✧ Small Probabilities

Extreme probabilities are hard for the human brain to understand and people tend to round up or down to a certainty. This can result in people making risky choices, interpreting a low probability event as actually impossible, and a high probability event as a sure thing.

✧ Loss Aversion

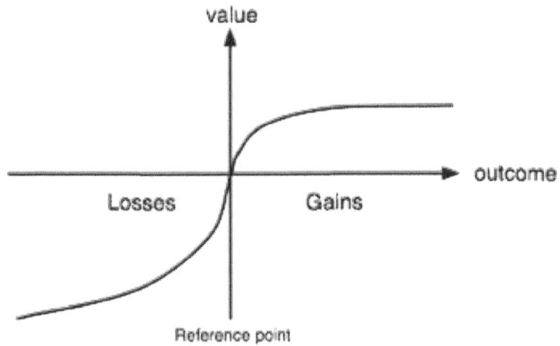

People are strongly loss averse, and we give losses more weight than gains. This is shown in the diagram, which maps psychological value against monetary outcome.

Loss aversion can cause examples of irrational behaviour in terms of mental accounting. For instance, an individual who gains $100 and then loses $80 may feel and behave like they have experienced a loss, rather than a $20 gain.

Loss aversion is so powerful it can be triggered simply by rephrasing a scenario:

Scenario A

You have just been given $1,000. You may now choose whether to gain a further $500, or take a 50% chance to gain a further $1,000.

Scenario B

You have just been given $2,000. You may now choose whether to lose $500, or take a 50% chance of losing $1,000.

The final states of wealth for the participant in either scenario are identical – at the end of the game, they will either be $1,500 richer, or they will have gambled and now be richer, either by $1000 or $2000. Despite the outcomes, in scenario A, the majority of people will choose the guaranteed option, whereas in scenario B, they will choose the gamble. The original gift of either $1000 or $2000 moves the reference point, so that a participant in Scenario A who gains $1500 will view the outcome as a gain, but a participant in Scenario B will interpret it as a loss, despite their identical profits. (See also the Framing Paradigm.)

✧ Relative Positioning

People tend to be more interested in their relative gains and losses as opposed to the actual benefits. This relativity applies both to their own state before the loss or gain, and to the difference between them and others (if the losses and gains affect others). Even if someone's income increases dramatically, they won't feel any better off unless their relative positioning changes. For instance, an individual who receives a 10% raise will gain more 'utility' from this benefit if their colleague neighbour does not receive the same raise. (We are using the word utility in the way economists do.) This relativity applies to other utilities that people value, like their position in a hierarchy, their happiness in a relationship, etc. The importance of relative advantage also applies to groups and tribes. In an experiment to test this, members of randomly selected groups were told to share cash between their group and another. Given the choice of splitting the sum in half, or of keeping less than half for themselves and handing an even smaller portion to the other group, they preferred the second option.[97]

The classical science of economics is largely based on Rational Utility Theory: the concept that a consumer will consider only the marginal utility of each possible option in a situation. For example, they will treat a gain of £11 as more significant than a loss of £10. In reality, the four behavioural characteristics described above overrule the rational 'Economan' response. These counter-examples are what led to the conception of Prospect Theory to take into account actual human irrationality. This is an important foundation of the new science of Behavioural Economics, where real psychology is integrated with theoretical economics to gain better insights into how humans make economic decisions. (See also the chapter on Rational and Reasonable.)

Tversky and Kahneman captured behaviours in situations of very high value losses and gains in their 'Fourfold Pattern' Model.[98]

Fourfold Pattern Tversky & Kahneman	Potential Outcome Framed as	
	LOSSES	GAINS
HIGH Chance Probable Effect	95% to LOSE $10,000 **HOPE** to avoid Loss RISK SEEKING Reject favourable Settlement	95% to WIN $10,000 **FEAR** of Dissapointment RISK AVERSE Accept favourable Settlement
LOW Chance Possible Effect	5% to LOSE $10,000 **FEAR** of Large Loss RISK AVERSE Accept favourable Settlement	5% to WIN $10,000 **HOPE** for Large Gain RISK SEEKING Reject favourable Settlement

Note:

❖ *The text in the picture is their original explanation of each extreme. The top line is the example* **prospect***. The second line shows the*

emotional response*. The third line describes the typical* ***behaviour*** *expected. The fourth line describes that behaviour in the example of somebody considering their lawyer's advice if this prospect was to happen in a courtroom setting.*[99]

The two scientists went on the measure how far a typical person's assessment of risk diverged from the rational measure of risk. They called this the Decision Weight. Using the published data from their experiments to measure Decision Weights (for moderate gains) we can see that it shifts to reflect an irrational optimism that small probabilities will become real. They christened this the 'Possibility Effect'. At higher probabilities, pessimism appears, in what they called the 'Certainty Effect'. I prefer to call this the Probable Effect, so that we have the Possible Effect versus the Probable Effect.

You can see this measured variation from rational probability in the graph below, based on their experimental results.

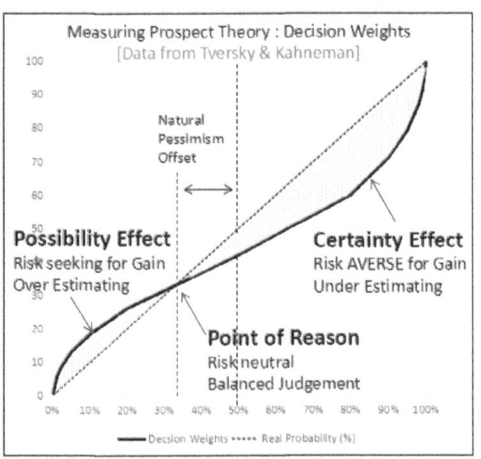

Taking account of prospective losses as well as gains, the graph is mirrored to show a negative probability. This is shown in the next diagram.

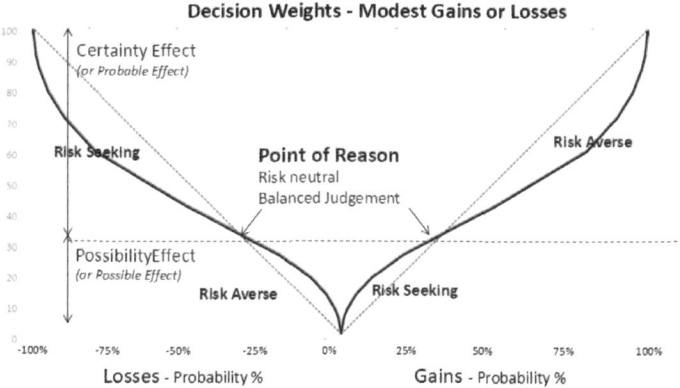

Because losses are more emotionally powerful than gains, the curve on the left-hand side (showing losses) is likely to be more exaggerated than it is shown here. More work is needed to determine the degree of change.

The Fourfold pattern suggests that the difference between the actual probability and the decision weight will get larger as the value of the gain or loss increases. To put this another way, the 's-curve' of decision weights will shift further from the straight line of reasonable probability. This is shown graphically in the following diagrams.

At LOW potential gains or losses The behaviour is rational and will be very close to real probabilities.
The curve is exaggerated by potential losses on the left.

At MEDIUM potential gains or losses. The behaviour is similar to low with just a small increase in deviation from natural probabilities

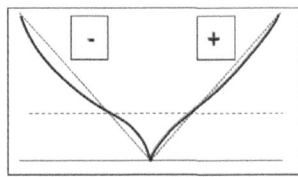

Low Loss/Gain

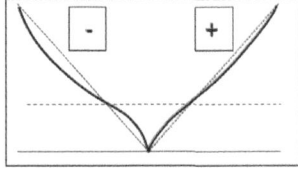

Medium Loss/Gain

At HIGH potential gains or losses The behaviour is exaggerated. We should expect a reasonable response only when the odds are close to certain OR when they are at the mid-point of Probable versus Possible

At VERY HIGH potential gains or losses, the behaviour is irrational on both gains and losses.
The behaviour can suddenly switch from risk advers to risk seeking based on a very small change in real probailities.

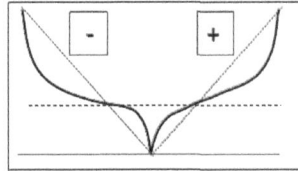

High Loss/Gain

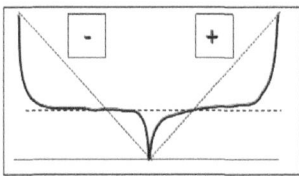

Very High Loss/Gain

Fourfold Risks Behaviour Model

I have combined the Fourfold Pattern and Decision Weights of Prospect Theory into one picture to highlight how behaviours switch as the individual reaches the extremes of choice. I call this picture, the 'Fourfold Field Risk Behaviours Model'. It is a creation of the author. I find it a useful model, and I know that others do too. However, I must emphasise that it is not taken

Appendices

directly from Tversky and Kahneman's work on Prospect Theory. It is not a standard, or widely known, interpretation of the theory.

The model is shown here:

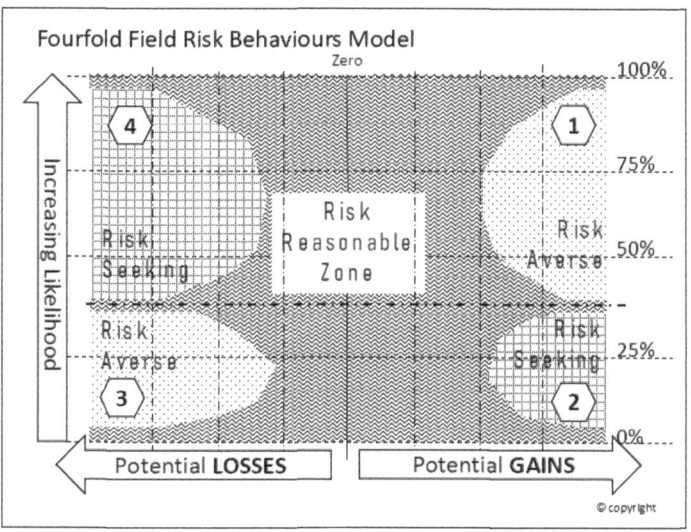

NOTE: *The diagram is conceptual only and it is not to scale. It is inspired by data collected by Tversky and Kahneman in experiments to measure Decision Weights and analysed by the author. While it is possible to design and run experiments to measure the correct proportions, this scientific research has not yet been done.*

It is useful to consider the model in the context of the four characteristics of risk behaviours identified by the scientists:

Certainty only appears at the top and bottom edge of the plane.

Small probabilities (close to 0% and 100%) occur at the top and bottom of the diagram.

Relativity has more impact as we move to the left or right from the centre. It is extreme on the left and the right of the diagram and reduces to zero in the centre. The value of gains and losses increases as you move from the centre, from low to medium, then to high, and finally to very high. This horizontal scale should be considered as a logarithmic scale.

Loss-aversion: The risk-reasonable area is asymmetrical around the vertical axis. Because expected losses have more impact than gains, the risk-reasonable area is smaller on the losses side of the picture.

The diagram is useful because it highlights some of the behaviours discovered in the development of Prospect Theory.

- ✦ The behaviour of people changes as the probability or large gains or losses moves from low to high on the vertical axis. This change is not gradual. At the extreme left and right of the picture (showing very large losses and gains) behaviour 'flips' from risk seeking to risk averse over a very small range of probabilities. This 'flip' happens below 50%.

- ✦ The Risk Reasonable Zone (where people make judgements which fairly closely match true probability) is asymmetric around the vertical zero gain/loss line. People switch into risk seeking and risk averse behaviours at lower value levels on the losses (left) side of the field.

- ⬥ People believe that low probability events are more likely to happen (the Possible Effect) and high probability events are less likely to happen (the Probable Effect) in both Loss and Gain scenarios. However, the Risk Seeking and Risk Averse behaviours are opposite from the loss to the gain side of the diagram.

- ⬥ The Risk Reasonable Zone in the centre is where assessment of probability is *closer* to the rational probability value. However, it will still diverge from the rational measure. Also, it will be affected by whether the risk is framed as a loss or a gain.

We can use a hypothetical court case to map example scenarios onto the model.

Imagine that two lawyers are explaining the possible outcomes of a case for damages to their clients and asking the client to decide which action they will take. The case is complete. Both sides have put forward their side of the story and the judge's decision is expected after lunch. In this imaginary sue and counter-sue scenario, both lawyers are experts and have a very good idea of which way this is going to play out.

At position '**1**' on the diagram, Client A's lawyer tells them that they have a very high probability of a win, and may gain a very large sum of money. In this position they become *risk averse*. They will be likely to accept an offer below their potential gains to resolve the matter immediately, rather than accept the small chance that the judge will decide against them.

Good Thinking, and Bad

Meanwhile, just down the corridor, Client B's lawyer is telling them that they are at position '2' on the map. They have only a very small chance of winning the large sum that they have sued for. Their reaction is to believe this slim possibility just might happen. Their behaviour is *risk seeking* so they will not accept a small gain if it is offered for an immediate settlement.

If we re-frame Client A to tell them that they have a very low chance of losing, they flip to the other side at position '3' and remain risk averse. Likewise, Client B will move to position '4' if framed as a loss risk.

We can see that, when there is a lot at stake and the odds are strongly stacked, the opponents will usually be in contrasting irrational positions: Risk Averse versus Risk Seeking. If the relative value of the outcomes changes, this can shift the dynamic. Let's say that Client B is very rich and the outcome of the case will make little difference financially. This will bring them into the risk rational zone and they might negotiate a good deal by taking advantage of the risk averse emotions of Client A.

In a high stakes, zero sum game, the dynamic will work against reasonable negotiations unless the probable outcomes are quite balanced. Because losses are more persuasive than gains, it is possible to move someone out of a risk averse or risk seeking position by re-framing the outcome from a loss to a gain.

If we replace the court case example with one of Generals advising Presidents at the starting point of a war, we can see that an understanding of how Prospect Theory affects judgements can be important in any high stakes scenario. We can expect that such an understanding would reduce the risks of Bad Thinking and unfortunate outcomes.

*If you want to teach people a new way of thinking,
don't bother trying to teach them.
Instead, give them a tool, the use of which
will lead to new ways of thinking.*

R. Buckminster Fuller - Scientist

References and Acknowledgements

1. Study published by Katarzyna Bozek and researchers at the Chinese Academy of Sciences and the Max Planck Institutes in Germany. PLOS Biology, 2014.

2. *Bifidobacterium Longum Subspecies Infantis: Champion Colonizer of the Infant Gut.* Mark Underwood et al. in *Pediatric Research*, Jan 2015.

3. *On the Evaluation of One Sided Evidence.* Brenner Koehler & Tversky. *Journal of Behavioural Decision Making*, 9 (1996).

4. Some would say that remaining perfectly still might be a better response than running in blind panic. Fleeing prey is attractive to big cats. This advice probably depends on whether you are running faster than other potential victims.

5. DECIDE: *A Decision-Making Model for More Effective Decision Making by Health Care Managers.* Guo K. L., Health Care Management (Frederick), 2008.

6. *Conjectures and Refutations: The Growth of Scientific Knowledge.* Karl Popper, 1963.

7. *Enhanced Understanding of the Microbiome is Helping Medicine.* The Economist, Nov 2017.

8. *An Embarrassment of Riches: Modelling Social Preferences in Ultimatum Games.* Bicchieri, Cristina and Jiji Zhang (2008) in U. Maki (ed) *Handbook of the Philosophy of Economics*, Elsevier.

References and Acknowledgements

9 *Cultural Differences in Ultimatum Game Experiments: Evidence from a Meta-Analysis.* Oosterbeek, Hessel, Randolph Sloof, and Gijs van de Kuilen (2004). *Experimental Economics*, 7 (2): 171–188.

10 *Drunken Ultimatums* by Christopher Shea, *The New York Times*, Published: December 13, 2009.

11 *Justice- and fairness-related behaviors in non-human primates.* Sarah F. Brosnan, 2013, Proceedings of the National Academy of Sciences of the USA.

12 *Thinking, Fast and Slow.* Daniel Kahneman, 2011.

13 *The Invisible Gorilla*, Christopher Chabris and Daniel Simons, 2010.

14 *Earth's Shifting Crust: A Key to Some Basic Problems of Earth Science.* Charles Hapgood, 1955.

15 The Identification/Response/Mode Model of Empathy. (Empathy_IRM) is very new thinking in the field. It is a synthesis of a lot of research, and it is a creation of the author who is currently testing it in discussion with some experts in the field. I find it much more useful than other models in current use. If you are familiar with another model, by all mean use that. If you like the Empathy_IRM Model, please use it and tell your friends about it. If you want to learn a bit more about it, there are links on the goodthinkingandbad.com website or go direct to prezi.com and search for 'Empathy: Love it or Loath it'.

16 *Why Most Published Research Findings Are False*, by John P. A. Ioannidis, 2005, PLoS Medicine.

17 *Evidence That Smaller Schools Do Not Improve Student Achievement.* Howard Wainer and Harris L. Zwerling. *The Phi Delta Kappan*, Vol. 88, No. 4 (Dec 2006), pp. 300-303

[18] *Will Invest for Food. The Economist*, 1 May 2014.

[19] *The Luck Factor* by R Wisemann, *The Magazine For Science And Reason*. Volume 27, No.3 ~ May/June 2003.

[20] *ibid.*

[21] *The Evolution of Reciprocal Altruism.* Trivers, R. L. (1971), *The Quarterly Review of Biology*, 46.

[22] *The Motivated Use of Moral Principles.* David A Pizzaro: *Judgment and Decision Making*, 4(6):479-491, October 2009.

[23] *Disgust and the Moralization of Purity.* Horberg et al., 2009. *Journal of Personality and Social Psychology.*

[24] *Conservatives are more Easily Disgusted than Liberals.* Inbar, Y et al., 2009 in *Journal of Cognition and Emotion.*

[25] *Marital Interactions: Experimental Investigations* by J D Gottman, 2013.

[26] *Effects of Group Pressure on the Modification and Distortion of Judgements.* Asch, S. E. (1952), *Readings in Social Psychology.*

[27] *The Perils of Obedience.* Milgram, 1974.

[28] www.mensa.org.uk/workout – Rough Guide to IQ

[29] *IQ Testing 101.* Kaufman, Alan S. (2009), New York: Springer Publishing.

[30] *Emotional Intelligence – Why it can Matter more than IQ.* Daniel Goleman (1994).

[31] *Balloon Analogue Risk Task (BART).* Lejuez et al., 2002.

[32] *Adolescents' Risk-Taking Behavior is Driven by Tolerance to Ambiguity.* Tymulaa et al. PNAS Magazine, 2012.

References and Acknowledgements

33 Jung Test Results (Similar to MBTI): from www.similarminds.com/jung_word_pair.html

34 *Cautionary Comments Regarding the Myers-Brigg Type Inventory* by Dr David J. Pittenger in *Consulting Psychology Journal: Practice and Research*, Summer 2005.

35 *MBTI Mapped to Famous Personalities and Characters*. www.personalityclub.com/personality-charts

36 *Adapters and Innovators* 1989, revised edition 1994, M. J. Kirton DSc.

37 *DECIDE: A Decision-Making Model for more Effective Decision Making by Health Care Managers* by Guo, K.L., Health Care Management (Frederick). 2008 Apr-Jun.

38 *Dilemmas in a General Theory of Planning.* Horst Rittel and Melvin M. Webber (1973) *Policy Sciences Magazine.*

39 *Wicked Problems and Network Approaches to Resolution.* Nancy Roberts (2000), International Public Management Review.

40 *The Structure of Scientific Revolutions*: Thomas Kuhn. 1962

41 *Sorting the Sky*: *The Economist* 24 Jun 2017

42 *Florida Effect Automaticity of social behavior: Direct effects of trait construct and stereotype activation on action. Journal of Personality and Social Psychology*, by John A Bargh, M. Chen and L. Burrows

43 *The Effects of Overt Head Movements on Persuasion: Compatibility and Incompatibility of Responses* by G.L Wells and R.E Petty. *Basic and Applied Social Psychology*, 1980

44 *Derren Tricks Shop Keepers To Let Him Pay With Paper – Trick or Treat.* www.youtube.com

45 *Putting Adjustment Back in the Anchoring and Adjustment Heuristic: Differential*

Processing of Self-Generated and Experimenter-Provided Anchors Epley and Gilovitch, (2000) *Journal of Personality and Social Psychology.*

46 *Superstition in the Pigeon.* Skinner, B. F. (1947) *Journal of Experimental Psychology.*

47 *The Structure of Scientific Revolutions*: Thomas Kuhn. 1962

48 *I knew it would happen. Remembered Probabilities of one future things.* Fishoff, B and Beyth R: *Organisational Behaviour and Human Performance* 1975

49 *The Black Swan: The impact of the highly improbable.* Taleb, N. N : 2007.

50 Svenson, Ola (1981). *Are we all less risky and more skilful than our fellow drivers? Acta Psychologica.* 47.

51 Kruger, Justin (1999). *Lake Wobegon be gone! The 'below-average effect' and the egocentric nature of comparative ability judgments. Journal of Personality and Social Psychology.* 77 (2): 221–232.

52 *Coping with Irrevocable Loss, Cataclysms, Crises, and Catastrophes: Psychology in Action.* Wortman, C. and Silver, R.C. (1987) American Psychological Association Master Lecture Series.

53 *Unskilled and Unaware of It: How Difficulties in Recognizing One's Own Incompetence Lead to Inflated Self-Assessments.* Kruger and Dunning (1999), *Journal of Personality and Social Psychology.*

54 *How (In)accurate are Demand Forecasts in Public Works Projects. Journal of the American Planning Association*, Vol 71 (2005)

55 *Overconfidence in case-study judgments.* Oskamp, S. (1965) *The Journal of Consulting Psychology.*

References and Acknowledgements

[56] *A progress report on the training of probability assessors.* (1987) Marc Alpert & Howard Raiffa in Daniel Kahneman, Paul Slovic & Amos Tversky (eds.), *Judgment Under Uncertainty: Heuristics and Biases.*

[57] *Blink* (2005) by Malcolm Gladwell

[58] *The Science of Intuition: How to Measure 'Hunches' and 'Gut Feelings'* by Cari Nierenberg, Live Science May 2016

[59] *Conditions for Intuitive Expertise: A Failure to Disagree.* Klien & Kahneman (2009) *The American Psychologist Journal.*

[60] *How sticky tape trick led to Nobel Prize*: BBC News : 5 October 2010

[61] Statista, The Statistics Portal, www.statista.com, Dec 2015

[62] *How Brands Grow.* Bryon Sharp Oxford University Press 2010

[63] *Construction Perceptions of Venerability: Personal Relevance and the Use of Experimental Information in Health Judgements.* Rotliman and Schwartz, (1998) *Personality and Social Psychology Bulletin.*

[64] Derren Brown: *The System*. Channel 4 TV Show, 2008.
www.youtube.com/watch?v=9R5OWh7luL4

[65] *The Market for Lemons: Quality Uncertainty and the Market Mechanism.* George Akerlof, 1970.

[66] *Coping with Irrevocable Loss, Cataclysms, Crises, and Catastrophes. Psychology in Action.* Wortman, C. and Silver, R.C. (1987) *American Psychological Association Master Lecture Series.*

[67] *Beliefs about beliefs: Representation and constructing function of wrong beliefs in young children's understanding of deception.* Heinz Wimmer, University of Salzburg and Josef Perner, University of Sussex.

68 Gale, Maggie; Ball, Linden J. (2002), *Does Positivity Bias Explain Patterns of Performance on Watson's 2-4-6 task?*, Proceedings of the Twenty-Fourth Annual Conference of the Cognitive Science Society, Routledge, p. 340,

69 *How Mental Systems Believe. American Psychologist*, 46(2), 107-119. DT Gilbert, 1991

70 *Ten years on from Norway's quota for women on corporate boards. The Economist*, Feb 2018.

71 *Experimental Tests of the Endowment Effect and the Coase Theorem.* Daniel Kahneman, Jack L. Knetsch and Richard H. Thaler. *Journal of Political Economy* 1990.

72 *Possession in Humans: an Exploratory Study of its Meaning and Motivation.* L. Furby in *Social Behavior and Personality: An International Journal*, Volume 6, Number 1, 1978.

73 *Cross-modality matching functions generated by magnitude estimation.* Joseph C. Stevens, JC and Lawrence E. Marks, Le (1980) *Perception & Psychophysics.*

74 *Priming and Communication: Social Determinants of Information Use in Life Satisfaction.* Strack, Martin & Schwartz (1988) *European Journal of Social Psychology.*

75 *How to Solve It, Mathematics and Plausible Reasoning.* Volumes I and II by George Polya (1990).

76 *Spontaneous Production of Figurative Language and Gesture in College Lectures.* Daniel P. Corts & Howard R. Pollio. *Metaphor & Symbol*, Vol 14, 1999.

77 *Mental Models.* Gentner & Stevens, Psychology Press, 1983.

78 *The Black Swan.* 2007, Nassim Nicholas Taleb.

79 *Thinking, Fast and Slow.* Daniel Khaneman (2011) Chapter 35, *Two Selves.*

References and Acknowledgements

80 *Judgement Under Uncertainty: Heuristics and Biases.* Tversky & Kahneman, in *Science* Vol 184 (1974).

81 *ibid.*

82 *At the bottom of Maslow's pyramid of human needs relative benefit is much less important. Is happiness relative?* Ruut Veenhoven (1991) *Social Indicators Research.*

83 *Uncivil Agreement* by Lilliana Mason, 2018, University of Chicago Press (Also referred to in *Prospect Theory Summary and Extension.*)

84 This picture, called the Fourfold Field Risk Behaviours Model is a creation of the author. It combines Tversky & Kahneman's Fourfold Model and their Possibility/Certainty effect graph into one image. Note that it is not a standard or widely known interpretation of the theory.

85 *Constructing Rich False Memories of Committing Crime.* Shaw & Porter *Psychological Science*, 2014.

86 *Common and specific brain regions in high- versus low-confidence recognition memory.* Cabeza and Hongkeun Kim in *Brain Research*, 2009.

87 *Fuzzy-trace theory: An interim synthesis.* V.F. Reyna & C.J. Brainerd in *Learning and Individual Differences* (1995).

88 *Can robots assemble an IKEA chair?* by F Suárez-Ruiz, Xian Zhou and Quang-Cuong Pham in *Science Robotics,* Apr 2018.

89 *Moving magnetoencephalography towards real-world applications with a wearable system.* Matthew Brookes et al in *Nature*, Mar 2018.

90 *Remembering one year later: Role of the amygdala and the medial temporal lobe memory system in retrieving emotional memories* by Florin Dolcos, by Kevin S. LaBar, and Roberto Cabeza in *PNAS*, February 15, 2005.

91 Li, Qi and Shu. *An Introduction to Science and Civilization.*

92 *The Structure of Scientific Revolutions*: Thomas Kuhn. 1962.

93 *Growth Share Matrix*: *The Economist*, Sep 11th, 2009.

94 *The Black Swan: The Impact of the Highly Improbable* by Nassim Nicholas Taleb (2007).

95 *Choices, Values, and Frames*. D Kahneman and A Tversky 1984 in *American Psychologist*.

96 My thanks to Sorren Sheedy who wrote a short paper on Prospect Theory while on a Behavioural Economics course in Cambridge in 2016 which provided an excellent foundation for this summary.

97 *Uncivil Agreement* by Lilliana Mason, 2018, University of Chicago Press.

98 The Fourfold Patterns and Decision Weights are explained with wonderful clarity in *Thinking, Fast and Slow* by Daniel Kahneman, 2011.

99 This representation of the Fourfold diagram here has been adjusted to show losses on the left and gains on the right. The original was reversed. This reversal does not change the meaning but having a left to right mapping to losses and gains is more intuitive.

INDEX

Adaption and Innovation, 72, 96

AI Artificial Intelligence, 254
    Plays Go, 254
    Black Box, 256
    Deep Thought, 254
    IKEA Furniture Assembly, 255

Akerlof, George, Market for Lemons, 188

AlphaGo, 254

Anchoring and Framing, 142

Angels' Advocate and Devil's Advocate, 73

Asch, Solomon, Groupthink, 71

AsTeEx, Intuitive Decision Process, 173

BART test, 83

Bayes, Thomas, Bayes Theorem 27

Bias compared to prejudice, 223

Biomene, 14, 32

Black Box, AI issue, 256

Bosnian Crisis, 194

Boston Matrix, 310

Brainstorming, 101, 302-303

Brown, Derren,
    Paper Money Trick, 141
    Horse Racing, 186
    Catz and Dogs, Adaption vs Innovation Diagram, 100, 325

Certainty Effect, 238, 333

Chabris & Simons, The Invisible Gorilla, 45

Consequential vs Principled Morality, 65

Conspiracy Theory, 136, 153

Continental Drift Theory, 47

Corts & Pollio, use of metaphors, 228

Covey, Steve, Seven Habits, 260

Crick, Francis, DNA, 226

Darwin, Charles, 130

DECIDE Model, 22, 112
    AsTeEx Diagram, 173
    DECIDE Diagram, 113

Decision Weight, 331-336

Deep Thought AI, 256

Degrees of Certainty or Standards of Evidence, 29, 323

Devil's Advocate and Angels' Advocate, 73

Disgust, effect on thinking, 69

DNA, Watson & Crick, 226

Doublethink, 31-33, 59

Dunning-Kruger effect, overconfidence, 161

Econs, 36

Edgeworth, Francis Ysidro, Hedonimeter, 234

Einstein, Albert, 47, 104, 210

Empathy, 49, 67, 193
    Empathy IRM Model, Identification, Response, Mode Diagram, 50

Endowment Effect, 204

EQ, Emotional Quotient, 80

Evolution, 18
    conscious evolution, 12

Falsifiable hypothesis, *Karl Popper*, 28, 38, 57, 200, 324

Florida Effect, Framing Experiment, 139

Focusing Illusion, 188

Fourfold Field Risk Behaviours Model, 239, 335
    Prospect Theory, 239

Fourfold Patten, 332-336

Framing and Anchoring, 44, 69, 137-146, 339

    Furby, Lita, Psychological Ownership, 206-207

Fuzzy Trace Theory, *Reyna & Brainerd*, 247

Gates, Bill, Gates Foundation, 58

Gilbert, Daniel, Effort to Disbelieve, 200

Gist and Verbatim Memory, 246

Gladwell, Malcolm, 'Blink', 168

Gottman, John and Julie, Married Relationships, 70

Groupthink. *Asch, Solomon*, 71

Guo, K L, DECIDE Model, 112

Hedonimeter, *Edgeworth, Francis Ysidro* , 235

Holmes, Sherlock, 300

Hume, David, 27

In Search of Excellence, 60

Innovation and Adaption, 96

Intuition, conditions for useful intuitions, 170

IQ, Intelligence Quotient, 79
    is IQ racist?, 79

James, William, pragmatic clock example, 28

Judgement, young people's brain development, 82

Jung, Karl, personality types, 87

Kahneman, Daniel, 252
    System 1 & 2 Thinking, 41
    Intuition (with *Klein*), 170
    Experience Utility, 234
    Prospect Theory, 237, 328

Kirton, M. J., KIA Kirton Innovator Adaptor index, 96

Klein, Gary, Naturalistic Decision Making, 170

Kruger, Justin
    Overconfidence, 157, 161
    Underconfidence, 163

Kuhn, Thomas, Structure of Scientific Revolutions, 129, 149, 301

Linnaeus, Carolus, Taxonomy, 128

Luck, 61, 159

Markus, George, False Memories, 245

MBTI, Myers Briggs Type Indicator, 88-92
    Criticism of MBIT, 91
    MBIT Thinking Styles Diagram, 94

Mental Models Theory, 211

Merkel, Angela, 65

Milgram, Stanley, Authority and Obedience, 71

Moral Psychology, 64

Munsterburg, Hugo, False Memories, 245

Myelination, brain development, 83

Nightingale, Florence, Triage, 119

Nixon, President, China and Russia visits, 150

O'Brien, Flan, The Third Policeman, 31

OCD, Obsessive Compulsive Disorder, 149

Index

Oracle of Delphi, Cyrus Prediction, 109

Orwell, George, Doublethink, 31

Philosophy, 25, 64

Pizzaro, David, Relative Morality 66

Plancius, Petrus, Cartographer, 226

Pólya, George, Problem Solving, 220

Popper, Karl, 27-28, 38, 58, 201, 303

Possibility Effect, 333

Prejudice compared to bias, 224

Principled vs Consequential Morality, 65

Prospect Theory, 146, 237, 328-339
    Fourfold Field Risk Behaviours Model, 239, 240

Psychological Ownership, three sources of, 207

Psychometrics, 87

Pyrrho (philosopher), 27

Railway Mania, 162

Rational Agent Model, Econman, 36

Rational Utility Theory, 237, 333

Reasonable and Rational Thinking Grid, 39

Reyna & Brainerd, Fuzzy Trace Theory, 247

Risk Register, 320

Risk Reward Levers in Prospect Theory, 243

Rittel & Weber, Wicked Problems, 123

Rotliman and Schwartz, Effects of cardiac risk, 181

Schumpeter, Joseph, Definition of Innovation, 97

Sedol, Lee, AI plays Go, 254

Skinner Box, Operant Conditioning Experiment, 148

Stakeholder Map, 81, 110, 315-316
    Degrees of Certainty or Standards of Evidence, 29, 323

Statistics. Sample Size Calculator, 56

Stern, William, Inventor of IQ, 78

Structure of Scientific Revolutions, *Thomas Kuhn*, 129

Sunk Cost, 205-206

Syllogism, logical test, 26

System 1 and System 2 Thinking, 41

Taleb, Nassim, The Black Swan, 151
    Ludic Fallacy, 231

Taxonomy, 17, 130
    Taxonomy vs Search 132

Thaler, Richard
    Econs, 36
    Endowment Effect, 205
    Ultimatum Game, 36-38

The Invisible Gorilla, *Chabris and Simons*, 46

Thinking Fallacies, 19, 128
    in intuition, 170

Triage, 21
    Decision Matrix Diagram, 125
    Decisions, 122
    in Medicine, 120
    in War Zone, 120

Trivers, Robert, Moral Psychology, 63

Ultimatum Game, 36-39

Verbatim and Gist Memory, 246-250, 258

Watson, James, DNA, 227

Watson, Peter, Confirmation Bias Term, 199

Weber, Max, Principled and Consequential Morality, 65

Wegener, Alfred, Continental Drift Theory, 47

WEIRD: White, Educated, Industrialised, Rich and Democratic, 64

Wicked Problems, *Rittel & Weber*, 123

Wimmer & Permer, Empathy Experiment, 193

Wiseman, Richard Lucky People, 61

PRINTED AND BOUND BY:

Copytech (UK) Limited trading as Printondemand-worldwide,

9 Culley Court, Bakewell Road, Orton Southgate.

Peterborough, PE2 6XD, United Kingdom.